WORLD YEARBOOK
OF EDUCATION 1996

World Yearbook of Education 1982/83
Computers and Education
Edited by Jacquetta Megarry, David R F Walker,
Stanley Nisbet and Eric Hoyle

World Yearbook of Education 1984
Women and Education
Edited by Sandra Acker, Jacquetta Megarry,
Stanley Nisbet and Eric Hoyle

World Yearbook of Education 1985
Research, Policy and Practice
Edited by John Nisbet, Jacquetta Megarry and Stanley Nisbet

World Yearbook of Education 1986
The Management of Schools
Edited by Eric Hoyle and Agnes McMahon

World Yearbook of Education 1987
Vocational Education
Edited by John Twining, Stanley Nisbet and Jacquetta Megarry

World Yearbook of Education 1988
Education for the New Technologies
Edited by Duncan Harris (Series Editor)

World Yearbook of Education 1989
Health Education
Edited by Chris James, John Balding and Duncan Harris (Series Editor)

World Yearbook of Education 1990
Assessment and Evaluation
Edited by Chris Bell and Duncan Harris (Series Editor)

World Yearbook of Education 1991
International Schools and International Education
Edited by Patricia L. Jonietz (Guest Editor) and Duncan Harris (Series Editor)

World Yearbook of Education 1992
Urban Education
Edited by David Coulby, Crispin Jones and Duncan Harris (Series Editor)

World Yearbook of Education 1993
Special Needs Education
Edited by Peter Mittler
Ron Brouillette and Duncan Harris (Series Editor)

World Yearbook of Education 1994
The Gender Gap in Higher Education
Edited by Suzanne Stiver Lie, Lynda Malik and Duncan Harris (Series Editor)

World Yearbook of Education 1995
Youth, Education and Work
Edited by Leslie Bash and Andy Green

WORLD YEARBOOK
OF EDUCATION 1996

THE
EVALUATION
OF HIGHER
EDUCATION
SYSTEMS

Edited by Robert Cowen
Series Editors: David Coulby and Crispin Jones

**KOGAN
PAGE**

London • Philadelphia

First published in 1996

Kogan Page Limited
120 Pentonville Road
London N1 9JN

British Library Cataloguing in Publication Data
A CIP record for this book is available from the British Library.

ISBN 0 7494 1777 3

Typeset by BookEns Ltd, Royston, Herts.
Printed and bound in Great Britain by Clays Ltd, St Ives plc

Contents

List of contributors

Note: Names here and at the head of the chapters are listed according to Western convention. In the Biographical Notes on Contributors at the end of the volume, both Western and Asian conventions are followed.

Masateru Baba, Shinshu University, Japan — *Chapter 9*

Ronald Barnett, Institute of Education, University of London — *Chapter 12*

Kai-ming Cheng, University of Hong Kong — *Chapter 8*

Boutheina Cheriet, Centre of Arab Women for Training and Research, Tunis — *Chapter 2*

Bob Cowen, Institute of Education, University of London — *Chapters 1 and 14*

Maria Figueiredo, Institute of Education, University of London — *Chapters 4 and 13*

Susan Douglas Franzosa, University of New Hampshire, USA — *Chapter 11*

Terri Kim, Institute of Education, University of London — *Chapter 10*

Denise Leite, Federal University of Rio Grande do Sul, Brazil — *Chapter 13*

John R Mallea, Brandon University, Manitoba, Canada — *Chapter 5*

Guy Neave, International Association of Universities, Paris — *Chapter 7*

Barry A Sheehan, University of Melbourne, Australia — *Chapter 3*

Isabel F. Sobreira, State University of Montes Claros, Brazil — *Chapter 4*

Tianxiang Xue, East China Normal University, PRC — *Chapter 6*

Preface

The creation and refinement of national systems for the evaluation of higher education systems is a relatively new activity, and it is a growth industry — or at least it is a growing industry. Whether it will lead to growth, either in economic or in academic productivity of a worthwhile kind, is one of the questions which most of the authors in this book raise. The real-life answers are still coming in, and the academics who have contributed the chapters in this book give cautious, sometimes sceptical answers. The evidence is still being generated in the behaviours of institutions of higher education, in the behaviour of academics in their professional groups, and in the behaviour of academics as individuals.

What is clear is that inventing national systems for the evaluation of higher education systems is a widespread activity, but it is not universal. There is an international trend in this area, but national level politics very much define why evaluation systems will be introduced and how evaluation systems should work.

The introduction of a national evaluation system for higher education is a matter of politics. Some political contexts prevent the introduction of measures of academic performance of the kind which are now visible in some parts of the northern hemisphere. Such systems are simply not possible in some places and in some political contexts for complex and serious reasons, a point which is made with great clarity in the chapter on Algeria by Cheriet.

Indeed, it is the historical and the political contexts within which evaluation systems are (or are not) introduced and work (or not) that are a major theme of this volume. Authors were invited to identify what was, say 20 or 30 years ago, the evaluation system for higher education — however informal or unsystematic — and to indicate what had become the major ways of evaluating the higher education system by the 1990s. Authors were asked to discuss what they took to be the forces of change which had produced, in their specific national context or geographic area, these new, more systematic ways of evaluating higher education systems. Finally, authors were invited, against a specification of how the new evaluation system is working, to identify the emerging short- and long-term effects of the new evaluation systems.

It was taken for granted that there would be wide variation in the precision with which such themes could be discussed. The analysis of the results or consequences of the new evaluation systems would, in some cases, have to be interpreted in the absence of clear research results given the newness of the innovations in some countries.

It was also taken for granted that authors from different cultures would write at different lengths, and from different perspectives and different assumptions: what is an important question in one country may not be even being asked in another. The evaluation systems and the authors' chapters, both, are influenced and partly defined by the political and historical contexts in which they were created.

The book illustrates some of the variations in those contexts in which national systems of evaluation have been created, or blocked. All the chapters in the book take up the tensions and contradictions which numerous actors have faced in creating or blocking evaluation systems; or in modifying what should happen next. This book by its accumulation of examples, rather than by deliberate editorial intent to affect practical policies, is part of that process of discussion and modification.

But like the discussions and the possible modifications to existing policies, the tensions and the contradictions are not the same everywhere. They could not be, as countries have different histories, different traditions of the relationship between the state and academe, different agendas of social and economic development, and different conceptions of civil society. They also have different traditions about how much control academics should have over their conditions of work, and their freedom to make their own definitions of excellence in academic production, a point well made in the chapter on Japan by Baba and in the chapter on Korea by Kim. In some ways the most interesting cases are where evaluation systems are not getting onto the state's agenda or, if conceived, are not being implemented as the state intended, a point well made by Leite and Figueiredo on Latin America.

However, there are some similarities amid the differences. Often there are tensions and contradictions between the historic tradition of 'the university' and those who hold positions in such institutions, and politicians and innovators in state agencies who, holding to new theories of accountability and quality control, are concerned with the reform of higher education systems. This point is very clear in the Australian chapter by Sheehan. But the tensions are not always of this kind. Sometimes the debate focuses very much on technique: in which ways should the productivity of the higher education system be measured; against which criteria of performance should academics be held to public account?

Particularly as a consequence of some of the crude techniques of measurement and the crude use of their results, academics are developing anxieties about the short- and long-term effects of the ways in which their productivity is measured, or is to be measured. Cheng makes this point very visible in his chapter on Hong Kong. It is perfectly clear from the evidence and interpretation provided in the chapters in this volume that evaluation systems reach down and into the smaller units of academic life, such as departments, and that evaluation systems are beginning to affect how academics work. In particular there is a tension, it would seem, between teaching and research, a point seriously explored by Barnett in his chapter on the United Kingdom; and research and teaching and community service. Which of these activities do evaluation systems measure, and what is the effect of an emphasis in an evaluation system on one of these activities (normally research) rather than the other activities?

The answers which academics are developing are complex. As organized public groups, academics are complaining, resisting, negotiating and redefining the demands of the evaluation systems which affect their professional lives. Figueiredo and Sobreira outline these forms of resistance in Brazil. In their departmental organization, academics are working out ways to survive – or even 'to win' – according to the new rules. And there are certainly hints in this volume of how individual academics are reorganizing their work patterns 'to beat the system': that is, performing sufficiently in accordance with public criteria to be seen to be coping, while they get on with the work their earlier professional socialization says is important.

Overall, it seems unlikely that several contemporary national systems for the evaluation of higher education will produce the results which are expected of them by governments. But it seems equally unlikely that academics will be able to retain the responsibility they have historically had, in many countries, for defining so many of the parameters of their professional production.

But why all the fuss? It is known that we live in an interdependent world, it is known that our nations are at risk, and it is known that we must all pursue competitive and comparative advantage in a world knowledge economy, and it is known that only the state has the resources and political clout to make such a major intrusion into the workings of (academic) institutions, protected for so long by strong ideologies of academic freedom and autonomy. Perhaps an important question is how is this known, to whom is this known, how much power do they have, and are they right? It is easy to destroy universities; it would be especially paradoxical to destroy them in the name of quality control and total quality management.

Rather less may be 'known' about the contemporary world system than confident politicans think, but there is indeed an international rhetoric, magnified or perhaps created by a number of reports from national or international agencies, which forms opinion and especially the opinion of politicians, and through the media, the opinion of a variety of publics. The point is made clearly for the United States by Franzosa. Both the States and Canada have exceptionally mature systems of evaluation, via accreditation agencies. What is very striking about the recent developments there is the way in which already complex systems of evaluation are increasing in density and in intensity, as in the Canadian case on which Mallea provides impressive detail. First reform, then understand, perhaps. So 'knowing' is perhaps not quite the right word; but whatever beliefs are held, they are certainly being acted upon. Some of the beliefs and ideologies of reform and their practical results are being written about in this book, and indeed elsewhere.

The literature on evaluation systems is growing rapidly. For several of the authors in this book, notably Guy Neave who writes on France, their chapter represents a particular contribution within a continuous concern for this topic in its social and historical context. But the productivity of scholars analysing something which is continuously changing makes the assembly of a general bibliography an exceptionally onerous task. Europe for example is especially well covered in several special issues of the academic journals, some of which are listed in the bibliography of the volume. My thanks go to Xanthi Karadima and Emmanuel Kanakis for having the courage to undertake the impossible task of making some selection from the literature.

My thanks also go to Rajee Rajagopolan for organizing me, another impossible task, as well as to Mary Griffin who transformed my interminable margin scribblings into legible text. My special thanks go to Jenny Fleming who word-processed just about everything at least twice, and again to Rajee Rajagopolan who on a day not lightly to be forgotten found a virus in the disks of the project – and dealt with it. My thanks also go to members of the Institute of Education computer Help Desk, Lindsay and Peter and Nigel, who rescued errant text, firmly assured a new printer that it could indeed print, and pulled things out of e-mail that had codes of behaviour which were very much their own. Maria Figueiredo translated foreign language material with great speed and accuracy and I am very grateful to her for that, among other things.

My final thanks must go to the authors in the volume who kept replying patiently to my faxes and to the General Editors whose sage advice, when followed, worked; and whose sage advice when not followed remained sage. I tried their patience on more than one occasion and I thank them for the cocoon of calm which they tried to create for me at the worst moments in a fascinating project.

Robert Cowen

1. Introduction: apex institutions, statuses and quality control

Robert Cowen

We have always known which were the best universities. They were Bologna or Salamanca, Coimbra or Cambridge, Oxford or Paris or al-Ahzar; or in a different time period, Berlin or Chicago; or, under specific conditions, Melbourne or McGill. The best national, even international, academics collected there. Clever children, if they were disciplined and lucky, were able to compete for entry, and graduates from those institutions were taken into the state's civil service, or served the church, or went, depending on time and place, into the higher ranks of politics.

Such institutions were also breeders and feeders for the academic profession itself. That is, they bred well-trained persons for research and teaching, and some of these persons later took up senior positions as heads of fields of study in less prestigious universities. This is one part of cultural dependency theory which works and it is possible to identify double metropoles, such as Edinburgh and McGill, or Paris and Rio de Janeiro, as well as the domestic dominance of Paris within France or McGill within some sections of Canada.

At its most extreme, as in the cases of the University of Tokyo, or Oxford and Cambridge for about one hundred years, a very small number of the best universities functioned as 'apex institutions': that is, they attracted children of high socio-economic status and children of talent, but through networks of influence and through their institutional reputation, they also ensured that important career lines were open to their graduates. Thus they were apex institutions in the sense that they were trainers of future nationally important elites.

They were also apex institutions in that they acted as guarantors of the definition of quality in the rest of the system of higher education both by exporting staff and by demonstrating in their public posture, and the quality of some of their research, what should be taken as good work. They provided role models, for both individual and institutional behaviour: they showed what proper academics — and proper universities — should value.

1

They also affected the secondary school system through their clear epistemologies about what was privileged knowledge (maybe philosophy and mathematics in France, or Latin and Greek in Germany or England). They even affected, as in the case of Tokyo, school examinations and how the national examination system itself was used; and took a remarkable grip on the minds and aspirations of teachers and parents for the children in their care. The impact of apex institutions — the theme of their dominance over other universities and their impact on the secondary school sector itself — can also be traced, with local variation, in the Republic of China (Taiwan), in the Republic of Korea (South Korea), Singapore, Hong Kong and Malaysia, and in Russia before the Revolution in the universities of Kiev, Moscow and St Petersburg. The University of London, with its extended examination service and later with its mentoring role, also acted as an apex institution for new colleges, later universities, in Africa.

Thus apex institutions were particularly visible definers of quality: for the state, for the rest of the academic industry, for the public through media exposure, and for parents and children. However, as quality control devices for a complete national system of higher education they work best in a limited range of conditions. And these conditions are not permanent.

The apex institutions worked best as quality control devices when they were part of a hierarchy of statuses; separated for example from technical colleges or teachers colleges or institutes of technology — as they were from 1945 in France, England, the Netherlands and in what was once West Germany. Even major efforts to disturb these hierarchies by the state, as in the former Soviet Union, were not immediately successful and the pattern of post-16 educational institutions has been a problem for governments since the 1960s, especially as governments have also been concerned with the production of useful knowledges from the higher education sector. It was mainly in the United States, with its invention of the Land Grant college movement, and the Wisconsin idea, that the lock was successfully picked.

As in the United States, it is the destruction of those status patterns within higher education which sets the scene for the new evaluation mechanisms. These status patterns can be destroyed by deliberate state action of a dramatic kind. This does not require a political revolution, such as the 1949 revolution in China and the subsequent secondary effort during the cultural revolution. It can, and has been done, within a continuous political framework as in England, albeit with some resistance, especially in Scotland, and it is being done in France and with slightly greater difficulty in Belgium and Germany.

What does help is a major expansion of the higher education system itself, either just in terms of student numbers, or in terms of institutional multiplication, as in Brazil, Japan, Korea and Venezuela for example. At some point, and the point seems to have been in the last decade, states consolidate and reorganize the higher educational system. This may be done at regional level, as for example in the early rationalization of the Californian higher education system. Now it is being done at the national level in many countries.

However, not only the status patterns are broken. The often traditional relationship (cf. the traditional University Grants Committee model extensively exported overseas from the United Kingdom) of cushioned distance between the state and the higher education system, especially its university sector, has been destroyed. And deliberately so. Whether through either of the two basic models of evaluation — accreditation systems or direct measurement systems — the state, through newly created agencies, has intervened to satisfy itself that account-ability is occurring and that quality is following.

To gain that control, almost everywhere where evaluation systems have been introduced it has been necessary for politicians to do two things: to re-work the vocabulary through which universities are perceived by electorates, and replace the traditional vocabulary of defence used by academics (academic freedom, autonomy, researchers and knowledge creators); and, second, to try to channel, manage and measure creativity. Resistance by academics has been strong and sophisticated in particular places, but in general the defence of the university has produced neither its martyrs nor public acceptance.

What is clear in the chapters which follow is that there are indeed 'circles of the mind': that is, a great deal of borrowing and copying is going on. Governments are looking at what other governments are doing in the evaluation of higher education systems and, through various networks, are establishing contacts, arranging for seminars for policy makers and adapting well or poorly the foreign evaluation policies which interest them. At the moment the metaphors of ideological and actual penetration are those of business and systems, especially information systems, and efficiency. Evaluation and higher educational systems will be 'managed'. It will be interesting and probably disturbing to see the institutional consequences of the management and routinization of creativity. The best universities, including the apex institutions, have managed — without much management — to make a remarkable historical contribution to human understandings and practices over several centuries. On the other hand, it now seems to be widely and confidently known that universities are chaotic. Perhaps a crucial question for governments to address as the grand narratives of modernity break up and as governments impose their very modernist evaluation systems, is the terms on which — and indeed, how — universities and higher education systems should be encouraged to remain contradictory, chaotic and creative in their professional cultures while simultaneously being measured as axial institutions in world alleged to be driven by knowledge.

2. The evaluation of the higher education system in Algeria

Boutheina Cheriet

Introduction

Writing about the Algerian higher educational system now must be conceived in terms of the formidable upheavals of a political and ideological nature that have been besetting this country for the last decade, culminating in their exacerbation in the form of a civil war illustrating a most fascinating power contest.

In the following text, there is an attempt to analyse the basic trends of higher educational policies, and developments which have both fed from, and into, the sociological changes that have pervaded the Algerian social formation, leading up to the emergence of a variegated civil society, facing an otherwise monolithic neo-patrimonial technocratic state.

The basic remark to be made about the higher education system in Algeria is whether it has evolved from a device of situational patterns in terms of social mobility and positioning of various social groups in a post-colonial dependent social formation, into a system of social reproduction of a more established nature. Discerning between the two is significant in terms of interpreting the present crisis, and locating the present state of play on the evaluation of the higher education system.

In addition to being structural and economic, the crisis in Algeria is a crisis of the system itself. It is above all a legitimation crisis, and a look at the higher educational process can help gauge the nature and extent of the crisis. Hence an attempt is made here to interpret the Algerian higher educational system as caught between its prime function of social reproduction within a problematic of new nation-state construction, and the retrospective pangs of an emerging civil society. By this latter expression, reference is made to the various claims, be they political or ideological, which stood up to and disturbed the monolithism of the state in Algeria.

4

State education as Frankenstein's son

In the aftermath of independence in 1962, educational policy formulation and implementation were to become the sole prerogative of the state. All the paraphernalia of the international discourse of Universal Primary Education (UPE) and the 'catch up' developmentalist obsession was eagerly adopted by the new authorities.

This was to mark the political and educational options. Despite a facade of revolutionism and nationalism, various schools of thought were to enter into incessant rifts, within the political nomenclature, or the intellectual groups or the administrative apparatus. Roughly, the ideational and social composition of the national movement on the eve of independence included a French educated military and political elite, an Arabophone nationalist elite mainly active in the ideological apparatus, and finally the natural heirs of the previous colonial administration embodied in a bureaucracy well trained in the best French traditions of Cartesian hierarchy. These groupings were to remain as players well after independence.

The implications of this composition of the elites meant in educational terms the adoption of a centralized educational organization, inherited from the French *école* and *lycée* up to the early 1970s, with a staggering financial burden ranging between 27 per cent and 30 per cent of the state budget. The period between 1963 and 1972 was dominated by the French educated with a clear leftist tendency. Hence the emphasis on the democratization of education, and the idea of self-management (of workers and peasants) in the economic arena.

However, this populist influence, while inspiring policies and programmes at the level of primary and secondary education, did not hold sway in the tertiary cycle. Indeed, despite early revolutionary euphoria, the French educated academics at the University of Algiers did not particularly welcome growing demands for Arabization by their Arab-educated colleagues.

A latent battle took place during this period between the Francophone Algerian professors, especially in the humanities, and Arabophone newcomers trained in Middle Eastern religious and secular centres of higher learning. The most interesting clash opposed Algerian teachers of Arabic language and literature trained in the French 'Orientalist' tradition of the *Bureaux Arabes* and the *Franco-Muslim Lycée*, and a monolingual Arab diaspora imbued with the 'oriental' learning traditions of Jami' al-Zeituna in Tunis, al-Azhar in Cairo and the more modern universities of Damascus and Baghdad. This eclectism in the educational field is but a natural corollary of the more comprehensive political and ideological option based on an ambivalent discourse purporting to bring together the local and the universal, the religious and the secular, the modern and the traditional so as to build the Algerian ideal city, strongly marked by the 1960s syndrome of developmentalism. All official documents and rhetoric have chanted the merits of this eclectism, remaining deaf to the stomping fury of the growing fundamentalist claim whose legitimacy was already embedded in the official discourse. Indeed, Islam has always been proclaimed the religion of state and the basic reference of Algeria's value system.

However, contrary to the widely held belief which ascribes to this latter group a cultural homogeneity, it is worth noting that they were separated by conflicting influences, still at play in the Arab world. These conflicting influences included the religious reformist legacy of higher religious learning inherited from the Arab Renaissance thinking which thrived at the end of the nineteenth century, and the more secular ideological discourse of Baathism as the epitome of Arab nationalist ideology as this developed in the early twentieth century. The first rejected Ottoman domination, while the second went a step further in rejecting Western occupation.

In the interplay of the above mentioned legacies in the field of higher education in Algeria, there was a dominant tendency to attempt to incorporate all of them, in the names of national unity and supreme state interest, especially during the 'reign' of the late President Boumediene (1965–78), when the technocratic elite had triumphed, making state construction a priority.

To serve this 'sacred' task in the terms of Boumediene, the educational system, especially in its higher levels, had to produce a 'technically and scientifically minded individual, open to universal knowledge', none the less connected to the Arab-Islamic cultural heritage.

However, while the techno-scientific dream was coming true with the promulgation in 1972 of a cardinal text, *La Réforme de l'Enseignement Superieure* (The Reform of Higher Education), two groups within academia were discontented. The Francophone school opposed the lifting of selective devices, warning against the dangers of mediocrity likely to affect the quality of educational services and content, and the Arabophones naturally felt discarded by the priority given to fields of learning taught primarily in French.

The first group felt nostalgic about the loss of the encyclopedic tradition of *culture générale* and the prestige of Cartesian training of which Algiers University was a part under the colonial administration. The second group warned against the 'second-class citizen' status likely to affect Arab educated students, mostly in the humanities. In fact, serious clashes had occurred in the early 1970s. Boumediene had tried to discard left-wing Francophone students imbued with the Marxian influence of their teachers by launching an extensive Arabization programme to be generalized to all social and human sciences. Clashes occurred between the left-wing students and those advocating an Arabization programme.

However, in addition to a quick and efficient repression of the left-wingers, cooptation was swift to arrive. The student movement of

Marxian perspective was incorporated in the support for another populist policy, that of the 'Agrarian Revolution' where they could pursue the idea, perhaps the illusion, of making Algeria's 'wretched of the earth' unite and take over power some day. Equally, however, the growing fierceness of the Arabophones was well domesticated through their participation in the administrative and legal arenas, with an extensive Arabization of legal studies and proceedings.

Social control vs quality control

One of the unmistakable manifestations of the delegitimation process was youths taking to the streets in October 1988, shouting slogans against the apparatchiks and all the state nomenclature, demanding the creation of a more 'egalitarian' system. The vast majority of protestors were aged between 15 and 25, and the official ideology they bitterly denounced was that of 'specific socialism', itself supposed to create 'egalitarianism'.

In the aftermath of the 1988 protests, the state initiated a process of economic liberalization and political democratization, just as it initiated policies of economic centralism, and 'educational democratization' following the gaining of independence from a no less centralist colonizer in the early 1960s.

The general educational options stemmed, as indicated earlier, from the international discourse of the democratization of education in vogue since the late 1950s but within a double problematic of the Cold War and the expansion of the capitalist system worldwide, as well as from the nature of postindependent nation-state formation with its inescapable dynamics of state controlled socialization, best insured through the educational process.

In Algeria, the newly independent state was to erect itself as the exclusive provider of educational services. Better, it was to give birth to an educational system – free and widely distributed – entrusting it with the 'sacred mission' of forming the ideal literate citizen imbued with values of 'rationalism, scientificity, and openess to universal knowledge' but none the less within the limits of the local cultural legacy, usually designated Arab-Islamic. This is not merely rhetoric. Serious efforts at institutionalization of local culture were made.

The *Bureaux Arabes* were implanted throughout Algeria at the end of the nineteenth century with a specific mission: that of establishing a consensus of the 'native muslim' population with its ethnic and tribal configuration. They were usually run by young academics and ethnologists who were trained in Arabic. For instance, Jacques Berque was head of a bureau in the 1930s. As for the *Lycée Franco-Musulman* they were roughly established around the same period, and were to train the administrative and intellectual elite of Algerian origin. Bilingualism was an essential feature of the institution, although Arabic was taught along translation lines, and French used as the main reference.

In higher education, the emphasis on the provision of scientific and technical knowledge neared that of an obsession, to the extent that almost all investment went into the construction of Universities of Sciences and Techniques in the major cities of the country as from the early 1970s. This is the period during which the state in Algeria came close to creating a monster by expanding the educational system as a whole, and the higher levels in particular.

Indeed, in addition to the formidable quantitative expansion at this level, purposefully non-elitist and non-selective, the formulators of higher educational policies in Algeria were determined to prove that through political will, a whole new society could emerge and provide convergence between a universal scientific legacy and local learning traditions. Hence the encyclopedic nature of curricula, and the rapid expansion of institutions of religious higher learning. These latter were granted as a token of the authorities' allegiance to the dominant Arab-Islamic component of Algeria's political and social culture.

One end result was the establishment of a dual higher educational system with schizophrenic underpinnings, dispensing modern sciences and techniques in French as the dominant foreign language in Algeria on the one hand, and all the spectrum of humanities, social sciences and religious sciences in standard Arabic, on the other. Attempts at 'Arabizing' some sciences, either gradually or fully, have by and large been mere exercises of political and ideological rhetoric aimed at curbing growing demands by an emerging Arabophone elite, rather than serious enterprises aimed at testing Arabic as a scientific vernacular.

The other end result was the training of a bicephalous university elite, later joined by a third group of PhD holders trained in various European (mainly former Soviet bloc) and American universities. However, the historic monopoly of the French educated of mobility within the sphere of higher education meant that the newcomers were not welcome as additions to processes of knowledge creation and reproduction in Algeria. As the French educated elite lost control over the direct channels of reproduction in the classroom, at least in the social and human sciences, the Francophone elite slowed down the mobility of PhD holders in academic promotion by blocking the granting of the so-called 'equivalence' of the Doctorat d'Etat. This situation prevailed until the late 1980s and dealt a serious blow to the state of scientific research in the country. In substance, French educated academics placed themselves as 'mandarins' over their colleagues from the Anglo-Saxon, Soviet and Arab universities, thus monopolizing definitions over 'quality control'. This situation has led in many cases to brain-drain phenomena in Algeria. Indeed some PhD holders from prestigious universities in the UK or the USA have had to wait for up to eight years to be recognized as Docteur d'Etat, while French doctorate holders were immediately granted the equivalence regardless of the reputation of their university. One of the most striking developments, in terms of attitudinal and behavioural patterns in Algerian academia, is postgraduate degree holders waiting at the Ministry of Higher Education trying to have an interview with the Directors of various departments in order to put forward their cases. The cost in research time was considerable.

It was through such processes that there was a metamorphosis of quality control into social control. However, the wheel of power was bound to turn in this most Khaldunian pattern of rapid albeit circular social change. Indeed, the violence of the civil war, and the nature of the main power contestant, namely religious fundamentalism, have caused a massive departure of Francophone professors and associate professors. Most of the assassinations of academics have been of persons in this category. The ensuing brain drain is unprecedented. Nearly 10,000 academics of doctoral rank (including medical doctors) have left Algeria in the last three years.

The early investments in the quantitative dimension of the educational system in general and the higher levels in particular, as well as the all too rapid training in the sciences and technological arenas launched in the 1970s, have come up with unexpected results. In a deeply egalitarian-oriented population, the appearance of new social categories, with disparate ideational and cultural references, was not internalized that deeply. The fact that the bulk of the followers of the fundamentalist claim are aged under 30 – which corresponds with 70 per cent of Algeria's population being aged under 30 – should be taken into account.

By dwelling on various traditions of cultural reference in their bid to construct a new individual and a new society, nation-state builders in Algeria have inadvertently caused the demise of their own legitimation devices. The return of Frankenstein's eclectic creature was bound to happen. The son of Frankenstein was by then fully formed, and before rebelling against its mental genitor, the creature's estranged organs started turning against each other. Serious clashes were reported in the mid-1970s between advocates of Arabization, usually of nationalist or Baathist obedience, and Francophone students of Berberist or leftist allegiance. The authorities crackdown fell on *both*, before subtly coopting *both* within populist measures, such as those indicated earlier: attracting left-wingers in the implementation of the 1972 agrarian reform, and associating the Arabophone nationalists in the Arabization of the primary and secondary educational cycles, as well as incorporating them in the administrative and legal arenas.

The return of Frankeinstein's son

By the end of the 1980s, higher educational institutions held nearly 182,000 students, and by the academic year 1992–93 the count was well over 240,000, of whom one third were enrolled in the exact sciences, technology and medical studies, respectively 17,655, 98,958, and 21,564, from a total national population of 27 million.

This evolution is not only staggering as higher education had numbered a mere 2,000 students in a national population of 10 million in 1962, but it also reflects the expedient nature of erstwhile populist political decisions, which had heavily invested in the educational process not only as a 'technical' training mechanism, but above all as social control. The more recent attempts at introducing more selective mechanisms in the early 1990s have met with staunch resistance by student unions of all disciplines, regardless of their political allegiance. In 1993 and 1994 the Ministry of Higher Education suggested that a system of elimination based on a minimum grading should be introduced, in addition to opening short cycle training of not more than three years to train higher technicians. While the second proposal was implemented, the first one was bluntly rejected by student unions who denounced it as being 'anti-democratic and anti-egalitarian'. Thus selection was accepted in terms of creating new social categories albeit of a subaltern nature, but not the blocking of higher education access to lower social groups.

The student union movement led a vast campaign in the spring of 1994 in order to oppose the new system of selection, brandishing the spectre of a general strike, the last thing the ministry wanted in these times of social unrest. The Minister of Higher Education in person promised that no major action would be taken without consulting the students.

University deans do admit in private that the main function of higher education institutions has become mainly that of social control. In order to avoid student unrest, word has gone to department heads throughout the country that wastage should be reduced to a minimum. On the other hand, an overloaded system of evaluation, (up to eight exams a year) bearing the sophisticated label of 'knowledge evaluation', has led teachers to inflate the success rate simply to avoid harrassment from students who have acquired the reflexes of a political pressure group, rather than those of consumers of a service.

In order to understand how such reflexes have developed amongst university youth, it is worth considering previous population control policies of the 1960s and 1970s which discouraged family planning. This has led to an exceptional increase of the resident population, from 12 million in 1966 to 23 million in 1987. The population growth rate reached a maximum of 3.21 per cent between 1966 and 1977, leading to a demographic configuration in a remarkable pyramid, with 70 per cent of the population aged under 30 in 1977, and 72 per cent aged under 30 in 1987.

In the late 1970s, such a pyramid could not but become the tomb of the Pharaoh, embodied in the charismatic leadership of late Colonel Boumediene who had imprinted the power structure with his grandiose vision of a young, vigorous, scientifically minded nation, marching toward the socialist millenium. Indeed, his death in December 1978 ignited the first legitimation crisis of the monolithic political regime, when timid whispers of economic liberalization started, only to be surpassed ten years later by louder shouts of discontented youth in unprecedented demonstrations throughout Algeria's major cities. In order to coopt traditional and religious opinion showing unrest with respect to the apparent secular content of educational programmes, the technocratic team in power under the late Colonel Boumediene in the 1970s decided to build centres of religious higher education in major cities of the country. The most well-known is the University of Islamic Sciences of Constantine, East Algeria, where a long tradition of reformist scripturalist thought thrived, initiated by Sheikh Abdelhamid Ibn Badis, himself a product of the nineteenth century Arab Renaissance movement. In 1992–93, national enrolment in Islamic sciences totalled 3,283 students.

In October 1988, hordes of young people took to the streets seemingly in protest against the political regime of the one-party state. They were the first riots of significant magnitude, which triggered off the democratization of political expression in the country. Previous contestations were confined to the spheres of professional and intellectual elites, be they of Islamist discipline, or feminist claims which had both been easily repressed in the early 1980s (Cheriet, 1992). Indeed, following the riots of October 1988, the bulk of arrested protestors were not activists of opposition political parties, but youngsters, most of whom were attending lycées and colleges, who were the future university cohorts.

Meanwhile, in the universities, students and lecturers organized according to allegiances that were seemingly new to the Algerian political and ideological scene. For the first time in almost three decades of independence, all allegiances were openly expressed, and there was a significant newcomer: the religious fundamentalist claim. Going a step further in their demand for an 'alternative' to the one-party nationalist state, they advocated the Islamic Republic as 'salvation' from all previous sins of what they denounced as the secular Republic, warning that the establishment of democracy was no less dangerous, precisely because of its secularism.

On the other hand, the Berberist leftist trend, which advocated a fully fledged democratic system based on the modern Republican model as 'the alternative', was also out in the open. The fundamentalist claim is primarily based on the ideal city of scipturalist orthodox Islam as a political discourse, and not as religious injunctions. The motto of 'the Islamic Alternative', *al-badeel al islami*, was clearly issued as a caveat against any other conception of political organizing, especially that with a secular coloration. Represented by a spectrum of parties and civilian associations, whose members were by and large products of the higher educational system, this group took a clearly confrontational stance towards the fundamentalist one, and while this latter addressed itself both in colloquial and literary Arabic to largely Arabized student and youth audiences, the first addressed the professionals and Francophone students, often using French as a vernacular. However, one has to handle this linguistic peculiarity with care, as it does not automatically infer a corresponding ideational configuration of political allegiances in Algerian universities.

According to the earlier classification of the student population of the late 1960s and 1970s, the natural heirs of the late 1980s and early 1990s should have emerged in the following manner:

- a largely Arabophone, literary-oriented fundamentalist option recalling a golden Islamic era, and purporting to revive it in the form of a puritan Islamic millenium,
- a 'Republicanist', democratically inclined Francophone option, imbued with the ideal of the universal millenium, clearly informed by Occidental enlightenment philosophies.

Nothing as predetermined has actually taken place. Whereas the democratic student movement invariably attracted Berberists and leftists of both Arab and French expression, mostly from the humanities, the Islamist groups gathered a substantial number of Francophone students trained in the scientific and technological higher education centres of the country. Of great significance is the fact that the cohorts aged between 19 and 24, which form the bulk of the graduate population, are mostly Arabophone in view of their totally Arabized training in the secondary cycle. Of no less significance is the educational background of Islamist activists, especially at the level of leadership which tends to be filled with students in medical studies and in physics. Thus the bicephalous educated elite has gone beyond the initial linguistic division to include a more subtle and complex expression of political and ideological plurality, as part and parcel of an emerging civil society in Algeria.

The reproductive dream of the technocratic elite in power, aimed at coopting all factions of the student population seems to have evaporated. In its place is a regressive retrospective assessment of the developmental millenium. An important transition point, among many, was 1986.

The acute economic crisis following the 1986 fall in oil prices deeply affected investments in various capital-oriented industries. It also seriously jeopardized the employment prospects of an increasingly qualified work force produced by the institutions of higher education, and ignited the legitimation crisis. In terms of employment, the national occupation rate averages a mere 20 per cent, which is remarkable in view of the exceptional youth of the country's population, their lengthy schooling and a very low rate of female employment, ranging between 6 per cent and 9 per cent.

In 1991–92 national figures released by the *Office National des*

Statistiques disclosed a university graduate population of 30,615, facing a depressed job market. Whereas in the 1970s and 1980s unemployment exclusively involved illiterate or poorly educated persons, in 1989 an unemployment rate of about 3 per cent was reported among higher education degree holders.

In retrospect, the higher educational system in Algeria has inadvertently led to the return of Frankenstein's son in the shape of more crisp and unambiguous political expressions of civil autonomy, and the demand for new millenia by a very young population. What is left to be done now is how to endow Algeria's social implosion with reflexes of systemic reproduction. The outcomes of the civil war will tell. In this context, evaluation styles of the kind visible in the USA or England are impossible.

References

Cheriet, B (1992) 'Islamism and Feminism: Algeria's Rites of Passage to Democracy', in Entelis, J and Naylor, P (eds) *State and Society in Algeria*, Boulder Colorado: Westview Press, pp 171–215.

Office National des Statistiques (ONS) (1994) *Annuaire Statistique de l'Algerie*, Alger: Imprimerie de l'Office.

3. The evaluation of the higher education system in Australia

Barry Sheehan

Introduction

The higher education system in Australia was established with the foundation of the University of Sydney in 1850, followed by the University of Melbourne in 1853. By 1913 each Australian state had a major metropolitan university based loosely on either the Oxbridge or the Dublin model. The Australian National University was established, at first under the sponsorship of the University of Melbourne, in 1946.

Up to that time only a small proportion of the age cohort successfully completed academic secondary schooling and a smaller proportion again matriculated and could afford the tuition and living expenses associated with a university education. Most were destined by virtue of their socio-economic status as well as by their education for careers in the professions or as industry professionals, or in the higher echelons of the commercial sector.

Many of the remainder of the age cohort educated beyond (or parallel with) the upper years of the secondary school, either academic or technical, went on to take an ever-expanding range of courses in a growing system of technical colleges, some of which achieved notably high status. The New South Wales Institute of Technology, for example, grew from technical college antecedents to be styled a university in 1949 and became the University of New South Wales in 1958.

Following World War II, a confluence of factors led to the establishment of a number of new universities. Educational initiatives to both absorb and cater for the vocational needs of thousands of returned ex-service personnel led to a rapid expansion and change in the student profile of the established universities. The baby boom following the war, together with the heightened educational expectations which went with economic prosperity and the accelerating growth in knowledge, led to the largely unanticipated and massive growth in schooling systems and to a heightened demand for secondary teachers, which in turn impacted on the university system. With the progressive

14

assumption of responsibility for the funding of higher education by the Commonwealth Government, these circumstances combined to create a climate in which the establishment and rapid growth of new institutions of higher learning became inevitable.

By the mid-1970s, the seven established capital city universities (including ANU) had been joined by a further 12 universities, all founded since 1946. Of these, seven were metropolitan universities, while the remaining five were set up in provincial cities. In addition, a binary system was formally established which included under the Commonwealth higher education funding schedule a system of degree-granting colleges. Some of these with technical antecedents generally became known as Institutes of Technology, and others formed from teachers' colleges; for them teacher education remained the chief focus. Other mono-purpose colleges served fields such as agriculture, pharmacy, visual and performing arts and, in some states, various branches of the health sciences. A number of new colleges were established in regional centres and, while they had broader course profiles, they focused chiefly on teacher education to provide teachers to meet the next anticipated wave of expansion in the school-age group.

In the early 1970s, the Commonwealth Government initiated a major consolidation, particularly of former teachers' colleges, and considerably reduced the number of small colleges in the system. After this consolidation there remained 17 universities, a few of which had amalgamated with contiguously located teachers' colleges, and almost 70 colleges, newly styled as Colleges of Advanced Education (CAEs), funded by the Commonwealth Government. A decade later the Commonwealth again initiated a push to reduce the number of small CAEs and by 1983, chiefly as a result of mergers, the numbers of CAEs had been reduced by some 30 per cent, to 47 colleges.

The next wave of major structural reform of the higher education system occurred in the late 1980s, when the Commonwealth Government again determined to embark on a programme of institutional amalgamations. Because education institutions in both the university and advanced education sectors fell within the constitutional control of State Governments, although funded by the Commonwealth, an extraordinary variety of outcomes emerged. Notably, the original metropolitan universities were involved in amalgamations, not with other universities (although some such amalgamations were seriously contemplated), but with colleges. While some amalgamations were structured in such a way that they could, if necessary, be dismantled, there is no question that, at the end of the process (which has only just been completed), the structure of the higher education system in Australia had been transformed — some argue destroyed — by the reforms of the former Minister, John Dawkins. Of the 59 institutions extant in 1987, there were 37, almost all styled 'university', in 1994. These 37 institutions constitute the Australian Unified National System which, together with two small private universities and three colleges, comprise the 'higher education system'.

A third tier of partly Commonwealth-funded post-secondary education expanded rapidly in the 1970s. This is the large Technical and Further Education (TAFE) system. While some TAFE activities are now structurally located in a number of universities (even the older ones) as a result of amalgamations with CAEs which had TAFE functions, TAFE is not regarded as 'higher education'. In a number of countries all post-secondary education is defined as higher education, whereas in terminology which is somewhat peculiar to Australia, the combined higher education and TAFE sector there is generally described as 'tertiary education'.

Traditional conceptions of excellence in the Australian higher education system

Higher education institutions – originally the six metropolitan universities – in Australia have always been concerned about a subset of quality, generally referred to as 'standards'. The refinement of the concept of quality in higher education is, of course, a recent phenomenon. The original professorate in most of these universities brought with it the conception of a standard of excellence established in the older British universities from which it came. There is little evidence that these professors made significant academic concessions to the culturally starved environment of their colonial students. Certainly, the quality of the first and upper second was of major importance to the professorate and appears to have been maintained.

Prior to the post-war expansion period, the growth of staff numbers in the charge of the professorate was through a tightly controlled apprenticeship system in which the values and norms of the traditional universities were well learned by acolytes who gradually worked their way up the academic hierarchy, with some notable indigenous achievers gaining chairs. The academic acculturation system thus worked in very much the same way as in the United Kingdom and Western Europe:

> [The] structure [was] inherently hierarchical... based on a system of patronage in which members of the non-professional class remained highly dependent on individual chairholders not merely for admission into academia but also for advancement once inside.
>
> ... In a stable academic ecology [non-professorial posts] had been a species of protracted apprenticeships that, with the fullness of time and suitable backing, would lead to professorial status... Socialization into academia.... took place through a master apprentice relationship (Neave and Rhoades, 1987: 211–12).

This acculturation system arguably served to perpetuate the standard of the good British first as a kind of 'absolute' yardstick in Australia. The single acceptable dimension of quality measurement resided in comparability with the British academic 'gold standard'. It is notable, however, that the English practice of using external examiners at the undergraduate course level to legitimate these standards has never gained favour in Australian universities, at least partly because of the tyranny of distance and the costs associated with it. Rather, a generous sabbatical leave scheme ensured that academics in Australia could maintain their international perspective. Only with the post-war explosion of the university student and staff population described above did the traditional system of what passed for quality control began to falter.

Again, the developing situation was not altogether unlike that in Western Europe. Neave and Rhoades argue that a deep rift between junior and senior staff began to emerge in Western Europe during the period of rapid growth, but that it was not so evident in the United Kingdom and the United States; although staff below the level of professor and reader did not spawn 'polarised groups of academics that separately represent their interests within or outside the academy'. Neave and Rhoades' analysis of the changing situation in Western Europe also largely characterizes the shift in Australia:

> The demographic explosion of the early 1960s coupled with the runaway demand for higher education exposed and exacerbated these underlying tensions. The rising tide of new students heightened tensions in two ways: it increased the teaching load borne by non-professorial staff ... and it unbalanced the 'ecology of academia' by the rapid growth in that same staff, brought in to teach the ever-rising influx of students. If chairholders still wielded power and influence, expansion in the lower ranks placed a severe strain on their patronage networks. And, no less important in moulding the expectations of younger academics, non-professorial positions expanded far faster than the professorial posts to which many had aspired. Expansion also profoundly changed non-professorial posts ... When the ecological balance was upset ... a new sub-class began to assume a permanent status and the traditional process of socialisation into academia became strained (Neave and Rhoades, 1987: 212).

In the early 1950s a significant and increasing number of bright young graduates from Australian universities looked towards North America rather than the UK for postgraduate opportunities. Many were assisted by the Fulbright scheme which, probably more than any other single factor, led to a change of international focus in Australian academia. This broader internationalization brought with it a new consciousness that there were 'other ways' of doing things — other ways which are still denigrated by some in the Australian higher education system as being of North American origin and therefore inappropriate in the Australian context.

Further, in the newer Australian universities in particular, significant numbers of staff allied themselves with radical causes during the period of student activism in the late 1960s to bring pressure on their universities to be more democratic, more egalitarian in outlook and to make their offerings more relevant and accessible. Even in situations where these pressures were for the most part resisted, there was a detectable shift in the attitude of junior staff, not least towards the professorate, some members of which were identified as 'entrenched obstacles to change'. The 'standards' applied by relatively new honours or postgraduate appointees, former school teachers and academic staff recruited from many countries to satisfy the rapid growth in student numbers, may have been valid in their own terms, but were certainly different from those upheld by the fully acculturated professorate of earlier years as described above.

Thus, with the rapid expansion of the higher education system in the post-war period, close adherence to the imported British standard shifted markedly, although allegiance continued to be given by all universities to notional 'international' standards. New staff appointed in increasing numbers to new universities, where the professorate was for the most part drawn from the older universities, were difficult to acculturate in the time-honoured manner. They had not served the traditional apprentice-ship to a professor and, in any event, came in large numbers from a different socio-economic background and with different political and educational attitudes which questioned many of the verities. Staffing the education enterprise at all levels also became a major vehicle for social mobility. Inherited notions of undergraduate standards, while still cherished by the established professorate in the older universities and many of their former apprentices in the new, inevitably lost their primacy in a new and expanded system.

The 'value-added' argument which began to emerge in higher education during this period was not a matter of concern to the well-established universities which could rely on an intake of good students (as assessed in the final year of schooling by Year 12 results, variously measured and named). The newer universities and the better colleges generally drew from the next lower echelon of students, with obvious overlap. In some areas the overlap was notable, however, in that some departments in colleges and newer universities developed a reputation for quality and attracted very high calibre undergraduate students, while some departments in established universities had weaker drawing power. Thus, there was clearly developing in Australian higher education a system not only of apex institutions as determined by the demand for entry from high quality students at all levels, but also apex departments, some of which stand out in institutions which may be described either as being of lower quality, or as having a different mission and objectives related to access rather than excellence, depending largely on the view of the observer. Among the observers are the various markets for the services of higher education. The emergence of the application of economic concepts such as 'value added' to higher education was the first clear signal that the traditional single 'output standard', which the international debates about the aggregate and individual economic value of higher education during the 1960s and 1970s had done little to diminish, was being subtly overtaken by broader concerns and that the quality debate was beginning to accelerate.

Although external examiners on the English model have rarely been used in Australian universities, in a number of fields — initially medicine and law — professional entry criteria imposed requirements on the university to meet demands about content and, at least implicitly, standards of performance acceptable to bodies external to the university. Over time, the professional entry requirements were formalized through systematic accreditation processes which are now applied at various levels in, among other disciplines, medicine, dentistry, law, engineering, architecture, accountancy and veterinary science. In this respect, the pattern in Australia resembles that in the UK. In addition, some universities have used external people in departmental reviews and, on occasion, to assist in the process of reviewing the future of a vacant chair or to consider the need to establish a chair in a new field.

In the former 'advanced education sector', on the other hand, which offered degrees which were 'equal but different' from those of the universities, and which were under significant control at the state level, courses were externally accredited for fixed periods. The structure and content of courses were approved by accreditation committees, normally with membership drawn from the college and from other institutions and from the professions served by the college, with recommendations being made to a state accrediting body. The committees usually examined documentary course and subject materials, discussed the course with relevant senior academic staff, and discussed the performance of the course, or any course which was being replaced, with students and former students. An accreditation 'industry' developed which made an impact at the broader institutional level but rarely appeared to have significant influence on what went on in lecture theatres, laboratories and tutorial rooms. Accreditation committees, while they almost invariably made recommendations on such things, had no power over resource allocation, the quality of staffing or the standard of the output. Even as an input model, therefore, accreditation boards were deficient in practice.

The pre-1987 universities (that is, those in existence before the wave of amalgamations in the wake of the Dawkins reforms) for the most part escaped state control over course content and structure, despite the state having constitutional responsibility for all education. Certainly, the universities required approval for the introduction of new courses, but the concern of the state authorities was not so much with the structure or content or standards of the course as with resource implications, potential duplication with other institutions, course length and likely demand for the graduate output of the proposed course.

In any event, 'standards' or 'quality' appear rarely to have been at issue. Thus, although the system was largely self-regulating in terms of standards — for the universities there were no accreditation requirements, no external examiners at the undergraduate level, no inspectorate — there continued to be an underlying and often explicit concern with the maintenance of 'international' standards operating through appeal to a shared understanding as to an invisible benchmark which was part of the mystique of the community of scholars. At the graduate level in the pre-war years it was normal for Masters theses to be examined by a least one scholar external to the university of the supervisor. The first doctorate to be awarded by an Australian university (The University of Melbourne) was conferred in 1947 and, as the research degree was becoming established, given the lack of research experience in Australian universities, it was common for at least one international external scholar to act as examiner. It is significant that, as the Australian Government began to establish and develop the scientific research base of the nation in the 1920s and 1930s, it did not turn to the universities for delivery of research. Rather, it sought the advice of eminent university people in setting up the Commonwealth Scientific and Industrial Research Organization (CSIRO).

The colleges and new universities which entered the system after the war appealed to some of the traditions of the older universities but, as indicated above, these were significantly diluted by attitudes within institutions which, quite apart from their different staffing mix, were created to ensure wider access to higher education and to increase participation rates from particular geographical areas and socio-economic groups. In some of these institutions, the term 'excellence' was (and is) associated with social and intellectual elitism and is rejected as embodying an unacceptable social concept. Even in the oldest universities there is ambivalence about the social connotations of a continuing push for 'excellence', or at least with the use of that word. The term has, however, been subtly redefined to refer not so much to the excellence of character, intellect, virtue and, implicitly, the social standing of the student, as the value-added excellence of the subjects, courses, teaching and research performance of the institution and its component parts. Not all observers of the system, however, have kept pace with this shift of meaning and continue to assert that those who strive for excellence and to maximize the intellectual gains for the student are, in fact, simply striving to reproduce the system of social and economic superiority. In addition, an area of contention developed around the standards (or standards of quality) to be required for disciplines such as languages as a 'beginners' subject at university level and of the emergent multidisciplinary teaching and research fields such as women's studies, ethnic studies, environmental studies, Asian studies and the like which, for the most part, developed initially in the newer institutions.

Emergent styles of evaluation and management

'Hallo!' said Piglet, 'what are *you* doing?'
'Hunting,' said Pooh.
'Hunting what?'
'Tracking something,' said Winnie-the-Pooh very mysteriously.
'Tracking what?' said Piglet, coming closer.
'That's just what I ask myself. I ask myself, What?'
'What do you think you'll answer?'
'I shall have to wait until I catch up with it,' said Winnie-the-Pooh.
(Milne, 1946:34)

While the older universities in Australia had a good deal of confidence in their perceptions of their own standards, and the newer universities and colleges promoted their perceived standards with vigour, the question of standards as a national policy issue began to emerge strongly only as the real per capita funding for students in Australian higher education declined steadily (by 11.8 per cent between 1983 and 1991) following an earlier period of severe constraint.

As the Vice-Chancellors, College Directors and Principals and the academic community at large became increasingly vocal about the threat to standards posed by cumulative underfunding, the Commonwealth became increasingly concerned about ensuring value for money and increasingly challenged the quality of what universities did with the funding they received and began setting about tightening things up. The theme of 'efficiency and effectiveness' came to underpin most government reviews, policy changes and structural reforms in higher education. In 1977 the separate Commonwealth funding bodies (for Universities, Advanced Education and TAFE) were amalgamated into the Commonwealth Tertiary Education Commission (CTEC), and within five years the reduction in the number of CAEs by one-third, as described above, had occurred. Between 1982 and 1987 higher education enrolments rose by 15.5 per cent while real operating grants rose by only 7.5 per cent. Soon after the Jarrat Report (1985) appeared in the United Kingdom, the Australian Government requested the CTEC to: 'initiate an enquiry into ways of improving the efficiency and effectiveness of the higher education sector' (CTEC, 1986:xv).

Prior to the efficiency and effectiveness reference, the CTEC embarked on a further initiative by commissioning Discipline Reviews. The first of several to be carried out in the second half of the 1980s was a review of the 12 university-based law schools which existed at the time. This was followed by a review of the nation's university engineering schools, accounting, and teacher education in mathematics and science respectively. The discipline reviews adopted comparative techniques and implicit notions of bench-marking. They were short lived, chiefly because they were extremely expensive to mount, but were seen by CTEC to be an essential part of the accountability process aimed at ensuring standards while eliminating waste and unnecessary duplication. The discipline reviews were clearly the forerunners of the institutional quality reviews introduced in the first half of the 1990s.

The first major explicit policy focus on quality issues *per se* in Australian education, however, was at the school level. The Report of the Quality of Education Review Committee (1985) on *Quality of Education in Australia*, known as the QUERC Report, was issued just before a major summit on taxation, thus ensuring that it would be quickly obscured. A clear agenda for the Review was to provide guidance on how Commonwealth funding to schools should be shared, although, at the formal level, the enquiry was directed towards achieving a higher quality of education in primary and secondary schools.

It was the report of the *Efficiency and Effectiveness Review* (CTEC, 1986), which followed QUERC, which provided the initial stimulus for a massive upheaval in Australian higher education. The Review distinguished between efficiency and effectiveness in the following terms:

> An efficient system is one which enables given outputs to be met at the lowest possible level of inputs or cost. However a system which is efficient in this sense will not be worth much if what is achieved is only of limited value. Hence, the effectiveness of a system − the extent to which the output achieves specified objectives − is also important. The phrase 'efficient and effective' is thus used to mean the achievement of the best, or most desired, outcome as economically as possible (CTEC, 1986:1).

The Review acknowledged that there is a wide variety of objectives in higher education, both within institutions and between them, and given this variety, 'it follows that there are rarely any simple criteria for measuring success in achieving objectives' (CTEC, 1986:2).

Issues of what should be measured and the time-scale accorded to such measurements were seen as major obstacles to assessment for both education and research:

> The operations of higher education institutions are not always amenable to detailed statistical and financial analyses, even assuming that necessary data are always available (CTEC, 1986:3).

The Review favoured an approach designed to change the climate in Australian higher education institutions so that, 'systematic evaluation of performance and assessment of quality can become routine activities' (CTEC, 1986:263) on the basis that:

> procedures for self-evaluation which are established voluntarily, and assume a professional approach to their task on the part of

academics, will be more effective in maintaining and improving the standards of academic activity than those which are the result of external pressure (CTEC, 1986:263).

The Minister of Employment, Education and Training, raised major questions about the *Review of Efficiency and Effectiveness*. While he thought it highlighted many of the major issues, it was also apparent that he believed the Review pursued soft options in its recommendations. Mr Dawkins abolished the CTEC in 1987 and set up a structure of Councils within the framework of a National Board of Employment, Education and Training (NBEET) and his Ministry, making higher education much more susceptible to ministerial involvement in both policy and operational matters and removing ministerial action from the likelihood of close parliamentary scrutiny. The Minister then took up the issues as he saw them in his Green Paper in December of the same year (Dawkins, 1987).

Mr Dawkins was committed to a resource allocation process which would focus increasingly on assessment of overall institutional performance in the context of promoting further growth in the higher education system and improving the 'nature and quality' (Dawkins 1987: 3) of higher education while simultaneously increasing access for disadvantaged groups. He saw the universities as ossified bodies offering ingrained resistance to change and indicated that the government:

has a responsibility to co-ordinate the national system of higher education effectively so that scarce resources are applied to their best effect at the institutional level (Dawkins, 1987: 47).

Dawkins established a new approach to the negotiation of educational profiles between higher eduction institutions and the Commonwealth, with an increasing focus on strategic planning and evaluation of performance.

These themes were taken up in the subsequent White Paper in July, 1988 (Dawkins, 1988). While the Committees of College Directors and Vice-Chancellors set about a pre-emptive attempt to define a 'soft' set of performance indicators for general application in higher education institutions, the Minister firmly indicated that:

The range of indicators to be developed should cover such issues as student demand and course completion rates, quality of teaching and curriculum design, relative staffing provision and measures of academic staff performance in various aspects of research, publication, consultancy and other professional services. Indicators of performance against equity goals and measures of organisational efficiency should also be included in this process. As soon as practicable, indicators which are agreed to be useful and appropriate will be incorporated into the Commonwealth's general funding arrangements for higher education (Dawkins, 1988:86).

From the first profiling exercise with the institutions in August 1988, the themes of efficiency, effectiveness and performance against the above range of measures, however imprecise, were stressed. It took a further two years, however, for DEET to produce a Report on *Performance Indicators in Higher Education* (1991). And the research group which produced the report confessed only that the range of indicators provided a useful starting point for monitoring institutional performance, backing away from applying quantitative performance indicators as a 'substitute for qualitative judgement', acknowledging them as but one of the sources by which such judgement should be informed (DEET 1991: xiv).

In the meantime, 'quality assurance' measures for research had largely been put in place with a substantial 'clawback' of funds from the then universities which all but eliminated their government-funded discretionary research expenditure and was intended to go some way towards 'levelling the playing field' both between universities and between universities and the institutes of technology, in particular by depositing those funds annually with the restructured Australian Research Council which would distribute the bulk of the funds as competitively-won research grants.

Only a short time before the eventual release of the Performance Indicators Report, the Higher Education Council had been confronted with a Senate Standing Committee Report on Employment, Education and Training, *Priorities for Reform in Higher Education* (Aulich, 1990). The Aulich Report was particularly critical of the quality of teaching and curriculum structure and content in higher education. The Higher Education Council responded by seeking the development of procedures within each institution so that high quality performance of academic staff could be appropriately rewarded, the recognition and rewarding of exceptional performance of senior staff who had reached the point of promotion being no longer available; the development of policies and the allocation of resources for academic staff development, especially in teaching; and by suggesting that the Australian Vice-Chancellor's Committee (AVCC) be invited to join with the HEC to:

> develop methods for assessing teaching quality which can be used within institutions for formal evaluation purposes after modifications to meet local requirements (Aulich, 1990: 19).

In a long-awaited formal response, Mr Peter Baldwin, a new Minister for Higher Education released *Higher Education: Quality and Diversity in the 1990s* (Baldwin, 1991), which suggested that institutions should define their own mission and objectives and assess quality in their own terms: 'The government has no intention of prescribing performance indicators to be used by institutions' (p. 32). But the government also signalled that it would assist institutions to establish and develop management information systems, including quantitative and qualitative indicators of performance. To this end the government sought to encourage and reward good teaching practices with grants of up to $250,000 per institution, with a further $300,000 available for institutional initiatives aimed at enhancing teaching quality. In addition, an independent National Centre for Teaching Excellence was proposed.

More notable, however, was the announced intention to provide $70 million of *additional* funds (about 2 per cent of operating grants) annually from 1994 for a 'quality assurance and enhancement program'. These funds would be allocated, 'in recognition of good performance in the use of all available resources to attain the best quality, including the achievement of equity objectives...' (Baldwin, 1991: 33).

There was also a clear intention, however, to have a national structure 'independent of the government' to report and comment on the application of effectiveness of quality enhancement measures developed by the institutions. In other words, the government was clearly interested in ensuring that the processes for the delivery of quality at the institutional level would be sufficiently responsive to the stimuli provided by government.

The Higher Education Council identified, as an underlying reason for its concern with quality, the general anxiety in the institutions that the foundations of quality higher education may have been shifted as the systems moved from elite to mass higher education. The inability to maintain quality staff, equipment and other facilities led to claims that quality had been impaired (HEC 1992:3).

In February 1992, the Council published a set of discussion papers on the quality of higher education preparatory to the HEC providing formal advice to the Minister on the quality reference later. The Council was asked by the Minister to examine the following aspects of quality in higher education: the characteristics of quality and its diversity; the relative importance of factors affecting quality; the strategies that may be developed by government and the higher education system to encourage, maintain and improve quality; the means by which changes in quality over time may be monitored and evaluated; and the nature of the relationship between resources and the quality of higher education (Baldwin 1991: 59).

The Higher Education Council largely bypassed the question of what is the meaning of quality, acknowledging the difficulty of defining it and pursuing the idea of establishing a framework which would encourage institutions to meet criteria understandable and acceptable to all the stakeholders, and to encourage them to strive for excellence – in Ball's words, to think again about the 'competence and capabilities expected (at their best) of the finest', while accommodating the national need for higher education to be accessible to more of the population than ever before (HEC, 1992). The Council saw the focus on outcome, *fitness for purpose*: 'as fundamental to understanding how each of the processes within institutions are organised and evaluated in order to ensure the quality of the outcome' (HEC, 1992: 6) and,

has ... adopted the following broad principles as the basis for its work:

- the attributes acquired by the graduates provide the ultimate test of the quality of the system to which they have been exposed;
- the judgements about the value of the individual processes that combine to lead to quality outcomes rest with the universities, their faculties or schools and their departments — the internal stakeholders, and to an extent, with the peers; and
- the major criterion to be applied to the judgement of quality of the individual elements of the learning programmes should be linked to the contribution that it makes to the staged development of the students (HEC, 1992:7).

The focus on the outcomes of higher education led the Higher Education Council to define the purpose of the major levels of award (Bachelor, Master and Doctoral); to describe the attributes the graduates should acquire (generic skills, a body of knowledge and professional or other job-related skills); and to assess the balance of attributes that graduates are likely to need. As a second step, the Council was concerned with the processes by which institutions organize opportunities for students to acquire the requisite attributes and only in the last stage would there be an analysis of the inputs.

While there is clearly a major change in the language of the quality debate since 1991, with analyses of fitness for purpose, value-added, inputs and outputs being the rule, it is not yet clear whether the substance of the debate has shifted to any great extent. The Higher Education Council acknowledges that regardless of the level of award, the attributes of a graduate are first, that he or she will have generic skills: skills that every graduate should be able to acquire regardless of discipline or field of study, including knowing how to learn, to solve problems, and to be able to think logically as well as laterally and independently, to be intellectually rigorous, to integrate information and to communicate effectively. Socially relevant qualities such as ethical practices and critical and evaluative skills are also required.

Second, the body of knowledge the graduate has to acquire has two main purposes: it should provide the graduate with knowledge of a discipline and its theoretical base and should act as a vehicle to inculcate the generic skills. Finally, there will often be some professional, occupational or practical skills which graduates can apply immediately in the framework of employment. Some such skills will be specific to an occupation, many will be more general (HEC, 1992:9).

This discussion of fitness for purpose is in a fairly straight intellectual line from Newman's *Idea of a University* and the utilitarian conflict, characterized somewhat superficially on the one hand by Newman's view of individual human potential and the ultimate capacity of the mind to develop intellectual constructs and to evaluate and test knowledge, with the purpose of education being to develop the mind and to replenish the cultural and human resources of society in a framework of largely non-material values; and on the other by Bentham's argument that knowledge alone would transform the institutions of church and state and fulfil human aspirations and that the purpose of the university is chiefly to ensure that students absorb and can reproduce the knowledge presented to them (see Penington, 1991).

> Name changing is an amusing parlour game, but scarcely addresses the real question: what is a university? Cardinal Newman was in no doubt. 'What an empire is in political history,' he wrote in *The Idea of University* (1852), 'such is a university in the sphere of philosophy and research. It is ... the high protecting power of all knowledge and science, of fact and principle, of inquiry and discovery. In Newman's humanistic vision, the role of the university was to train the mind of the governing classes and tend the intellectual soul of the nation. And that vision has kept its grip on the collective imagination....
>
> Just as the polytechnics exemplify all that is modern, sleek and efficient, universities have a mystique rooted in the dimly remembered past. The bond of which Newman wrote between power and intellect is as old as the privileges granted to medieval scholars by their rulers... (*The Times*, 19 June 1992).

In Australia, as elsewhere, the quality debate is confused by terminology — the attributes and immediate objectives of quality (eg, fitness for purpose) often being tangled with questions relating to the measurement of those attributes in a given context and to their usefulness or comparability (evaluation), questions relating to appropriate processes for quality assurance (eg, promotion and management), and the issue of the broader purpose of the exercise (eg, accountability). Much academic and bureaucratic energy has been expended on arguing about operational definitions in a political context in which it seems apparent that the object is to ensure that politics and the Department of Employment, Education and Training 'drive' the process, but that the universities eventually (and hopefully enthusiastically) 'own' it. Government is well aware that the institutions have no option and will go to considerable lengths in policing themselves to avoid the possibility of more direct and intrusive government intervention.

A 1992 publication of the Australian Vice-Chancellors' Committee indicates that, despite a gentle caveat, at least one side of the equation was falling into place even more easily then DEET could have hoped:

> Many of the concepts associated with contemporary quality theory in other spheres — continual improvement, teamwork, close attention to initial design (of courses and teaching), control at the work face rather than in the hierarchy — are concepts which are in principle at the heart of Australian universities. The Australian university system actively supports them. The AVCC, for instance, has adopted and advocated to its member universities the following principles of quality improvement:
> * all universities in the Australian university system should be

publicly committed to continuous quality improvement, entailing systematic procedures for assessment and monitoring of processes and outputs;

- universities have a major responsibility to all interested parties, whether students, staff, professional bodies, employers, government or the wider community, to provide assurance that quality and standards are preserved and enhanced;
- responsibility for quality assessment and improvement should be located as close to the point of delivery as possible and involve individual academics, departments, faculties and centres; and
- there must be a real commitment to the maintenance and improvement of quality from those responsible for resourcing the system as well as from the academic leaders of each institution. Diversity, and the security such diversity provides, will be jeopardised if inadequate resourcing forces a choice between continued diversity and quality (AVCC, 1992: 7–8).

By 1992, every higher education institution in the country was involved in the quality debate, not only because of policy discussions at national level, but also because there was a number of enabling and reinforcing factors at the university level. In 1988, in an industrial settlement commonly known as the 'Second Tier', a process was first agreed for dealing with inadequately performing academic staff. While the mechanisms are cumbersome for the institution and give considerable protection to the staff member, they nevertheless make the notion of tenure as a defence for inadequate performance obsolete. However, while *mechanisms* are established, and a Head of Department can trigger the process simply by naming the poorly performing person, the question is begged as to what constitutes inadequate performance (and, more importantly in terms of the quality debate, its obverse), thus bringing institutions to grips with a range of issues at the staff level.

Second, as a result of a further industrial award in July 1991, the Industrial Relations Commission upheld as being consistent with the award an Academic Staff Appraisal Scheme geared to annual appraisal against duties and objectives in teaching, research and administration mutually agreed between the supervisor and the staff member. Because of its acceptance by the Commission, this process and variants of it were adopted by universities all over the country. Third, the Industrial Relations Commission determined that incremental salary progression should not, as in the past, be automatic on an annual basis, but should be given for performance assessed as 'satisfactory'.

At the national level a further dimension gathered strong impetus, with the support of government, the Department of Employment, Education and Training, the Australian Council of Trade Unions and many employer and professional groups. The notion of competency-based approaches to skill training and education, at all levels, is clearly intended to have an impact on matters such as university entry and credit transfer in a systematic national approach which would diminish a strong plank in the concept of university 'autonomy' – the power to decide who teaches what, how, and to whom. At least part of the competency agenda is to get more people into higher education on the basis of assessed achievements of other than an intellectual kind or of a different intellectual kind, measured by different people and legitimated by different agencies than those with whom the universities are accustomed to dealing.

The old concept of matriculation – the passing of an end of secondary school examination followed by the signing of a register to enter higher education – wherein the rite of passage was assured, has long since disappeared. In the pre-war era, when some 10 per cent of the eligible cohort went on to higher education, the passing of the Year 12 examination provided a guarantee of entry. With the explosion of numbers described earlier, entry has become highly competitive. It is still widely believed, however, that a 'pass' in the Year 12 examination, however styled, does or should constitute a qualification to enter university. Unmet demand, estimated each year by the Vice-Chancellors' Committee, is defined as those qualified to enter higher education who fail to gain a place. On this measurement, all of those who pass (with pass in many instances reflecting a very low level of achievement) are deemed 'eligible' for entry, thus reinforcing anew the old matriculation expectation.

Government initiatives to increase TAFE rather than higher education places are, therefore, a justifiable option. The Government appears conscious that the reduction of inequality in higher education institutions creates cost-inefficiency: the cost per place to the government for the additional TAFE load, even funded sufficiently generously to please the managers of the sector, would be less than half the average cost of places in universities and, even were the places to be funded generously in higher education, the Vice-Chancellors would still be complaining publicly about per capita underfunding. Such expansion would not be at odds with the competency approach (seen by the universities as being more appropriate to TAFE) and would not of itself offer any greater threat to the universities. It is, however, the subject of considerable ambivalence for many of the nation's 37 Vice-Chancellors and their advisers. Some newly amalgamated institutions appear to be relying on growth to stabilize their institutions regardless of the quality of the student intake which constitutes such growth. The institutions in higher student demand, on the other hand, which in any event rely somewhat less on the funding earned from undergraduate school-leavers, tend to see the transfer of the 'tail' to TAFE as at least some immediate protection against a perceived push towards further deterioration in the standards (quality?) of higher education, if not longer-term protection against the threat embedded in the competency approach.

The first 'quality round' took place amid considerable fanfare and not a little confusion in 1993, when institutions were invited to submit portfolios substantiating their claims to quality performance and quality assurance processes in teaching, research and community service. In 1994, the quality review was confined to teaching, and in 1995 to research and community service. In the first round, universities were categorized into six bands (criticized as a 'league table') and in the second round into three bands which provided the basis of the distribution of the substantial 'quality funds' referred to above. Assessment of the efficacy and validity of the process would be premature, but two things are clear. First, the process has brought about a major cultural shift towards a 'client focus' within institutions, as emphasis in performance measurement has focused on outputs as much as on inputs. Second, the process has empowered management, possibly at the cost of some elements of collegiality or institutional democracy.

It can be argued that the university Vice-Chancellors and college Directors and Principals of the 1980s did much to bring the current quality thrust to the sector. They continued to complain bitterly about the rate of funding, whether marginal or average, and to bemoan the continuous fall in standards which was the inevitable result of the declining quality of infrastructure and deterioration in staff:student ratios, thus incontrovertibly establishing a public relationship between per capita resource levels and the quality of the product. They also continued to take the money and increasing numbers of students ('our social responsibility') and, furthermore, to take additional unfunded students by over-enrolment. In an era when industry and government were seeking to become more cost-efficient and were seeking to identify 'fat' in their own systems, what were they to think of the rhetoric, as against the evidence, coming out of the higher education sector?

Explaining the 'quality phenomenon'

The quality movement has clearly become an international phenomenon in higher education. An obvious question to ask is, why it is happening? The equally obvious answer is that the movement is about 'accountability'. But even were we to explain to whom universities are to be accountable, as the AVCC (1992: 7–8) attempts to do, after the style of Frazer (1991: 9–11) and for what, we do not have an adequate answer to the question, which goes to motive and to the politics and economics (if not the political economy in the classical sense) of the movement. The narrower analysis of accountability issues focusing on value for government or societal investment is unlikely to explain the international nature of the movement. A different analysis may offer some clue to a potential undergirding for comparative perspectives and for explanation of both the commonalities and differences of approach internationally.

The antecedents of the quality movement appear to reside in what are believed to be powerful new tools for the management of productivity in highly competitive commercial markets. While the focus of, for example, Total Quality Management (TQM) is on a happier (more fulfilled) and more productive workforce and continually improving service to the client, the 'bottom line' is always measured by profitability, and it is reasonable to assume that if other socially acceptable, but different and even conflicting methods were demonstrably to improve productivity and profitability at a greater rate, then they too would become fashionable. Here, the thinking of liberal organizational theorists and 'progressive' management notwithstanding, the criterion for the judgement of success is chiefly, though not exclusively, on a financial cost/benefit relationship at the enterprise level. It is not difficult to see in hindsight that (terminology aside) elements of the TQM approach were appealing to government and not too affronting to higher education, and were adopted to overcome the shortcomings of more direct methods to control unit costs.

Labour governments in Australia have traditionally been dominated by concerns about distributive justice in the context of relatively high levels of national prosperity, based in turn on the availability of and markets for natural resources over long periods. With a severe recession, decline in natural resources markets, mounting foreign debt, and the obvious lack of a manufacturing and research and development base, questions of potential economic inequality were buried in political rhetoric about Australia as the emergent 'Clever Country'. This emergence, in the view of the former Minister, Mr Dawkins, is to be stimulated by education, especially at the post-secondary level. Economic regeneration and sustainable growth comprise the new political holy grail.

The political economy of the changes which have occurred in Australia – and which may be applicable elsewhere – has not so much to do with the complexion of the government in power as with coming to grips with what are viewed as new economic realities and subordinating purely politico-social goals to these imperatives. The old rhetoric (on both sides of politics) remains however, possibly to serve the appearance of stability and continuity, because a fundamental shift in philosophies is not yet quite apparent. Again, it appears that, internationally, governments are promoting 'brain game' productivity as the way forward in an increasingly competitive world market environment of major trading blocs where, to establish or maintain a favourable balance of trade, leadership in information technology applications, plant and animal biotechnology, and the like, will be necessary. The need to lay strong foundations for the potential to generate economic growth both currently and in the longer term is a driving imperative for infrastructural, macro and micro economic reform in Australia and other countries and for which a strong contribution from higher education is seen as necessary.

A major difficulty, however, is that higher education has become one of the mechanisms in society that not only impacts upon aggregate economic rewards to the society, but has also been influential in shaping the structure of rewards — that is, in meeting the Labour charter for distributive justice. The principles adopted by Labour left theorists seem to owe more to Rawls' difference principle than to utilitarian philosophies. The difference principle is a conception of distributive justice which advocates selecting reward structures that favour the disadvantaged — the people at the bottom rung of the ladder — as much as is feasible, taking into account the opportunity costs of the cooperating parties and their responsiveness to incentives. To utilitarians, on the other hand, the reward structure is best that yields the greatest sum total of human happiness. It would be acceptable, for example, to widen incentives further as long as the gains to the gainers outweigh comparatively the losses to the losers. (Rawlsian theorists respond by arguing that it is not right to trade away one person's reward for the sake of a larger reward for another person irrespective of the size of the gain compared to the first person's loss.)

Thus, the powerful neo-egalitarians in the Australian Labour movement adopted a view of fairness (equality of outcomes) which implies that endowments should be divided equally prior to any economic activity. This creates a complication for a professed social reform government which has also had to acknowledge a basic axiom of welfare economics and a rationale of cost-benefit analysis: if the aggregate benefits from a collective action would equal or exceed the aggregate burdens of paying for it, and if any losers from the project were actually going to be compensated by the gainers, then it would be justifiable for the government to go ahead with the project, other things being equal. No one would be worse off with the project than without it and some might be better off. If the aggregate benefits exceed the aggregate burdens and the losers are compensated without turning any gainers into losers, then some would be better off and none would be worse off. With some better off there would be a *social improvement*, called the 'Pareto Improvement'. The axiom that Pareto Improvements are a good thing has not been seriously disputed in Western political economy, although a contrary view appears in some powerful factional groupings within particular political parties.

Now that the potential demand for higher education in Australia, as in other countries, has pushed against the limits of resources available, political/economic decisions are being taken against a prevailing rhetoric of access to higher education based on distributive justice theories, and less publicized knowledge that sustained economic regeneration requires an approach more committed to building a hierarchically structured competitive skill base. In this process a number of trade-offs can be distinguished, one of which is the quality movement aimed at optimizing the aggregate value added for the investment in each part of the system. It cannot be argued that this is the outcome of a coherent long-term plan.

It is rather the outcome of a forced shift in philosophy. In effect, with the government announcing that TAFE will significantly increase intakes with a commensurate increase in resources, the likely introduction of new student support arrangements, the equally likely introduction of increasingly market-based access, and changing Year 12 examination systems and university selection processes (in some states), a new and cheaper binary system is being created with potentially significant repercussions for the fundamental tenets of traditional Labour policy. A change of government in 1996 would not necessarily make a very significant difference to the underlying principles, only a difference in emphasis, including the likelihood of a stronger push to a market-based deregulation of the higher education student intake.

References

Aulich, T (1990) Senate Standing Committee on Employment, Education & Training. *Priorities for Reform in Higher Education*, Canberra: AGPS.

Australian Vice-Chancellors' Committee (AVCC) (1992) *Australian Universities in a Changing World*. Report for the 1993–95 Triennium, May.

Baldwin, P (1991) *Higher Education: Quality and Diversity in the 1990's*, Canberra: Australian Government Publishing Service.

Commonwealth Tertiary Education Commission (1986) *Review of Efficiency and Effectiveness in Higher Education*, Report of the Committee of Enquiry, Canberra: Australian Government Publishing Service, September.

Dawkins, J S (1987) *Higher Education a Policy Discussion Paper*, Canberra: Ministry of Employment, Education and Training, Commonwealth of Australia, December.

Dawkins, J S (1988) *Higher Education a Policy statement*, Canberra: Ministry of Employment, Education and Training, Commonwealth of Australia, July.

Department of Employment, Education and Training (1991) *Performance Indicators in Higher Education*, Report & Recommendations, Report of a Trial Evaluation Study, Commissioned by the Commonwealth Department of Employment Education and Training, Canberra: AGPS, vol.1, June.

Frazer, M (1991) *Quality Assurance in Higher Education*, Hong Kong CAA, International Conference, July.

Higher Education Council (HEC) (1992), *The Quality of Higher Education: Discussion Papers*, Canberra: AGPS.

Jarratt Report (1985) *Report of the Steering Committee for Efficiency Studies in Universities*, Committee of Vice-Chancellors and Principals.

Milne, A A (1946) *Winnie-The-Pooh*, Australia: Pilven & Stephens, p 34.

Neave, G and Rhoades, G (1987) 'The Academic Estate in Western Europe', in Burton R Clark (ed) *The Academic Profession*, California: University of California Press.

Penington, D (1991) *Introduction to the Conference Theme: 'Quality in Higher Education'*, Presentation to the National Invitational Workshop on Quality in Higher Education, Centre for the Study of Higher Education, University of Melbourne, 10 August.

Quality of Education Review Committee (1985) *'Quality of Education in Australia – Report of the Review Committee'*, Commonwealth of Australia (Fyshwick A.C.T). April.

4. The evaluation of the higher education system in Brazil

Maria C M de Figueiredo and M Isabel F Sobreira

Introduction

The Brazilian university system is relatively new; consequently efforts towards evaluation of the system are very recent. Indeed it may be doubted whether there was a 'system' of higher education until the tremendous expansion of higher education in the 1960s and 1970s. Thereafter a concern emerged: how to guarantee quality in the midst of such a rapid and relatively unorganized expansion of enrolments and of higher education institutions.

Of course some centres of excellence developed during the twentieth century (Cowen and Figueiredo-Cowen, 1989). Institutions such as the University of São Paulo, the Federal Universities of Rio de Janeiro, and of Minas Gerais, and the Paulista Medical School, among others, were well known for the quality of their teaching and for expertise in research in specific areas. But their reputations were established by word of mouth, by the views of 'insiders'.

No formal system for the evaluation of higher education existed until an experiment to evaluate and improve graduate education in the 1970s, which proved both controversial and effective. But only in the 1980s has the issue of evaluation become a matter of discussion among members of the academic community – staff, students, unions – and government circles.

Higher education evaluation in Brazil has therefore a trajectory. This chapter will attempt to analyse the different moments of this trajectory and especially how it has been shaped by the nature of the university system itself and within the context of social and economic policies in the last 30 years.

The chapter will first look at the antecedents of the current evaluation system, ie, the university reform of 1968. Second, it will examine the emergence of the university evaluation system in the late 1970s, through the CAPES national evaluation programme for graduate education. Third, the chapter will discuss two government-sponsored programmes for

34

evaluation at the undergraduate level, as well as scattered initiatives at the level of individual institutions, during the 1980s. Fourth, the emergence of evaluation as a 'system' in the 1990s will be discussed. In the final part of this chapter an attempt will be made to show how the system of evaluation is now working, and what the short-term effects are likely to be.

Brazilian higher education and the evaluation system: antecedents

Unlike other countries in Latin America, where the universtity system goes back as far as the sixteenth century, the Brazilian university system was only established in the 1930s. What existed previously was a number of professional schools set up in the early nineteenth century in order to prepare cadres for public administration needed after the transplantation of the Portuguese Royal Household to Brazil in 1808. The model for these schools was the Napoleonic system of the Grandes Écoles in France. Later, when a new Ministry of Education and Health was created in 1931, legislation was introduced to define the model of a university system for the country. The Universidade do Rio de Janeiro, reorganized in 1939, was thought of as that model for the whole country.

Only in 1968 was the Brazilian university system to be redefined through a major educational reform known as the University Reform Law, or Law 5,540/68. The reform resulted from two Reports: the *Meira Matos Report*, and the *University Task Reform Report* which analysed the nature of the Brazilian higher education system in order to propose action for its improvement. In force up to the present time, the model of university implemented in 1968 was very much inspired by the prestigious American research universities. It was also conceived of as a powerful instrument of economic development, geared to the production of manpower (Arapiraca, 1982; Figueiredo, 1986; Freitag, 1979).

The reform was controversial: it had a specific modernizing intent in line with the model of development favoured and adopted by the military government after 1964. This model of development, in the 1960s and 1970s privileged investments aimed at producing sophisticated consumer goods for the internal market and for exportation. This new economic scenario required the reorganization of civil and political society. The state undertook new, 'modernizing' policies, first establishing control over the ideological apparatus, eg, unions, media and education, and second, the state undertook a role as the creator of economic expansion. With the setting up of multinational companies in the country, the state had to provide training to prepare the skilled work force necessary for economic expansion. At the same time, another phenomenon became apparent: the mechanisms for social mobility among the middle classes were transferred from private business to occupational hierarchies in bureaucracies which expanded and multiplied in both the private and public sectors (Cunha, 1977; Figueiredo, 1987). For these new positions, formal education and formal educational qualifications were necessary.

The educational system responded to these two pressures, ie, the demand for education and the demand from the economic sector for the training of human resources. These demands activated the need for restructuring the higher education system. Fearing the student movements and radical proposals for higher education reform, the government decided to act quickly so any innovation would not endanger the structures of power, and the newly adopted economic and political ideology (Cardoso, 1979; Schneider, 1971; Skidmore, 1977). The University Reform Law was therefore quickly formulated and implemented in 1968 at the government level.

Economy and productivity – business principles – were dominant in the reform. The consequence was rationalization of institutional structures and of resources. The idea of quality was less relevant than the role of higher education as an instrument of development. The academic community, which was not consulted, was soon formulating criticisms mainly about the authoritarian nature of the reform (Berger, 1977; Romanelli, 1978).

Within this general policy and the new definition of the relationship between education and development, the state implemented policies regarding graduate education. The model of graduate education in Brazil had been defined earlier in 1965 in a government paper (MEC, 1965). This model, which was based on the American system as pointed out earlier, was intended for the whole country. Policies were gradually implemented by the government from 1968 ownwards. In early 1974 a National Council of Graduate Education was established. This Council published, the following year, the *First National Plan of Graduate Education*. With this plan, the first step toward the creation of an evaluation system for higher education in Brazil was taken.

The first moment in the trajectory of the evaluation system

The University Reform of 1968 produced conflicting results. It consolidated a new national system of higher education. It also led to a rather disorganized expansion of the whole system which permitted both the proliferation of 'isolated' institutions of higher education – stand-alone professional schools – and the recruitment of full-time poorly qualified staff. The number of graduate courses available increased dramatically. Before 1966, there were 26 masters courses and ten doctoral programmes; in 1975, the figures were 490 masters and 183 doctoral courses; in 1980, the numbers rose to 710 masters and 272 PhD programmes (Figueiredo, 1986). In 1995 graduate education includes up to 1,220 masters and 600 PhD programmes.

This rapid expansion met two purposes. For the government, expansion (at both undergraduate and graduate levels) fitted well the entrepreneurial conception of education, and of university education, which was very clear in the governmental plans of Brazil from 1964 until the mid-1980s. As already indicated, according to these plans there was a close relationship between national development and human resources. Conceptualized as an instrument for development, education had its aims implemented in quantitative terms. The role of higher education was to be an instrument for manpower training, as a strategic instrument for development; and as an element in policies informed by human capital theory (Figueiredo, 1986). Graduate education became mandatory for promotion in academic careers. Positions outside the university system (in enterprises, industries, and institutes of research, for example) also privileged graduate education which was viewed as compensating for the training offered at undergraduate level, mostly in private higher education institutions of very variable quality.

Criticisms of the status quo became very difficult politically – in the immediate period after both educational reforms, academics and teachers were under severe ideological control. Acts of repression were fully in force (Figueiredo, 1986).

It was only in the late 1970s with the political 'opening' (*abertura política*) that the issue of quality re-emerged. Under the difficult conditions of the 1960s and 1970s such debate as there was about the university in academic circles was on autonomy, freedom and democracy. When concern for quality and efforts to implement a system for the evaluation of higher education were made visible in the late 1970s, it was only at the level of graduate education; and by then it was safe, with no political implications, and the debate was partly generated at governmental levels.

The first initiatives and practices started with CAPES – *Fundação Coordenação de Aperfeiçoamento de Pessoal de Nível Superior* (the Agency for Higher Education Staff Improvement) linked to the Ministry of Education. CAPES is a governmental agency responsible for the advanced training of human resources; it is also responsible for the formulation of national policies on graduate education. In the early 1970s, CAPES introduced an institutional programme for the training of higher education staff. The programme, called PICD – *Plano Institucional de Capacitação de Docentes* (the Institutional Plan for Staff Qualification) – was very ambitious. It aimed at the implementation of a planning system, at the national level, for the upgrading of university academic and administrative staff. It defined its own goals in five year plans. In the decade 1970 to 1980 the number of scholarships (in Brazil and abroad) distributed by CAPES/PICD increased from 804 to 8,539 (MEC/CAPES, 1971; 1981). Each university was entitled to participate in the programme. However one of the requirements was a diagnosis of the institution and a subsequent staff development plan (Brasil/SESU/ CAPES, 1979). These were the first ingredients of a simple but steadily developing evaluation system. With the successful implementation of the PICD, and the rapid expansion of graduate courses, in the late 1970s CAPES sought to devise mechanisms which would enable follow-up and evaluation of masters and doctoral programmes nationally.

The main reason for devising and implementing an evaluative process was practical. Financial resources were being distributed (for research and as grants for graduate students) to different graduate courses in different regions in the country. Except for the traditional, well-known courses, very little information existed about the quality in an increasing number of masters and doctoral programmes. The process of evaluation gained impetus under Claudio de Moura Castro, a former Director of CAPES. Some graduate courses graded as weak would face the possibility of being closed down or of having very few financial resources, which happened in some cases. Claudio Castro was fired as a result of pressure from Vice-Chancellors in whose universities the graduate programmes were considered weak. However, the system developed, has been refined over the years, has been taken up as a model by UNESCO, and has influenced other systems of education in Latin America.

For the evaluation of graduate programmes, CAPES used and developed a matrix of indicators of quality for academic staff. Those indicators include: number of publications per staff, staff qualifications, staff research output, number of theses, as well as institutional criteria such as library content and research equipment. The frequency of evaluation was at first once a year; since 1982 it has been every two years. Classification is through grades from A to E. The profile of a A course, for example, is a course which has staff qualified with a doctoral degree, and with a good record in publication in national and international journals. The curriculum structure and the research activities must be coherent and related to the areas of studies on offer. The completion rate of masters and doctorates must be reasonable, within a normal, expected timetable. The other extreme − courses graded E − do not have conditions to offer acceptable graduate training; if a restructuring is not undertaken, the course has to be closed down (Castro, 1985; INFOCAPES, 1994).

Evaluation is carried out by members of the academic community. The members of the Committee of Evaluation are appointed from a list of consultants. Each member must have experience in the training of masters and doctoral students, have substantial publication output, and experience in academic and scientific consultancy. Visits by consultants to the courses in the process of being evaluated are mandatory (INFOCAPES, 1994).

From the beginning it was understood that controlling the expansion of courses would be ineffective if the institution did not maintain a permanent system of information. This system would in turn be very useful in policy formulation, strategy operationalization, and resource allocation. So information systems were set up and each course now produces detailed data annually. These data are structured in categories such as course, staff, curriculum structure, flow of students, and scientific production (INFOCAPES, 1994).

The results of the evaluation were initially from 1982 used only within the appropriate course. Since 1992, the results have been made accessible, through the Pro-Rectors, to all graduate courses and to the press. There are now efforts being made to improve the quality of data, a greater emphasis is being placed on the qualitative aspects of evaluation and greater accessiblity to relevant data for the academic community (INFOCAPES, 1994).

There is little doubt that the system of evaluation implemented and developed by CAPES for nearly 20 years has been quite successful and relevant for Brazil. However it has been argued that the system is an example of authoritarianism in educational policies in Brazil: it was devised at the central level of administration. Nevertheless the system has worked, and has contributed to emerging discussions about systems of evaluation at the next stage in the trajectory of the Brazilian higher education evaluation system.

The second moment in the trajectory of the evaluation system

In the 1980s, a shift in higher education evaluation activities took place. Interest was centred around the evaluation of the higher education system as a whole. There were two strands of action. The first was represented by two governmental programmes, via the Ministry of Education: the Programme for the Evaluation of the University Reform (*Programa de Avaliação da Reforma Universitária* – PARU), and the Executive Committee for the Reformulation of Higher Education (*Grupo Executivo da Reforma da Educação Superior* – GERES). The second strand was represented by emerging but isolated experiences developed in a number of different higher education institutions.

The enormous increase of enrolments in higher education and in the number of institutions during the 1970s, led to a concern with the quality of teaching in the 1980s. This concern motivated CAPES to implement the Programme for the Evaluation of University Reform, which was an initiative of the Federal Council of Education. In 1983 a Coordinating Commmittee was appointed jointly by the Federal Council and the Ministry of Education with the objective of evaluating the University Reform of 1968. It was expected that the Committee would carry out studies about the implementation of the reform – although 15 years after the event.

The Committee, chaired by CAPES, chose a strategy of work

involving analysis of, and debate about, the condition of the universities; it also sought the formulation of alternatives. The academic, administrative, financial and political conditions under which teaching, research and extension activities took place in the different institutions all over the country were to be analysed. The extra information to be collected referred to questions of: power structure and the decision-making process; financial, administrative and academic autonomy; and personnel policy. The way the programme was conceptualized implied that a complex programme would be carried out over a long period of time. It aimed at formulating different alternatives for the improvement of Brazilian higher education (Figueiredo, 1986).

However, PARU lasted only until 1986. Whether or not PARU produced useful outcomes remains to be fully analysed. The programme was never fully implemented; rather it was rejected by the academic community because it had been devised by the central administration, the Ministry of Education. It was, *ipso facto*, judged to be authoritarian (Saul, 1988).

The second attempt to launch a national programme for higher education evaluation, which also failed, was the Executive Committee for the Reformulation of Higher Education — GERES. The Council of Vice-Chancellors of Brazilian Universities (*Conselho de Reitores das Universidades Brasileiras* — CRUB) at its Annual Conference in 1986 took up the responsibility to encourage each university to evaluate performance. The recommendations contained in the CRUB Report (*A New Policy for Brazilian Higher Education*) were understood by the Ministry of Education merely as a group of propositions that needed to be scrutinized (MEC/SESU, 1987). Therefore, the Ministry set up the Committee for the Reformulation of Higher Education — GERES.

There was great controversy around the work of the committee: the scientific community and the universities were divided. The Secretariat of Higher Education within the Ministry then decided to sponsor seminars about evaluation so that the universities could become more receptive to the idea. In 1987 four important seminars took place in different regions of the country; one university was the organizing institution with the participation of institutions of that geographical area. In the North of Brazil, the Federal University of Pará was the hosting university; in the South, the Federal University of Santa Catarina; in the Southeast, the Paulista State University; and in the Northeast, the Federal University of Ceará. In addition to this series of meetings, the Secretariat of Higher Education also supported activities associated with evaluation. Two of them are singled out here for what they represented in terms of later intensive action on evaluation. One was the Galileu Project. It aimed at developing managerial indicators in higher education institutions. The other was a project associated with the Agreement between the Ministry of Education and the Interamerican Bank of Development (MEC/BID III Project). The project recommended that all the 11 universities involved should implement a Centre for Evaluation, preferably linked to the Pro-Rector of Planning (Paul *et al.* 1992).

However, GERES' proposal for the reformulation of higher education based on an evaluative process was rejected by the academic community (Cardoso, 1991). This was the point of departure for an intense debate about evaluation with alternative proposals from other segments of academia, notably the National Association of Higher Education Staff – ANDES (*Associação Nacional de Docentes dos Ensino Superior*) and the Council of Vice-Chancellors of Brazilian Universities (CRUB).

Around the same time, in the late 1980s, evaluative initiatives started to develop locally in a number of higher education institutions. The state University of Rio de Janeiro, the Federal of University of Ceará, the University of Campinas, and the Federal University of Pará are examples. An extensive analysis of these experiences was made by Paul and colleagues who classified the evaluation activities in three levels: (a) institutional; (b) undergraduate teaching; and (c) courses. A large number of evaluation projects were geared to the redefinition of the global project of the institution. This redefinition was very different from institution to institution, varying from curriculum reformulation to the identification of the institution's profile. Other projects were related to the university entrance examinations, the high rates of dropout and failure, and political and pedagogical redefinition of courses. Some other projects, dealing mainly with analysis of curriculum, and with bio-psychological and socio-economic profiles of students, were much less specific, with unclear results.

In their analysis, Paul *et al.* (1992) point out a number of weaknesses in these emerging evaluation activities. The indicators used were not of a comparable nature, so the methodology could not be transferred to other institutions. Some difficulties were faced by the institutions themselves. For example those in charge of the evaluation process in individual institutions had conflicting views regarding quantitative and qualitative evaluation. In some other cases the difficulty lay in the level at which evaluation should take place: the whole institution, the individual school, or the department. A serious problem came to be the absence of a system of information with reliable data.

In contrast to this was the experience of evaluation at the University of São Paulo, traditionally viewed as a centre of excellence. In the 1980s USP underwent two experiences with different results. The first one was a disaster, politically. The evaluation exercise, later known as 'the list of those academics who do not publish' (*a lista dos improdutivos*), had been encouraged and carried out from the central administration, under the leadership of Jose Goldemberg, then Vice-Chancellor. The publication of the list in major newspapers became a matter of great controversy. The staff rejected the evaluation exercise, particularly the way in which the process was carried out. They argued that the only acceptable form of evaluation would be self-evaluation (Goldemberg, 1992).

Goldemberg however had in mind to create a 'culture' of evaluation, and sought other ways of achieving that. The second attempt consisted of data collected over a period of four years (1985–88) about the activities of the different departments and units of the University of São Paulo. The data would be entirely quantitative, aiming at obtaining information that could act as indicators of performance of the individual units. The data were then used by the central administration to justify new initiatives and proposals, and to inform decision-making policies. It seems that the experience made members of the university aware of the need for such a practice (Goldemberg, 1992).

Two points need to be raised in relation to this second moment in the trajectory of higher education evaluation in Brazil. First, the outcome of the various projects implemented in different institutions, no matter how amateurish they may have been, was, in general, positive. Second, there was an awareness of the relevance of evaluation in the struggle for the improvement of the higher education system, both by the government and by the academic community.

The idea that evaluation was relevant to the new project of the Brazilian university became clear in the debates around the 1988 Constitution. Of course the new Constitution emphasized the principle of university autonomy. However, since then all proposals discussing the new Law on the Directions and Bases of Education (*Projeto de Lei das Diretrizes e Bases da Educação*) have advocated in different ways the principle of evaluation as a necessary instrument for the improvement of the higher education system of the country.

Indeed it was true that the government itself took the initiative, on different occasions, to set up committees for evaluating the university reform with a view to proposing alternative models of the university. The major reason behind these initiatives was to block any radical proposals for evaluation from coming forward.

In the late 1980s and early 1990s a shift in the higher education evaluation system occurred. Activities in higher education evaluation flourished. They included: national and regional seminars and conferences on the theme; the establishment of Centres for the Evaluation of higher education in a large number of higher education institutions; and, most importantly, a 'softer' and more flexible attitude from the Ministry of Education (Secretariat for Higher Education) about ideologically radical proposals for a system of evaluation. This shift may be understood in terms of other shifts in the social, economic and political scenario in Brazil. These shifts, and the impact on the system of higher education evaluation, will be sketched next.

The third moment in the trajectory of the evaluation system

In the 1980s the restoration of liberal-democratic social structures was under way. In 1982, for example, democratic elections for state

Governors took place, after a gap of 17 years. Political movements supporting democratic election for the Presidency of the country in 1984 became widespread – the campaign, launched by the Workers' Party (*Partido dos Trabalhadores*) was soon adopted by all political parties. This movement also had very strong participation of the masses, and is considered to be the biggest mass movement in the history of Brazil so far (Lamounier, 1991).

In the late 1980s, the country was facing serious problems which had been building up during the previous military governments. These problems included: the low productivity of investments, high levels of financial speculation, an economy in recession, very high inflation, and a bankrupt state. Politically, the government was concerned with the promotion of the so-called transition to democracy. This implied the elimination of all arbitrary and authoritarian legislation of the military regimes, and the recreation of a more democratic tradition. A new constitution was urgently required. Economically and socially, the governmental task was even greater. It had to adopt measures that would ensure a reduction in social inequalities. To achieve that, specific and major problems would have to be tackled immediately: recession, inflation, and the low rate of economic growth (Lamounier, 1991).

By the mid-1980s re-democratization was fully in progress. The majority of the authoritarian legislation had been abolished. Press censorship was finally eliminated. The number of political parties expanded, including the re-legitimation of the traditional radical left-wing parties. The major trade unions were also re-legitimated. The 1988 constitution was democratic and liberal, tending toward decentralization. With the new constitution, for example, the individual and collective rights of the citizen were guaranteed; the rights of workers were expanded; financial and administrative autonomy of the individual states was increased; and the country was preparing for presidential direct elections for the first time in 29 years (Lamounier, 1991).

Brazil had become the country which had been able to make the fastest progress in industrialization through import substitution in this century. It had become the tenth country in terms of GNP in the world; it contained the largest industrial park among Third World countries; it was producing almost all the consumer goods and 90 per cent of the machinery and equipment it required.

However, the other, negative, scenario showed a country with 40 per cent of the population without medical assistance, 25 per cent of the population illiterate, and with a high percentage of infant mortality. Economic 'packages' like the Cruzado Plan (1986), Bresser Plan (1987), and the Summer Plan (1989) did not work out. In the late 1980s, control over the economy was lost; inflation soared, reaching the rate of 90 per cent a month. There was a crisis of the state, made manifest through low wages and salaries, strikes, rural land invasions, urban looting and widespread urban violence, and corruption.

In this political and socio-economic context, the debate on university autonomy and democratization gained both strength and depth. The crisis of the university became a more visible issue (Figueiredo, 1986). The debate about academic freedom versus state control which dominated the 1970s and early 1980s became less relevant; it was now mainly about the movement for the re-democratization of the country. Also important were the discussions about university management at the political and administrative levels, with implications for issues of costs and maintenance. Fewer resources, lack of definition of priorities, and internal inefficiency were other issues characterizing the crisis in the university system. Higher education staff associations such as the National Association of Higher Education Staff (*Associação Nacional de Docentes dos Ensino Superior* — ANDES), and the National Association of Heads of Federal Institutions of Higher Education (*Associação Nacional dos Dirigentes das Instituições Federais de Ensino Superior* — ANDIFES), as well as other professional associations like the Brazilian Society for the Progress of Science (*Sociedade Brasileira para o Progresso da Ciência* — SBPC) played a major role in these debates (Figueiredo, 1986).

Discussions about the crisis in the university in the 1980s have had several different intellectual perspectives and conceptual positions, but centred on two main themes: (a) the search for an identity; and (b) the struggle for democratic forms of governance (Figueiredo, 1986). If the boundaries were in general muddled, the complexity of the crisis in the late 1980s was even deeper. Subordinate (but no less important) to the issues of identity and of democratic governance were two concepts. The first was the idea of the university as a social institution of public interest, ie, the university ought to be free and financed by the state. The second dealt with the need for evaluating higher education (Belloni, 1989). These were the core points of the project for higher education proposed by the National Association of Higher Education Staff — ANDES.

As conceptualized in the ANDES project, autonomy and democracy are necessary ingredients for the university to perform its social function. Within this frame, it becomes an important instrument: it will lead to the improvement of quality of higher education and, therefore, evaluation can contribute to the development of a critical and productive university (Cardoso, 1991). This issue was central in the discussions among higher education staff movements in various seminars, specifically those organized by ANDES in 1986 (in Curitiba), in 1988 (in Londrina), and in 1990 (in Rio).

In terms of content, the debate about evaluation reflects the discussions, in the mid-1980s, on the crisis of the university. At that time, there was a clear boundary between the offficial discourse, ie, the government through PARU, CRUB and GERES, and the critical discourse, ie, arguments put forward by academics from the left (Figueiredo, 1986).

In the 1990s the boundary is greatly reduced, largely because of the establishment of the National Programme for the Evaluation of Brazilian Universities (*Programa de Avaliação Institucional das Universidades Brasileiras* – PAIUB). PAIUB was set up in 1993, when the Secretariat of Higher Education of the Ministry of Education appointed a National Committee for the Evaluation of Brazilian Universities. The Committee members were drawn from among educational bureaucrats and representatives of a variety of higher education associations, following a proposal from the National Association of Heads of the Federal Institutions of Higher Education – ANDIFES.

Thus, PAIUB emerged from suggestions by members of the academic community and its stated aims and principles are very much in accordance with ideas about critical discourse. Issues such as seeing the process of institutional evaluation politically, setting up a 'culture' of evaluation, looking for legitimacy, building up the programme through participation, are all there. PAIUB argues that evaluation is a process for developing academic performance; it is a tool for management and planning in the sense that it helps to identify and to formulate policies and actions, and it is a process of accountability. The programme has encouraged the universities to put forward projects on evaluation. In 1994 a considerable number (56) of universities had integrated with the PAIUB, and have had their projects on evaluation approved by it.

The PAIUB has been very useful in the extent to which remaining resistance from the institutions over evaluation has been reduced. This resistance is understandable given the fear that the results of any evaluation would affect, for example, financing. PAIUB has also been highly focused: it has targeted only undergraduate courses, concentrating efforts over a period of 18 months, after which graduate education and research activities will enter the process of evaluation.

PAIUB has a strategic role in the future development of the evaluation system. Perhaps the force behind the programme, and the system, will be ANDES, the National Association of Higher Education Staff. ANDES was advocating a system for higher education evaluation as far back as 1982. It has kept the debate on the theme alive. It has come up continuously with relevant critiques of, for example, the concept of evaluation, and the political nature of the system (Cardoso, 1991). ANDES has also rejected models of evaluation which are now favoured by the PAIUB. One criticism raised by ANDES is that the utilitarian approach to programmes of evaluation is likely to confirm and stabilize educational and financial policies rather than change them (ANDES, 1994).

Other criticisms raised by ANDES are related to the general nature of evaluation projects in individual institutions. First, evaluation processes are individualized and fragmented – lecturers, departments and courses are evaluated without any kind of articulation which leads to a loss of the social meaning of results. Second, the procedures are imposed by higher echelons in the central administration, distant from academic activity itself, which leads to the loss of autonomy by practising academics. Third, the link between evaluation and budget can become a powerful and dangerous instrument given the increasing tendency towards privatization of Brazilian education as a whole (ANDES, 1994; Cardoso, 1991).

ANDES (CONAD, 1994) has had clear theoretical views about education, and about evaluation. Their project for education, and for a system for higher education evaluation, differs considerably from the neo-liberal governmental approach to education. The idea of Total Quality Management as developed in business enterprises (Deming, 1982; Ishikawa, 1965; Ishikawa and Kondo, 1969) has framed the neo-liberal concept of quality in education. Within this concept, quality is a matter of educational management; the socio-political and cultural variables of the educational problems become irrelevant; and quantitative methods are privileged, as well as technical instruments for the solution of educational problems. Against that neo-liberal view of education, and of quality in education, is ANDES' concept: a pattern of quality implies the establishment of basic conditions to be fulfilled by all institutions, public and private; evaluation is an instrument for democratization, and quality must be understood as social quality; differentiation among institutions must be understood contextually (ie, in geopolitical and historical context). Finally, higher education evaluation has to be socially and historically contextualized; participative and emancipatory, and both quantitative and qualitative. Evaluation is meaningful only if it contributes to the idea of the emancipatory and critical university.

Specific activities of evaluation have been implemented in different higher education institutitions. They are linked to the PAIUB programme but most of them are very much within the theoretical perspective of ANDES. Two examples – the University of São Paulo and the Federal University of Rio Grande do Sul – will briefly illustrate the point.

At the University of São Paulo, evaluation takes place at the level of the department conceived as the academic cell where common languages and concepts in the areas of teaching and research are discussed. That way, the departments have been given the task of looking for reformulation and improvement in relation to performance. The process of evaluation is coordinated by a Permanent Committee of Evaluation. It has two major components: internal and external evaluation. The department carries out its self-evaluation, through a report in which its performance, policies and philosophy in the last five years are analysed. Afterwards, the department is visited by a committee of external assessors who write up a report about teaching and research activities, and services to the community. The report, which must include a list of recommendations for the improvement of the department, is only approved by the relevant board if it is critical in content. The University of São Paulo uses evaluation as an instrument that will enable the institution to reach the standards of the best universities in the industrialized countries. That is its ultimate goal (MEC/SESU, 1994).

The project of institutional evaluation at the Federal University of Rio Grande do Sul, in Porto Alegre, linked to PAIUB, was implemented in July 1994. The programme's proposal is to rethink and to improve the different practices of evaluation carried out in the last few years. The focus of the work is around undergraduate education. The interrelations among academics, administration and students will be considered in the analysis, as well as the other interrelations in teaching, research, services and management (Leite and Bordas, 1995).

Like the University of São Paulo, in the Federal University of Rio Grande do Sul there is also a Central Committee of Evaluation. A new element has been added however: this Central Committee has attached to it an Executive Board for the Evaluation Programme. This Board is responsible for carrying out the process; the organization and the development of the evaluation process is the responsibility of Boards for Evaluation set up in each school. This is thought to guarantee the participation of the members of that school or of the course (Leite and Bordas, 1995; UFRGS, 1995).

The programme being carried out now involves five strategies of action. Awareness is the first one; it is permanent and it deals with seminars and workshops necessary for the discussions about evaluation. Diagnosis is the second strategy; it is supported by the use of indicators. Third, there is internal evaluation, the central strategy of the process. The next strategy is the external evaluation. Finally, the process is fed back with a re-evaluation. In the whole process the involvement of all members of the individual institute or course is fundamental, as well as the participation of the community represented by clients, users, unions, entrepreneurs and alumni. The final product is a plan of action for the improvement in quality of the institute or of the course.

Those two examples of systems of evaluation, as in the other 54 universities integrating with the PAIUB, are still at a very early stage of implementation. There can be shifts in the ways they have been conceptualized and operationalized. The balance towards a more 'official'/neo-liberal or 'radical'/emancipatory approach will always depend on the political orientation of those in charge of the process.

Conclusion

Radical changes have happened in Brazil in the 1990s. First, in 1990, a President took office after the first free election in 29 years, although this democratically elected President (Fernando Collor de Mello) lost his position at the end of a very long impeachment process in 1993. Second, the masses, in the name of democracy and participation, have been playing a key role in the political scenario of the country. Third, with the newly elected President – Fernando Henrique Cardoso – the socio-political and economic agenda of the country has been energetic; although the political alliances between the first left-oriented academic as President and the conservative Liberal Front Party/PFL and the centre-left Brazilian Social Democratic Party/PSDB are not widely liked. Fourth, euphoria is high with the *real* – a newly introduced currency that is remaining strong – and with the apparent stabilization of the economy at a low level of inflation.

The educational agenda in the 1990s, has also been quite dramatic. Discussion about the Educational Bill under debate in Congress and in academic circles is one item on the agenda. Quality in education is another. In the name of quality, educational projects have been implemented everywhere. In the individual states, plans for improvement in basic and secondary education, with the support of the World Bank, have been implemented. In institutions of higher education, the evaluation 'culture' is now in force. In the central administration (the Ministry of Education and the Ministry of Science and Technology) new evaluative experiences are flourishing.

Nevertheless, that educational agenda is far from any consensus. The agenda is permeated by contradictions. One contradiction deals with the polarization sometimes found in the discussions about evaluation. Principles such as democracy and academic freedom have clashed with the apparently objective principles of the evaluation of institutional performance.

Another contradiction is in the vacuum in the qualitative evaluation of undergraduate programmes. Only in 1995 has the issue been addressed by the Ministry of Education (MEC, 1995; Pinto, 1995). There are suggestions that attention will now be turned to undergraduate courses. But the first experience to be launched later this year does not look very promising. It is sectorial and the instruments for measuring quality may not be appropriate. Students from the area of sciences will be sitting for an examination after their graduation. The exam will cover the different subjects in the different years of higher education training. How many would fail such an exam? If they fail, then what? In any case, the Ministerial project has been rejected by the academic community even before it has taken place, as another example of authoritarianism (*Jornal da Ciência Hoje*, 1995).

A third contradiction is related to two research projects from CAPES and from CNPq recently implemented in undergraduate courses – the Special Training Programme (*Programa Especial de Treinamento* – PET) from CAPES, and the Scientific Initiation Project (*Projeto de Iniciação Científica*) from CNPq, according to which students are selected to work full-time with a lecturer on a research project of common interest. The objective is to offer a more solid training in research so the quality of undergraduate work may improve. However there are problems of principle, and of distribution. How many undergraduate students can benefit from the programmes? Which areas of knowledge are more likely to be privileged? Are the programmes likely to favour centres of excellence to the detriment of those institutions which badly need improving?

Similar questions may be asked about two of the most recent programmes implemented by CNPq: SABE and PERT, although they have clear potentials. The first programme, System for the Evaluation of Brazilian Students Abroad (*Sistema de Avaliação de Bolsistas no Exterior* – SABE) was launched in May this year by José Tundisi, Head of CNPq; it is intended as an analysis of the quality (and limitations) of CNPq's graduate education programmes abroad. The second programme, Programme for the Return of Talents (*Programa de Estimulo ao Retorno de Talentos* – PERT) was jointly implemented by CNPq and the Ministry of Foreign Relations in December 1994. The objective of this programme is to provide Brazilian students abroad:

> ... with the opportunity of interchanging with Brazilian institutes of higher education and research, or with business institutions involved with the social, scientific, and technological development of Brazil (CNPq/MRE, 1994: 2).

The emphasis on quality is clear: the graduate students will visit institutions, in both private and public sectors, to become acquainted with the most advanced industries and with the centres of excellence in Brazil. But this idea of quality improvement lacks the political and social dimensions embedded in the discussions and proposed projects of the academics.

Overall then, evaluation undoubtedly is the key issue in academic and governmental circles now in Brazil. Approaches to evaluation differ though. For the government, evaluation should be linked to cost-benefit theories. For most of the academics, evaluation should incorporate an educational, critical and emancipatory vision. The two views are difficult to reconcile – and are still contending.

References

ANDES (1994) *Relatório Final do XIII Congresso da Andes – Tema III*, Viçosa: ANDES.

Arapiraca, J (1982) *A USAID e a educação brasileira*, São Paulo: Cortez.

Belloni, I (1989) 'Avaliação da universidade: por uma proposta de avaliação consequente e compromissada politica e cientificamente' in Vieira, S (ed.) *A Universidade em Questão*, São Paulo: Cortez.

Brasil/SESU/CAPES (1979) *Manual do Programa Institucional de Capacitação de Docentes*, Brasilia: CAPES.

Berger, M (1977) *Educação e dependência*, Rio: Difel.

Cardoso, F (1979) *O modelo político brasileiro*, São Paulo: Difel.

Cardoso, M (1991) 'A Avaliação da Universidade: Concepções e Perspectivas', *Universidade e Sociedade*, 1(1) pp. 14–24.

Castro, C (1985) *Ciência e universidade*, Rio: Zahar.

CNPq (The National Council for Research)/MRE (1994) Protocolo de Ação Conjunta para o Estímulo ao 'Retorno de Talentos', Brasília.

CONAD (1994) *Relatório Final do XXVIII CONAD*, Recife: ANDES.
Cowen, R and Figueiredo-Cowen, M (1989) 'Educational Excellence: The Case of Brazil', *Higher Education Policy*, 2(3) pp. 14–17.
Cunha, L (1977) *Educação e Desenvolvimento Social no Brasil*, Rio: Francisco Alves.
Deming, W (1982) *Quality, Productivity, and Competitive Position*, Cambridge: MIT.
Figueiredo, M (1986) 'Academic freedom and autonomy in the modern Brazilian university: a comparative analysis', unpublished PhD thesis, University of London.
Figueiredo, M (1987) 'Politics and Higher Education in Brazil: 1964–1986', *International Journal of Educational Development*, 7(3) pp. 173–81.
Freitag, B (1979) *Escola, Estado e Sociedade*, São Paulo: Cortez.
Goldemberg, J (1992) 'O impacto da avaliação na universidade', in Durham, E and Schwartzman S (eds) *Avaliação do Ensino Superior*, São Paulo: USP pp. 91–104.
INFOCAPES (1994) 'A avaliação da CAPES', *Boletim Informativo*, 2(1) pp. 17–20.
Ishikawa, K (1965) 'Recent Trends of Quality Control', *Reports of Statistical Applications and Research*, 12 (1) pp. 1–17.
Ishikawa, K and Kondo, K (1969) 'Education and Training for Quality Control in Japanese Industry', *Quality*, 4, pp. 90–96.
Jornal da Ciência Hoje (1995) IX (317) pp. 6–7.
Lamounier, B (1991) *Depois da transição: democracia e eleições no governo Collor*, São Paulo: Loyola.
Leite, D and Bordas, M (1995) 'Avaliação na UFRGS: a qualidade da diferença e a diferença de qualidade', *Educación Superior y Sociedad*, Venezuela: CRESALC/UNESCO (forthcoming.)
MEC (1995) *Provisional Document no. 1018*, 8 June, Brasilia: Ministério da Educação.
MEC/CAPES (1971) *Annual Report*, Brasilia: CAPES.
MEC/CAPES (1981) *Annual Report*, Brasilia: CAPES.
MEC/Federal Council of Education (1965) *Opinion no. 977/65*, Brasília: Ministério da Educação.
MEC/SESU (1987) *Relatório GERES*, Brasília: Ministério da Educação.
MEC/SESU (1994) *Programa de Avaliação Institucional das Universidades Brasileiras (PAIUB)*, Brasilia: Ministério da Educação.
Paul, J, Ribeiro, Z and Pilatti, O (1992) 'As Iniciativas e as Experiências de Avaliação do Ensino Superior: Balanço Crítico', in Durham, E and Schwatrzman, S (eds) *Avaliação do Ensino Superior*, São Paulo: USP, pp. 141–66.
Pinto, P (1995) 'MP cria teste para conceder diploma', *Folha de São Paulo*, 15 de março.
Romanelli, O (1978) *História da Educação no Brasil (1930/1973)*, Rio: Vozes.
Saul A (1988) *Avaliação emancipatória*, São Paulo: Cortez.
Schneider R (1971) *The Political System of Brazil — Emergence of a 'Modernising' Authoritarian Regime: 1964–1970*, New York: Columbia University Press.
Skidmore, T (1977) *Brasil: de Getulio a Castelo*, Rio: Paz e Terra.
UFRGS (1995) *Programa de Avaliação Institucional da UFRGS — PAIUFRGS*, Porto Alegre: Uni-Copy.

5. The evaluation of the higher education system in Canada

John Mallea

In a rapidly changing Europe, evaluation in higher education has become a critical issue for academics, administrators and politicians. The immense expansion of higher education systems, increasing financial constraints in the public sector, demand for accountability, and a general tendency towards decentralisation are factors behind the demands for evaluation. (Ingemar Fagerlind, Director, Institute of International Education, University of Stockholm; Foreword, in Chinapah, 1992: v.)

Introduction

Marked interest is also being shown in the evaluation of higher education beyond the borders of Europe. It is a phenomenon to be remarked upon throughout the OECD countries, including Canada. Here, as elsewhere, explanatory factors include concern over declining resources, demands for greater accountability, and a continuing search for excellence. And, while contexts and approaches vary, the assessment of student achievement follows a fairly common pattern, as does the traditional peer-review assessment of faculty. Of interest is the extension of the latter to evaluation at the institutional and system levels. The expanded use of performance indicators is also apparent and increasing attention is being paid to output as well as input measures.

The monitoring and evaluation of Canadian higher education provides an interesting case study given the varied historical roots, traditions, institutional models and cross-border influences that have helped shape its institutions and given rise to its diversity. For example, higher education in French-speaking Canada has drawn upon French traditions; institutions of higher education in English-speaking Canada have patterned themselves on Scottish, Irish and English models; and US colleges and universities (especially land grant institutions) have exercised an important influence. Over time an array of institutions,

51

many organized along federal lines and reflecting their distinctive origins, came into existence. Today, they form an association of colleges and universities serving a bilingual, multi-racial, multi-cultural, federal society in which constitutional responsibility for education rests in the hands of ten provinces and two territories.

How these institutions are evaluated depends to a considerable extent on the answers to three basic questions:

Who is evaluating whom?
What is being evaluated? and
For what purpose?

Nevertheless, over time, some rather general prestige rankings have emerged with institutions viewing themselves, and being viewed by others, as possessing excellence in either research, teaching and community service or some combination of these. Increasingly, too, institutions are assessing themselves in terms of international norms and standards.

Student achievement

In Canada, as in North America generally, the academic year is normally divided into academic terms or semesters. The latter usually run from mid-September to late January and from February to May; in some cases, a summer semester, June through August, is added. The former approach consists of two terms: September–December and January–April plus a summer term July–August; increasingly a fourth term, Intersession, is being added in the months of May and June.

Academic courses are normally organized on a self-contained but sequential basis and run for one or two terms or semesters. Evaluation consists of coursework, essays, papers, short tests, mid-term and final examinations. Marks achieved are aggregated into a cumulative grade point average and serve as the major indicator of a student's academic performance. Concerns over issues such as the appropriate balance between course work and examinations, the impact of grade inflation, and the quality of subject matter integration are frequently expressed.

Peer review

The peer review approach to faculty evaluation occupies a central and highly valued place in Canadian higher education. It is one in which the quality of an individual's scholarship and research is judged by a jury of peers. It is an approach that is firmly embedded in the evaluation procedures of higher education institutions and one that is increasingly being applied at the institutional and system-wide levels.

Individual level

Peer assessment plays a pivotal role in the appointment, retention and promotion of faculty at all levels. By the time an individual attains full professor rank, he/she is likely to have been assessed in this way at least five times. The criteria and procedures applied, moreover, are formally and systematically outlined in detailed institutional policies and/or collective agreements. The transparency of the process is considered important, and external as well as internal peer evaluators are employed.

A similar process is used in the award of individual research grants coming from the institution, or research councils, or government or private agencies. Scholars of international stature frequently participate in the judgement and selection process, and their presence is a virtual requirement for grants associated with centres of excellence or strategic research priorities at the national, bilateral and multilateral levels. Increasingly, too, the number of citations in international (as well as national) journals in a scholar's field of study are taken into account.

Individual professors are also provided with feedback on their performance in instruction, via one or more of a wide range of evaluation mechanisms applied by department heads, directors and deans. These include student evaluations of teaching as well as assessments made by colleagues and/or administrators. Service to one's profession and/or the community is gauged by annual reports detailing one's activities and achievements in these spheres.

The peer-review process of monitoring and evaluating achievement is also applied to the performance of academic administrators. The latter are usually selected from within the ranks of the faculty by committees on which faculty wield major influence. Selection committees are established for initial appointments and renewal of terms of office which normally last from three to five years. Senior academic administrators – Directors, Deans and Vice-Presidents – may be assessed annually by the President, with the written evaluations being submitted to a college or university's lay board as evidence that the President is effectively monitoring the management and administration of the institution.

Institutional level

Implementation of the peer-review process at the programme or institutional level is of more recent vintage but is now widespread. It assumes a variety of forms but in essence consists of a set of procedures providing for collegial assessment of academic programme offerings. These are assessed at the departmental, school or faculty level with reviews occurring at regularly specified intervals, usually every five to seven years. An internal review of a programme will frequently be carried out first. The report of this review will then serve as background information for a team of external examiners selected on the basis of their subject matter expertise in the area(s) being examined.

The external review team will normally make one or more on-site visits. It will interview students, graduates, faculty, staff and academic administrators; seek clarification of matters covered in the internal review; request further information; and raise key issues and concerns. It will then prepare a draft report and submit it to the unit under review so as to ensure accuracy of factual information. Once these steps have occurred, the external review team will write its final report and submit it to the institution's academic decision-making body for considered discussion, recommendation and action.

Programme reviews of this type, and those carried out by the accreditation bodies of professional associations, form an important part of an institution's overall planning process. They help shape its mission, goals, strategic directions, operational and financial plans. The monitoring process is usually cyclical with at least one component of an institution's programme being reviewed at any one point in time. It is a process that many funding sources, not least governments, consider necessary for the maintenance of an institution's credibility and integrity.

System level

Utilization of the peer-review assessment process at the system level is infrequent but not unknown. In Canada it has assumed a number of forms over the years. The membership of provincial government commissions established to review their higher education system is frequently drawn from academe. Some provinces have carried out system-wide peer reviews of undergraduate programmes in selected disciplines. At least one province, Ontario, has also undertaken them at the graduate level. Here the process has been used in connection with the funding of proposed new programmes (taking into account factors such as societal need, student demand, and intrinsic merit). In addition, all existing graduate programmes must meet periodic quality appraisal standards in order to qualify for continued funding (Skolnik, 1989).

The procedures and criteria applied in Ontario place great emphasis on the quality of faculty as this is assessed in terms of peer-adjudicated publications, research grants, etc. Other criteria include library and computing resources, curriculum and programme requirements, and grade point requirements for admission. The criteria do not include evaluation of instruction, student supervision, student outcomes, or public and professional service.

The process is not without its critics. Skolnik (1989) writes of a preoccupation with quantity as opposed to quality of publications, differences of opinion concerning the appropriate balance between evaluation of instruction, research and service, student development outcomes, constraints on the development of new paradigms of scholarship such as 'the reflective practitioner', and inadequate consideration of relevant admission factors other than marks or grades.

His most severe criticism, however, is reserved for the system-wide application of the connoisseurship model. In the Ontario case this consists of an appraisals committee drawn largely from the natural sciences, which 'works to suppress diversity, innovation, and non-conformist approaches in the search for knowledge' (Skolnik, 1989: 638).

In Skolnik's view, and he makes a valid point, the mutual interdependence of different parts of the university, and their common commitment to the search for truth, would 'be enhanced considerably by a decentralisation of the appraisals process in which the autonomy of multiple centres of connoisseurship were recognised' (Skolnik, 1989: 640).

Performance indicators

The use and misuse of performance indicators is a topic of contentious public and professional debate in Canada. The level of the debate was heightened by the publication of university rankings in *Maclean's*, a Canadian weekly magazine, in October 1991 and November 1992. Its rankings were based largely upon the use of input measures.

Input measures

Input measures have been widely used by provincial governments to help them develop appropriate funding mechanisms. They have been employed less frequently by individual institutions but perhaps the initiative of one university (Queen's University, 1992) will be followed by others. In Queen's their use was primarily driven by information dissemination and resource needs. The university stressed the fact that prospective students want better information on which to base their decisions and that funding sources increasingly stress the need for greater accountability. The institution itself, moreover, observed that it sought more objective bases on which to link allocation decisions to strategic priorities. Four broad categories of performance were assessed: students, professors, research and the learning environment. Indicators employed for the student category included undergraduate and graduate demand, prior educational performance levels, gender balance, geographic diversity, scholarships and student assistance. Honours and awards constituted the performance measures for faculty, with sponsored and peer-adjudicated funding being used to assess institutional research intensity and performance. The quality of the learning environment was measured by class size, student : faculty ratios, student services, library acquisition expenditures, the number of library volumes per student, and central computing expenditures as a percentage of total operating expenditures.

Output measures

Honours and awards for students and faculty can be considered as output as well as input measures of performance. However, the institutional use of more detailed output measures to assess educational outcomes is rare. Probably the most comprehensive treatment of outcome measures in Canadian higher education can be found in a study by Evers and Gilbert (1991) who observed that 'Apart from the type of university degree and the final grade average, universities know little about other specific outcomes of education such as cognitive and affective consequences' (p. 54).

In their study, these authors analyse data from two independent research studies assessing student outcomes: Career and Education Achievement in the Study Environment (CEASE) and Making the Match (MTM). They investigated a range of outcomes but focused on the skill development process as estimated by students and graduates.

In the CEASE study, students were asked how they rated their level of competence on the following skills: thinking and reasoning, problem-solving, decision-making, planning and organizing, time management, communication, interpersonal and social, quantitative/mathematical, independence and supervisory. They were also asked to indicate their development on the University of Guelph's stated Learning Objectives: literacy, including reading, writing and oral communication skills; numeracy, including qualitative or computational skills; sense of historical development/historical consciousness; independence of thought; desire to continue learning; creativity; global understanding; a sense of wider international and cultural contexts; moral maturity, including an understanding of moral and ethical choices; aesthetic maturity, including acquaintance with literature and the arts; understanding of forms of inquiry, including an appreciation of science and other methods of inquiry and their limitations; and depth and breadth of understanding focusing on substantive in-depth knowledge of a field of study (Evers and Gilbert, 1991: 62).

In the MTM study, the first phase looked at the perceptions of managers and university-educated employees of large Canadian corporations about the adequacy of university education for corporate employment; the second phase examined the skill acquisition of individuals from early university years until ten years out in their careers. Skill competency levels were based on more than 60 items condensed into summary measures of competence representing 18 broad skill areas for graduates and 17 broad skill areas for students. These included many of the same skill areas found in the CEASE project but gave greater specificity to listening, conflict management, visioning and leadership/influence skills.

The findings of the two studies are discussed in detail. Of most interest here, however, are the conclusions reached. Managers rated creativity, visioning and leadership as the top three skill areas in greatest demand in future corporate employment (Evers and Gilbert, added written communication). Graduates considered the only dimension of their development, where university instruction played the most important role, was in the ability to conceptualize. For students, on the other hand:

> Formal university instruction is considered to be a major source of development for thinking and reasoning skills, problem-solving skills, planning and organisation skills, time management skills, ability to conceptualise, learning skills and quantitative, mathematical and technical skills... [It] is not considered to be the major source of development for independence, interpersonal and social skills, supervisory skills, risk-taking, managing conflict, leadership/influence, and creativity/innovation (Evers and Gilbert, 1991: 74).

University experiences were also not considered important influences on such outcomes as cultural, artistic, global, historical and political sensitivities/awareness, and caring concern for others.

Commentary

I believe that the monitoring and evaluation of higher education in Canada will assume greater rather than lesser importance in the years to come. Important stakeholders – students and their families, governments, employers, labour and the tax-paying public – will press for it in increasingly vocal fashion. Discussions, both lay and professional, will increasingly take place within the broader context of higher education's contribution to local, regional, national and international economies. Higher education's role in the creation and dissemination of knowledge will be reassessed and its links to science, technology and innovation systems stressed.

Research in the universities is coming under increasing scrutiny. The Royal Society of Canada conducted a review in the late 1980s. At least one national research council is examining how excellence in research might be better monitored and assessed. In Alberta at the beginning of 1995 the Minister of Advanced Education and Training established a review of that province's universities with the intention of developing a policy framework which would recognize the relationship of research to the advancement of knowledge, the economic benefit of Alberta, and the quality of life of its citizens.

It is anticipated that some form of national reference points for the purposes of comparison will be identified, and that these are likely to include an institution's success rate in peer-adjudicated research awards, measures of the economic impact of its research, research dollars received, and the number of publications in peer-reviewed journals.

In addition, pressures will be brought to integrate research and development in higher education institutions with that carried out by governments and the enterprise sector. Education training will increasingly be viewed in terms of its contribution to human resource development, especially at advanced levels.

The nature, scope and intensity of these pressures for greater integration will vary from system to system, institution to institution. But as these pressures are applied, institutions of higher education will seek to strengthen and expand monitoring and evaluation systems that are transparent, credible and effective. As they do so, the process will raise issues of specific institutional goals and functions in a far more explicit fashion than hitherto. Indeed, the process is already well under way.

More attention, for example, will be drawn to the professional and public service functions of higher education institutions. Thus some colleges and universities have already carried out studies of the economic impact of their institutions on their communities. Others have established centres of technology transfer and/or applied research institutes of special relevance to regional needs and development. Still others have published, in readily available and attractive formats, texts listing the expertise and professional public service contributions of their faculty and staff.

These activities are of course valuable. But they raise unanswered questions for the monitoring and evaluation of individual and institutional performance. How are they to be assessed and weighted in terms of an institution's overall mission? How do they figure in an institution's reward structure? What assessment mechanisms and procedures are available? How are they to be applied? What of those areas of higher learning that are not readily accessible to assessment? More broadly, and more importantly, what are the cumulative effects on autonomous institutions of becoming more fully integrated into the economic life and knowledge base of a society? These are complex questions, and they add to the difficulties of monitoring and evaluation practices in colleges and universities.

Notwithstanding these difficulties, however, it is increasingly recognized that institutions of higher learning can and should be monitored and evaluated, that a growing array of useful but incomplete tools exist to do so, and that expectations regarding their use are on the increase. Most important of all, there is the growing recognition within the higher education community that these expectations possess substance and legitimacy and that, if higher education is to avoid being seen simply as a service sector for the economy, it must assume responsibility for expanded methods of self-assessment and respond to external pressures with appropriate openness, objectivity and independence.

Acknowledgements

An earlier version of this chapter appeared in the Proceedings of the OECD/PHARE Seminar, on Monitoring and Evaluating Educational Systems, in Bratislava, Slovakia, 15–16 March 1993; Paris: OECD Centre for Cooperation with Economies in Transition.

References

Chinapah, V (ed) (1992) *Evaluation of Higher Education in a Changing Europe: Report from the UNESCO Seminar on the Evaluation of Higher Education in a Changing Europe, Stockholm, May 1990*, Stockholm: UNESCO and the Institute of International Education, University of Stockholm.

Evers, F T and Gilbert, S N (1991) 'Outcomes Assessment: how much value does university education add?', *Canadian Journal of Higher Education*, XII (2), pp. 53–76.

Queen's University Alumni Review (November–December 1992) Special Supplement, pp. 14–21.

Skolnik, M L (1989) 'How Academic Programme Review can Foster Intellectual Conformity and Stifle Diversity of Thought and Method', *Canadian Journal of Higher Education*, 60 (6), pp. 619–643.

6. The evaluation of the higher education system in the People's Republic of China

Tianxiang Xue

Introduction

In adapting to the emerging structure of the socialist market economy for the time being, China's higher education is committed to gradually develop an autonomous system under the government's general guidance. And the evaluation of higher education is now playing an increasingly important role in assessing education quality, the efficiency of running educational institutions and teaching efficiency within government guidelines. So it is necessary to summarize our experience in evaluation practice and strengthen the study of the evaluation theory to bring China's higher education evaluation up to a new level.

Evaluation of higher education is defined as a process in which the value of activities of higher education is judged through data systematically gathered, so as to achieve the cardinal goal of strengthening the links between higher education and society and accelerating overall quality progress. In its essence, evaluation of higher education is to evaluate such themes as the quality of management running educational institutions, education quality, discipline quality and students' achievements. Thus evaluation of higher education quality and evaluation of higher education are equally treated in this chapter.

The main purpose of this chapter is to get an overall and systematic view of studies about higher education evaluation within mainland China in the light of the influence produced by traditional Chinese culture. Also I will briefly deal with the existing problems, and what we have accomplished, and put forward my own point of view on trends for China's higher education evaluation.

Studies about evaluation of China's higher education

The evaluation of China's higher education has gone through quite a long period of time, but only has a short history in its modern meaning.

We might date it back as far as 4,000 years ago if we take the academic achievement test into consideration. But for one reason or another, only when New China was founded in 1949, did studies of evaluation of higher education get a chance to develop in their modern sense.

Preparatory stage (1978–1985)

There were three reasons for the quick development in modern education evaluation in China during this time:

- we needed to evaluate the reform of bringing order to higher education shortly after the so-called 'Great Cultural Revolution';
- new disciplines, especially evaluation theory, were introduced to China from the West;
- the government's line 'to seek the truth, to emancipate the mind helped pave the road towards the evaluation of higher education in China.

Major activities during this time were studies of evaluation of higher education which were undertaken in some regions and departments. For example, in 1982, the Ministry of Hygiene carried out an evaluation of teaching quality in its subordinate colleges of medicine by means of a unified examination. Also, to meet the demand for theory study, some foreign academic achievements were successively introduced to China. But on the whole, the study of evaluation at this time was still dispersed rather than coherent.

All-round development stage (1985–1990)

The promulgation of the Central Committee's Decision on Reform of Education Structure in May 1985 marked a fruitful era for China's modern system of evaluation. Major activities in this period included:

- The first national session on the evaluation of higher education held in Jingpohu, Heilongjiang province in June 1985. Follow-up sessions were held in Hefai (Auhui province), Beijing and Tianjin to continue studies of the nature of evaluation of higher education, especially its purposes, principles, processes and criteria.
- Multi-level education evaluations were brought into full play in which at least eight Ministries or Commissions, six Education Committees at provincial and municipal levels and 500 regular higher education institutions were involved.
- External exchanges concerning evaluation of higher education were stressed. Two Sino-American symposia on education evaluation were held and inspection groups were sent to the USA and Canada as a part of collaboration projects with these countries.
- A number of theory advances were made and academic periodicals were published during this time, for instance, *Education evaluation:*

Theory and Technology (Chen Yukun, 1987) and *Reports on Evaluation of Higher Education* which was first issued in 1988. This is now the periodical *China's Higher Education Evaluation*.
- By the end of the seventh Five-year Plan, a capable cohort of higher education evaluation researchers had been formed in which higher education administrators, experts on higher education, and faculty on campus were the backbone.

Deeper research stage (1991 to date)

The State Education Committee's Provisional Regulations on Evaluation in Regular Higher Education Institutions in October 1990 set a framework for China's higher education evaluation system, serving as a landmark for deeper research in this area. Another important impetus to the development was Deng Xiaoping's talk during his tour of south China in 1992. The socialist market economy system goal set at the fourteenth National Congress broke with the convention of the planned economy and provided a good environment for educational evaluation in China. The main activities in this period included:

- The fifth National Session on evaluation of higher education which was held in Changchun, Jilin province, in January 1994 at which the Higher Education Evaluation Society was founded, the first of its kind in China.
- A symposium on evaluation of higher education in countries around the Pacific Rim was held. National evaluation of higher education lectures and a Sino-American Evaluation Seminar on higher education were also sponsored in the same year, which were of benefit to Chinese scholars.
- In 1994, an Appraisal Committee on universities and colleges evaluated the newly booming non-state universities and colleges, six of which were approved.
- In July 1995, the State Education Committee organized a group of 140 experts and scholars from various universities and colleges all over China to appraise as many as 2,700 monographs, papers, reference books and research reports published during the past decade. More than 500 items were given the grading of 'Academic Excellence'.
- New progress was also made in theoretical study. More than one thousand papers on the evaluation of higher education were published. The following distribution shows the themes and topics of articles carried in the magazine *China's Higher Education Evaluation* (up to the end of 1993).

Comprehensive	73
Teaching	52
Discipline	10
Curriculum	20
Student	7
Scientific	3
Management	9
Teacher	5
Moral Education	3
Library	3
Total	185

Additionally, interpretations of the evaluation of higher education in China by Professor Chen Yukun (1993) and a few monographs on the topic of evaluation became widely read. Against this background of effort and productivity in thinking and research, there have remained some problems.

Some problems facing China's evaluation of higher education

Some negative effects were produced when a lopsided approach was taken to the rankings which were a result of evaluation, especially as some studies neglected scientific methodology in the evaluation of processes. This problem is rooted in a feature of Chinese culture which puts too much emphasis on the goal rather than the process.

Second, too much stress was laid on macro-research such as the government's role in managing a university, while neglecting micro-research like teaching goals, students' achievement, etc. This was somewhat in correspondence with traditional intuitionism and the concept of 'wholeness,' but for the examination of details, such ways of evaluating proved to be too abstract, vague and thus neither scientific nor useful in providing applicable results. This evaluation style also had something to do with the older leadership style in China. Evaluation of higher education used to be carried out under the direct guidance of the different levels of Education Committee, and of course the authorities took more interest in macro aspects of evaluation than micro ones.

Third, researchers focused on evaluation indicators or indicator systems rather than on the purposes and functions of the evaluation of higher education. From the very beginning, due to the concept of so called 'social self' in Chinese culture, indicators or indicator systems were placed high on the evaluation priority list, which led to two extremes: stressing the integrity of the indicator system, while ignoring individual diversity in the evaluation objectives, and thus leaving a gap between the evaluation and the reality; second, there was too much stress on seeking the measurability of evaluation objectives while overlooking the purposes, functions, methodology and attributes of the evaluation. Sometimes quantity instead of quality became the aim which was concentrated on.

Fourth, there was a lack of experts from such areas as pedagogy, psychology and sociology. This limitation in personnel resources blocked the evaluation of higher education from achieving maturity and further development. Partly due to traditional thinking by analogy and reasoning based on experience, we could do a good job in dealing with data, but were less good at exploring the philosophy behind these data.

Fifth, quantitative analysis was used much more often in the methodology than qualitative analysis. To some extent, such a phenomenon was in contradiction to the Chinese traditional way of thinking, 'intuitionism', but it was also a tradition that people would take a respectful approach towards the academic authorities, which maybe derived from older traditions of 'worship of the sage'. So it is not strange to note that Chinese scholars indiscriminately imitated the Western 'advanced' evaluation theories, methods and evaluation indicator systems at the early stage of development of these techniques in China.

Some current trends in the study of China's evaluation of higher education

There is an effort being made to incorporate social demand evaluation, with individual demand evaluation, to contribute to the coordinated growth of society. In China, priority was given to the idea of integrity and maintenance of the interest of the whole rather than individual or partial interests. What made the thing worse was too much political intervention in evaluation. Individual elements are now expected to be strengthened during the process of China's evaluation of higher education reform and in the process of transforming the traditional culture.

An effort is being made to incorporate formative and summative evaluation to allow the achievement of quality goals in China's higher education. Different kinds of evaluation will be used to serve different purposes. It seems to be a custom that theorists pay more attention to formative evaluation while administrators care more about summative evaluation. One explanation is that in the former case the purpose is to 'improve' and in the latter case, to 'prove'. Two problems should be avoided here: increasing and high costs brought about by delay in the summative evaluation; and creating barriers to the practice of formative evaluation in China.

It is important to incorporate macro-evaluation with micro-evaluation to enhance the effectiveness of teaching and management. In my view, without evaluation of details such as discipline, teaching, students' achievement and so on, macro evaluation will end up achieving nothing.

It is also necessary for evaluation theories to be linked with practices in creating a theory of evaluation of higher education with Chinese characteristics and absorbing Western theories and experience. In our history, we have had successful experience in making the West service China and have drawn lessons from the so-called 'wholesale Westernization'. Mutual understanding of each nation's circumstance is the precondition of mutual benefit. Equal attention should be paid to 'case research' and 'basic research' in order to make breakthroughs in both areas. But we should be careful. We need more specialists in evaluation and a licence system should be introduced as a qualification for 'evaluation experts', as we train more qualified and capable evaluation personnel.

References

(The original references are in Chinese.)

Chen Yukun (1987) *Education Evaluation: Theory and Practice*, Guangzhou: Guangdong Higher Education Press, pp. 344–55.

Chen Yukun (1993) *On China's Higher Education Evaluation*, Guangzhou: Guangdong Higher Education Press.

China's Higher Education Evaluation, (1988–1993), Issues 1–16, Shanghai.

7. The evaluation of the higher education system in France

Guy Neave

Introduction

Amongst the many developments that shaped higher education in Western Europe during the course of the 1980s, few have been more central than the rise of the so called 'evaluative state' (Neave and van Vught, 1988, 1991). This term stands, not unnaturally, as a species of shorthand and as such acts as a summary for a number of interlinked processes and procedures which, taken together, add up to a very radical and substantial revision to established relationships between government and higher education. Put succinctly, the rise of the evaluative state is a phenomenon grounded in three concerns which are highly pragmatic in nature, even though the imagination of political parties, advisers and their followers is often tempted to wrap them in an ideological tinsel. These three concerns are the constraint on most Western economies to sustain an increasing burden of social expenditure, a continued and spectacular demand for higher education and, last but by no means least, the realization amongst the technicians of government that the ability of higher education to meet widescale post-industrial and occupational change is no longer served by close and detailed control of central administration over the tactical running of the nation's system of higher education.

The rise of the evaluative state is then a way of meeting these medium-term difficulties by a combination of measures which, *grosso modo*, involve on the one hand, the delegation of responsibility for institutional planning down to the individual university and, on the other, confining the area of central government responsibility to setting the broad goals and guidelines of national policy; in short, replacing what some policy analysts have interpreted as the heavy hand of 'state control' by a less interventionist relationship with the world of academia, grounded in the notion of 'state supervision' (Neave and van Vught, 1991; 1994).

In this new distribution of power, influence and responsibility between

66

the strategic overview exercised by a hopefully slimmer central Ministry and the setting out by institutional management of the ways in which individual universities will implement national goals, the process of evaluation is a central and vital policy instrument. Irrespective of the technical details involved, or of the precise nature of individual indicators employed to identify 'the good and faithful servant' or to point the finger of financial scorn at the more laggardly, the process of evaluation is the prime vehicle by which central government obtains an overall — and up to date — picture of what is happening within its system of higher education and that at a time when diversity of demand and variation in individual response have reached a complexity without parallel in the history of that institution.

Evaluation acts then as that essential instrument of articulation between the formulation of national strategy by central government acting on behalf of the nation's authoritative representatives and the interpretation, implementation, performance — and thus fulfilment — of that strategy at the level of the individual university. Through the utilization of procedures of review, assessment and objective indicators of performance, the state manages to combine in remarkable parsimony three functions which lie at the heart of higher education policy. These are verification, assessment of performance and control over costs and output. To be sure, these functions have always existed. But by tying them together — and even in certain instances of which Britain is one — by relating budgetary allocation explicitly to institutional performance, the evaluative state now has at its disposal a coordinate instrument of policy in many ways far more powerful than the historic practice of control by legal fiat, ministerial circular or administrative decree.

The evaluative state, whatever the ideological presentation that surrounds it, is more powerful than the 'state control' model which it replaces for the very simple reason that it involves placing the basic obligation of proving the good husbandry or efficiency of higher education upon individual establishments, held to be directly answerable to the public rather than passing through the intermediary of the Ministry itself. It is no less powerful for being based on a practice which, in earlier times, was the prime device for distributing what the American sociologist of higher education Burton Clark has called 'the gold coin of academic exchange' — to wit excellence and repute and standing (Clark, 1983) — by means of peer review. The evaluative state has, in effect, transformed peer review from being the private instrument of intelligence-gathering for the academic community into a public tool by which academia is itself weighed in the balance. Academia, like Shakespeare's unfortunate artificer, is indeed 'hoist upon its own petard'.

The drive towards the evaluative state

If Britain has often been amongst the leaders in this drive to set up the evaluative state, it is far from being alone. Australia (Meek, 1994) Belgium (VLIR, 1993) the Netherlands (van Vught, 1989) and, more recently, Sweden (Furstenbach, 1992) and Spain (de Miguel *et al.*, 1991) have each embarked on the road that leads on to regular and systematic evaluation of the performance, productivity and output of their institutes of higher education, university and non-university alike. And on this monument to a revigorated academia, France is no exception. On the contrary, standing as it does as the quintessential expression of a higher education system historically rooted in the 'state control' model of relationship between government and university, the path which successive governments have beaten towards a French edition of the evaluative state is not without its particular interest, not least because, in many respects, it is a tale, once again, of that nation's originality and exceptionalism.

Structure and administrative oversight of French higher education

It is not far short of a banality to say that systems of evaluation reflect not simply a nation's goals for higher education and the ways in which it is thought they may be achieved, but also the structural idiosyncrasies of the higher education system itself. Here it is important to bear constantly in mind several features which are unique to higher education in France.

The first of these is that the university *stricto sensu* is not the elite sector. Rather the path that leads on to honour and 'high preferment' in both state service and in the private sector resides in the 200 or so *Grandes Ecoles*, ferociously selective in their admissions policy (Durand-Prinborgne, 1992: 217–24) and exercising a degree of influence over public life far beyond what their numbers would otherwise justify. In the first round of the Presidential elections of March 1995, three of the main candidates – the Socialist Lionel Jospin, the ex-Premier Edouard Balladur, and the then current Head of State Jacques Chirac, were all graduates of one of the best known amongst the *Grandes Ecoles*, the *Ecole Nationale d'Administration*. Finally, there is what is sometimes called 'short-cycle' higher education in the shape of the two-year University Institutes of Technology of which there are 53 and their predecessor, the Higher Technicians' Sector which is located atop certain specialized *lycées*, though deemed to be part of higher education provision.

The second feature of French higher education which follows from this institutional differentiation is its highly segmented nature which is as evident in the degree of selection for admission as it is with respect to the overall administrative responsibility a particular Ministry will exercise over a given sector. Certainly, the Ministry of Higher Education and Research is the major *ministères de tutelle* (Friedberg and Musselin, 1991) for Engineering Schools, Universities and University Institutes of Technology (Durand-Prinborgne, 1992: 220). But alongside this classic configuration runs another line of control passing through other Ministries and even local authorities and Chambers of Commerce. Into this somewhat heterogeneous area of administrative oversight fall such establishments as the national agronomic institutes and schools under the Ministry of Agriculture; the Ministry of National Defence has sway over St Cyr — the equivalent of Sandhurst — and over the august *Ecole Polytechnique* which has no equivalent in Britain; health service training establishments come under the Ministry of Health; and the Paris Chamber of Commerce exercises tutelage over the *Ecole des Hautes Etudes Commerciales*, France's counterpart to the Harvard Business School.

The third feature of French higher education is the relatively marginal role played by the private sector, both in respect of the numbers of students enrolled and in respect of the degree of independence it enjoys *vis-à-vis* the decisions of central administration (Durand-Prinborgne, 1992: 219). In 1988–89, for example, total enrolments in the private sector — perhaps best described as the 'non-state sector' of higher education (Neave, 1985) — were of the order of 118,885, including private business schools, engineering establishments and higher technician studies: less than 10 per cent of all national enrolments in higher education.

It is against this backdrop of a state which, if greatly centralized in its control over higher education, is far from enjoying an administrative tidiness that many foreign observers attribute to it, that one must set the overhauling and refurbishing of France's systems of evaluation. It is, I think, clear that what passes today as an unprecedented novelty, whether it is termed 'quality assurance' or evaluation, involves the extension of new techniques of assessment, new criteria if not a new mentality, all three largely derived from private industrial practice, into the workings of the public domain with the purpose of lending a new precision and suppleness to an old function. That function is to ensure that access to and the transmission of knowledge are carried out according to the conditions that the nation, academia and the economy are prepared to endorse and to support.

Just as there are unique characteristics in the structure, administrative responsibility and social standing of higher education in France, so too one finds exceptions in the expanded system put in place to evaluate it. Historically, control over quality and over the conditions under which academic work was carried out has been part and parcel of the overall span of administrative control exercised by the Ministry of Education or by its counterpart in higher education.

Since 1976, the hiving-off of higher education into a separate Ministry or State Secretaryship has been one of the more delightful, if confusing features of higher education policy in France. Generally speaking, right-of-centre governments tend to split-off higher education from primary and secondary education, whereas the left tends to take the view that education, as a service of the nation, should remain, like the Republic, one and indivisible. Under this way of looking at things, higher education is simply a sub-set of a vast National Ministry of Education, a view that could well owe much to the fact that school teachers are one of the more powerful interest groups in left-wing coalitions, whereas university teachers tend to have a similar weight in their right-wing counterparts.

Functions which, in systems grounded on the Anglo-American model of state/university relations, would fall into the purlieu of the individual university remained firmly in the hand of central authority. Amongst them, nomination to posts of individual academics and their promotion, as well as control over the process of validation of degrees, are the most significant (Starian, 1992: 19). In short, to revert to contemporary jargon, one of the main characteristics of higher education in France was that administrative control also involved quality control through the setting down of national norms for appointment to post, and for procedures of staff selection and promotion. Similarly detailed conditions were laid down governing the right of individual universities to award national diplomas as opposed to university degrees.

This duality between national diplomas and university degrees is not, however, unique to France. It is, for instance, also to be found in Belgium and in the Federal Republic of Germany (Neave, 1986). The basic difference between the two types of degree is that the quality and standards of state, national or, in the Belgian case, 'legal' as opposed to 'scientific' degrees, are both underwritten by central authority and confer the formal right on their holder to be considered for posts in public service. Those holding degrees and diplomas awarded by the individual university alone do not benefit from this right. National diplomas act then as a powerful device for homogenization on the one hand and as an instrument of formal control from the centre on the other and are all the more influential for the fact that they are deemed to be more valuable on the labour market by both students and employers.

Earlier instruments of evaluation and control

If the ultimate responsibility at national level for appointment and promotion were matters for the Higher Education Personnel Department inside the Ministry of Education and the award of national diplomas and validation remained the concern of the National Council of Universities, such procedures were largely *a priori* to the extent that once the conditions required had been fulfilled, they were rarely the subject of any follow-up assessment. To be sure, central authority retained the right, in the case of courses leading to national diplomas, to withdraw recognition. But this was rarely used and then mainly on administrative grounds – for instance, insufficient numbers of students – rather than grounds of either individual or institutional productivity and output.

One such instance of withdrawal of recognition for Masters'-level programmes took place in the latter days in the Giscardian régime in 1979. But its timing (it was implemented during the summer vacation) its speed and its extent suggest that it was more in the nature of a settling of academic scores between the then Ministry of Higher Education and certain university presidents than the outcome of a careful exercise in formal evaluation. The decision was later overturned by the *Conseil d'Etat*. This incident alone should remind readers that 'evaluation' can also serve as a weapon in conflicts related to issues other than quality as well as bringing to their notice that other feature of decision-making in French higher education, namely its high degree of politicization (Premfors, 1980).

This is not to say that procedures of evaluation relating to academic productivity shone wholly by their absence. Such procedures did indeed exist but applied almost exclusively to the research sector which, in France, is organizationally separate from the university with its own career structure, conditions of recruitment and grades, even though physically sited in universities (Clark, 1993; 1995).

Thus, in France, the state did indeed exercise a species of administrative evaluation which may be described as being in an 'initiatory' mode. This mode is not dissimilar to the investigations, inquiries and assessment employed by the erstwhile (British) Council for National Academic Awards prior to conferring the right to award CNAA degrees on individual establishments in the polytechnic sector. According to this procedure, universities in France were expected to submit proposals in line with 'national templates' (*maquettes nationales*) in which duration, the number of hours of study and the broad outlines of the syllabus were set forth (Guin, 1990: 123–46). Evaluation was thus limited to either the launching of new courses, or to the substantial revision of those already in place. Paradoxically, for a country where centralization has been the dominant administrative form, the initiatory mode left the basic decision to apply for national degree status in the hands of the individual university. If the state exercised a curtailed form of evaluation as part of its overall command over higher education, this is far from being the same thing as the evaluative state. Why then did French authorities embark on the road towards the evaluative state and what form did it take?

Strategic considerations in the move to the evaluative state

If the generic purpose of systematic evaluation is broadly similar across countries – that is, to render transparent accounts to the public of what has been achieved in terms of student output, qualification, prospects of employment, institutional good husbandry and academic productivity – the circumstances in which it is launched are very different. Unlike either Britain or the Netherlands where the prime issue from the early 1980s onward was spiralling unit costs and financial constraint generally, the main issue in France was the drive substantially to expand student numbers in higher education and radically to overhaul the higher education system in keeping with what is seen as France's key position as one of the two leading nations in the European Union. The putting in place of a systematic *a posteriori* mechanism of evaluation stood as part of this overall strategic effort. Already by 1984, the then Socialist administration was fully committed to doubling the numbers of students in higher education over the ensuing 16 years: in effect to increase the student population to over two million. Despite successive changes of government, this ambition has remained intact and is well on the way to being realized. Student numbers, which were 1.32 million in the academic year 1989–90, reached 1.67 million by 1993–4 – a rise of slightly over 25 per cent in five years (*Rapport au Président de la République*, 1994: 33). No less important, since it fundamentally altered the relationship between secondary and higher education, was the parallel goal to raise the number of school leavers reaching a level of achievement equivalent to the Baccalaureat to around 80 per cent of the appropriate age group. The objective, first mooted in the mid-1980s and enshrined in the Education Guideline Law of 1989, was to be realized in the course of the following decade (*Ministère de l'Education, de la Jeunesse et des Sports*, 1989).

Clearly, any higher education system – even the most successful – under such pressures to expand could not do so and maintain established patterns of administrative control. Furthermore, increasing evidence was to hand which could no longer be ignored that if detailed state control exercised from the centre might have been adequate for elite higher education, its dysfunction was all too painfully obvious once that stage had been surpassed. With the prospect of a massive influx of students into higher education, with larger numbers of students than ever before coming from backgrounds without family experience of higher education, the reality of diversity of demand coupled with the need to adjust to structural change in both industry and commerce broke asunder the basic assumptions on which both French higher education and its particular administrative patterns of control had long rested. The basic assumption that central government could uphold the legal fiction of homogeneity of provision across the nation and irrespective of geography – the touchstone of French education since the time the Imperial University was launched in 1808 – was thus called into question by the sheer scale of the enterprise.

New priorities, new assumptions

The setting up of the National Committee for Evaluation in 1985 fulfilled numerous purposes over and above the technical exercise of regularly evaluating the overall activities of individual establishments of higher education. At a time when the essential diversity of the student population, as regards ability, as regards its occupational intentions, and thus as a consequence, the corresponding diversity in types of courses put in place to meet their needs, whether vocational or academic, short course or fast track, was a matter of record, evaluation provided a two-way flow of intelligence, to government no less than to academia on the condition of higher education, a condition which could no longer be assumed simply to fall into what legislative intent and ministerial circular stipulated. In the French context, evaluation of higher education was part and parcel of a rather broader and fundamental revision in the relationship between central, regional and local government which not only involved the 'off-loading' of certain core functions hitherto vested in central administration. Evaluation stood as a new element in policy formation and an equal shift in 'policy style' from what has variously been identified as a species of 'stop/go' model in which the central administration acted under pressure of the threat of crisis (Premfors, 1980) to one in which individual establishments possessed an increasingly significant area of latitude to formulate, justify and implement their own programmes of action, rather than waiting on the *ukase* and pleasure of the Prince.

There are, then several specific features which set aside the French drive towards the evaluative state from either its British or its Dutch counterparts. In the first place, it was not so much a reform determined by internal factors bearing down on higher education. It was rather an initiative taken within higher education to meet widespread change in the political system and more especially in the distribution of financial responsibility between central and local government. To be sure, the setting up of the National Evaluation Committee can be explained by referring to conditions internal to higher education; the increasing complexity of having to run what official jargon at last recognized as a system based on a 'a variable geometry' (Guin, 1990: 123–46) rather than adhering to the powerful myth of 'legal homogeneity' (Neave and van Vught, 1994). And, no less, to the challenge, substantial in itself, of putting in place suitable instruments of steering higher education through a government-induced expansion of higher education without precedent since the early 1970s. Where both internal and external factors came together was in the precise role that central government ought to play in managing a system in which diversity of demand and delegation of control were to be the governing watchwords. Here, two elements intervened in favour of altering the role of central administration, the first political and the second, not unexpectedly in view of the likely cost involved in expansion, financial. Both turned around reassigning responsibilities away from the centre and strengthening the capacity for taking initiatives at regional and establishment level.

Political and administrative decentralization

The political argument in favour of decentralization was the result of the perverse effects of centralization itself. One of the by-products of centralization is to create a degree of dependence – some would say an unhealthy reliance – on formal hierarchy to decide even the most routine matters. Not only does this situation create immense 'decisional overload' on the central administration, it also tends enormously to obscure the possibility of a 'strategic vision' by immersing the centre in the short term and drowning it in the routine. Furthermore, central control often tends to politicize decision-making as particular interests seek to break through the slowness of formal procedure by resource to the political arm. Politicization of decision-making has long been an outstanding feature of higher education administration in France (Premfors, 1980). Arguably, it has also contributed mightily both to the endemic gridlock that many observers have noted (Crozier, 1972) and thus to further politicization as local interests fight through their disputes at national level. By increasing the bounds of institutional autonomy, not only were establishments encouraged to look to their own ingenuity; by the same token, central administration could assume a more strategic role.

The second argument in favour of decentralization was largely fiscal, and its consequences were of prime importance in redefining the relationship between central government and regional administration. Doubling student numbers, plus additional equipment and building costs, were doughty burdens on national expenditure. By sharing with regional authorities part of the responsibility for financing higher education and bringing in other 'partners' such as municipalities and industry, the burden could be spread. Though a cunning solution in as much as it obliged local authorities to raise taxes whilst allowing national authorities to avoid the odium of increasing *theirs*, the price to be paid politically was not negligible. If regions assumed the cost of the upkeep of buildings and the development of branch campuses, they also assumed a major role as a stakeholder in the enterprise of higher education. Some idea of their increasing importance can be grasped when one adds up their financial contribution to higher education. Between 1990 and 1994, regional and local authorities injected FFrs 16.2bn (£2.093bn) into the university infrastructure (*Rapport au Président de la République*, 1994: 36). Regional authorities, whether in the person of the Chief Education Officer (*Recteur d'Académie*) or the *Prefect* took over formal responsibility, the first for coordinating regional needs and developments across the various sectors of the higher education system and the second for the financial implications that followed from the first (Neave and Kaiser, 1994: 124–125).

The strengthening of the regional layer of higher education administration, hitherto generally held to be of minor importance (Clark, 1983), the creation of Regional Outline Plans (*schémas régionaux d'aménagement*) and the granting of financial teeth to regional authorities can, of course, be interpreted as the 'denationalization' of a state system of higher education. But it can also be seen as part of that inevitable process which the setting up of the evaluative state also involves, namely a multiplication in the number of public authorities with which the university has now to deal. From a French point of view, the ending of what can be seen as a monopoly of the central state over finance and the creation of partnerships between region and centre, were far from being disadvantageous. Diversity in the sources of funding, even though they did remain overwhelmingly within the realm of the public purse, seemed to hold out greater promise of a real degree of institutional latitude even if this was not always seen in terms of autonomy.

The rise of contractual financing

The final step in the abandonment of national homogeneity has been to place the financing of individual universities on a contractual basis. This had been foreseen in the Higher Education Guideline Law of 1984, though in point of fact it remained a dead letter until the *Loi d'Orientation* of five years later. Contractual financing imposes a special obligation upon the individual university as part of the negotiating procedures, to draw up a 'detailed mission statement' covering the resources to hand, the objectives to be fulfilled and the resources required to carry them out. Equally, contractual financing demands at a minimum that the individual university has both know-how and experience in exercising internal self-assessment, a feature of which the least that can be said is that it was not encouraged by the more traditional means of centralized control.

If we have gone into the anatomy of reform in French higher education, not all of which bears directly on the issue of evaluation, it is to provide a backdrop against which to set the particular mechanisms involved in this process of reconstruction. In addition, it is also to furnish a broad context which allows a better purchase over, and understanding of, some of the unique features that go to make up the French version of the evaluative state.

As we have seen, the drive to expand higher education in France has, since 1984, been consistently grounded on the basic assumption that expansion required a major recasting of the fundamental relationship between central administration and the individual university – the principle of negotiated contractual financing – between central administration and regional authorities — the principle of 'partnership' rather than formal administrative subordination — and finally, the explicit link between universities and the regional interest.

A rare self-denying ordinance

It is one thing to proclaim change by legislation. It is quite another to break away from long engrained habits of thinking and acting. The basic issue underlying the introduction in French academia of systematic and rolling evaluation of individual institutions was, curiously, how precisely to prevent evaluation from becoming yet another device for perpetuating a centralist mentality? Or, put slightly differently, how could it serve to stimulate initiative and innovation at institutional level and thus give solid grounding in institutional behaviour to the intentions of the legislator to promulgate what, from the standpoint of an historically powerful and highly centralized administration, amounted to a rare example of a self-denying ordinance?

This particular conundrum has exercised a predominant influence in shaping evaluation in France and most particularly in determining both the siting of the National Evaluation Committee in administration and its underlying strategic purpose (Staropoli, 1987). If the National Committee is an official body, it stands aside from the traditional loci of power and control in central government. It is not answerable to the Minister of Higher Education; on the contrary, as a gauge of its independence, it is chaired by a prominent member of French academia whose mandate is for five years. And, furthermore, the National Committee reports directly to the President of the Republic. While half of its 16-member Board without counting the President is composed of academics, the remainder are drawn from what might best be described as institutions that act as independent watchdogs over government; for example, the Council of State, the Audit Court and the Economic and Social Council.

The political symbolism of other countries is never easy to grasp. Suffice it to note that the Council of State is an independent review body which pronounces on the constitutionality, and thus formal legality, of administrative acts and whose decisions are binding. The Audit Court bears a certain similarity with the British Comptroller General's Office. It too exercises independent review and oversight in the usage of public funds. The Economic and Social Council is the main review body for social and labour legislation and brings together the three 'social partners' — government, employers and labour. Each institution stands as a species of 'transversal organ', cutting across the administrative responsibility of individual Ministries. Together, they constitute a form of check and balance against administrative arbitrariness.

Thus, the French version of the evaluative state drew both symbolic and real lines between the function of evaluation and the realm of control, whether exercised through normative procedures of recognition and validation or through the attribution of resources, whether human or financial. State and evaluation are, in effect, kept asunder.

Evaluation à *la Française*

From the first, the style of evaluation undertaken by the Committee has deliberately eschewed the inquisitorial and, since the allocation of resources is not tied to the outcome, it avoided too that unfortunate equating of evaluation with chastisement and penalty, a feature that other systems have perhaps been less sensitive in observing. The basic unit of analysis is the individual institution in its entirety and the range of the Committee's activities covers the whole of the higher education system: university, *Grandes Ecoles*, University Institutes of Technology, Business Schools *e tutti quanti*. The French edition of institutional evaluation does not involve the assessment of individual academics, still less of students, individual courses or individual research output. Officially, it is argued that individual evaluation of performance falls under the purlieu of other bodies, students being evaluated by their teachers, academics by peer review undertaken by the National Council of Universities, while researchers have long been subjected to the rigours of the National Council for Scientific Research, of the National Institute for Health and Medical Research or, more recently, of the National Committee for Research Evaluation (*Rapport au Président de la République*, 1994: 14).

No less astounding is the outright rejection of evaluation based on teaching programmes. The refusal to draw up lists of comparative performance between different programmes, and thus to indulge in national league tables of disciplinary performance across different universities, has been just as resolute as the determination not to erect performance indicators into a be-all or end-all of evaluation. Certainly, performance indicators have their part. But they are embedded in the qualitative analysis of the particular institution. Indeed, one of the current developments has been to *reduce* the number of performance indicators for teaching, research and administration, while retaining a minimum degree of continuity that will eventually permit an evaluation across time of a given establishment (*Rapport au Président de la République*, 1994: 17).

The procedure of evaluation is not dissimilar to the time-honoured practice both in Britain and in the Netherlands, of Visitation Committees of experts nominated by the National Evaluation Committee to evaluate a stipulated university. It is a detailed and time-consuming process which requires anything between 12 to 18 months from start to finish. The choice of establishment to be evaluated is the responsibility of the National Committee. A typical evaluation exercise takes place across two separate phases. The first gathers general background information and analyses facts and figures in conjunction with the University President or the institute director. The report that results from this visit is analysed by experts, again nominated by the Committee, and the results presented to the Committee itself. The first phase and its follow-up serve to draw up a number of guidance documents (*momentos*), one for members of the review team specialized in governance and administration, another for those concerned with a particular sector, eg, Health Services, University Institutes of Technology. Each guidance document is organized into three parts: information on the institution brought together and analysed by the permanent Secretariat; basic questions raised by members of the National Committee; and specific elements within the field the expert has been nominated to examine (*Rapport au Président*, 1994: 15–16).

A second visit takes place roughly a year after the start of the exercise at which the questions raised in the guidance documents are pursued in greater depth in dialogue with institutional leadership, with representatives of academic staff and students on site. The final report which emerges from this visit is discussed by the full Committee. Subsequently, a copy is sent to the University President for his/her observations. The report is then published under the authority of the National Committee.

As of May 1994, the Committee has evaluated some 91 higher education establishments. Over the ten years of its existence, it has reported on 77 universities – virtually the whole university sector, with the exception of the University of the Pacific and the seven new universities set up since 1991. Attention is now turning towards second-round evaluations. These will differ in certain notable respects. They will focus on cross-sectoral evaluation, that is, reviewing the provision of higher education within a given conurbation as opposed to individual establishments within a given sector eg the university as opposed to Engineering Schools or *Grandes Ecoles*. Greater emphasis will be given to the specific environment – geographic, historic and administrative – within which the individual university is set. Just as important will be the links developed with other institutions as well as its relations with the political, social cultural and economic milieux (*Rapport au Président*, 1994: 16–17). In parallel to follow-up evaluations will be increased attention to the evaluation of individual disciplines. Already in 1989, the Committee turned its gaze to geography, in 1993 to information and communication sciences and the following year to dentistry.

Though the evaluation of disciplines is as yet in its early days, that the Committee has been able to turn its attention to this aspect is, to a large extent, a reflection of the degree of confidence which it now inspires in academia. Two characteristics set off reviews of disciplines from the evaluation of institutions, though clearly the one builds on information gathered in the course of the earlier exercise. The first is the use of foreign experts to place French specificities within the international context of the discipline. The second is the introduction of a four-point scale, ranging from excellent (4) to insufficient (1) to assess the quality of the individual department (*Unité de Formation et de Recherche*).

If a brief account of procedures and progress are *de rigueur*, they do not of themselves explain the underlying tensions and long-term objectives which have shaped them and to which such procedures are themselves a response. Though evaluation implies judgement it does not always have to be harnessed to an ideology of competition, nor does it inevitably lead on to a culture of compliance. The French model of evaluation contained in the workings and methodology of the National Committee is summative in its purpose. Both at national and institutional levels, it is, as its main objective, geared to achieving a closer understanding of what the issues are, what objectives have been achieved, those which have not and why, of a higher education system in the throes of a quite massive overhaul. It is knowledge based on the grounded experience of individual institutions as perceived by those institutions. One of the most striking features in setting up this new evaluatory mechanism in France has been the sheer pragmatism of the undertaking and coupled with this, the careful attention paid to preserving good relations between National Committee and academia by constant consultation on such sensitive and controversial matters as criteria to be evaluated, modes of evaluation and methods to be employed. Such sensitivity to the grassroots is perhaps all the more amazing for the fact that in France, the culture of administrative compliance has long been the norm. But precisely because the French policy-making style has tended to rely on change by decree (which is perhaps an elegant euphemism for administrative compliance) (Premfors, 1980) any attempt to nurture the delicate plant of institutional initiative by old methods would, like as not, merely have resulted in preserving the old vices, not to mention old rigidities.

Envoi

Foreign observers may well express misgivings about the holistic nature of institutional evaluation, French style. But such misgivings tend to forget that one of the essential features of the spate of reforms through which higher education in France has passed, is the unprecedented shift towards negotiated relationships, between state, region and individual higher education establishment. It would be somewhat illogical as well as being highly dysfunctional if the mechanism which was designed to instill new ways of behaving, to strengthen institutional initiative and to foster amongst universities an enhanced capacity for shaping their own futures, did not endorse this same precept. Evaluation is also a pedagogical exercise which is not simply limited to the introduction of new techniques, novel methods or the gathering of new information. It also implies a new perception of institutional role and responsibility, what means are necessary to build on an institution's strengths, what resources it has and what the options are for their realization. It is perhaps one of the more delightful paradoxes that, in France, the purpose behind the creation of an evaluative state was not to bring the overly autonomous to public account and to financial rectitude so much as to create that spirit of confidence in academia that it could negotiate with the increasing range of stakeholders in higher education from the position of strength which partnership required.

References

Clark, B R (1983) *The Higher Education System: Academic Organization in International Perspective*, Berkeley, Los Angeles: University of California Press.

Clark, B R (1993) *The Research Foundations of Graduate Education*, Berkeley, Los Angeles: University of California Press.

Clark, B R (1995) *Places of Inquiry: Research and Advanced Education in Modern Universities*, Berkeley, Los Angeles: University of California Press.

Crozier, M (1972) *La Société bloquée*, Paris: Editions du Seuil.

de Miguel, M, José-Gines, M and Rodríguez, S (1991) *La Evaluacion de las Institutiones universitarias*, Madrid: Consejo de Universidades.

Durand-Prinborgne, C (1992) 'France' in Clark, B R and Neave, G (eds) *The Encyclopedia of Higher Education*, Oxford: Pergamon Press (4 vols) vol.i. *National Systems of Higher Education*, pp 217–24.

Friedberg, E and Musselin, C (1991) *Le Gouvernement des Universités: Perspectives Internationales*, Paris: L'Harmattan.

Furstenbach, John (1992) 'When Pyramids crumble', *Higher Education Policy*, 5, (3), pp. 55–9.

Guin, J (1990) 'The Re-awakening of higher education in France', *European Journal of Education*, 25 (2) pp. 123–47.

Meek, L (1994) 'Higher Education Policy in Australia' in Goedegebuure, L *et al.* (eds) *Higher Education Policy: an International Perspective*, Oxford: Pergamon Books for International Association of Universities.

Ministère de l'Education, *Jeunesse et des Sports* (1989). Paris: Ministère de l'Education.

Neave, G (1985) 'The Non-State sector in education in Europe: a conceptual and historical analysis', *European Journal of Education*, 20 (4) pp 321–39.

Neave, G (1986) 'The all-seeing eye of the Prince in Western Europe', in Moodie, G C (ed) *Standards and Criteria in Higher Education*, Guildford: SRHE and NFER-Nelson, pp. 157–70.

Neave, G (1988) 'On the cultivation of quality, efficiency and enterprise: an overview of recent trends in higher education in Western Europe 1986–1988', *European Journal of Education*, 23, (1–2) pp. 7–25.

Neave, G and Kaiser, F (1994) 'Higher Education Policy in France', in Goedegebuure *et al.*, *Higher Education Policy: an international perspective*, pp. 104–31.

Neave, G and van Vught, F A (1991) *Prometheus Bound: the Changing Relationship Between Government and Higher Education in Western Europe*, Oxford: Pergamon Press.

Neave, G and van Vught, F A (1994) *Government and Higher Education Relationships Across Three Continents: the Winds of Change*, Oxford: Elsevier for International Association of Universities.

Premfors, R (1980) *The Politics of Higher Education in a Comparative Perspective*, Stockholm: Department of Political Science.

Rapport au Président de la République (June 1994) Paris: Comité National d'Evaluation.

Starian, P E (1992) 'Accreditation and quality assurance in higher education', *Papers on Higher Education*, Bucharest: UNESCO-CEPES.

Staropoli, A (1987) 'The French National Evaluation Committee', *European Journal of Education*, 22 (3).

Vlaamse Interuniversitaire Raad (1993) 'Quality assessment in higher education: the Flemish universities' *Working Paper No.1*, Brussel, VLIR (xerox).

van Vught, F A. (1989) *Governmental Strategies and Innovation in Higher Education*, London: Jessica Kingsley.

8. The evaluation of the higher education system in Hong Kong

Cheng Kai-ming

Introduction

In late 1993, Hong Kong started the first and so far the only research assessment exercise for higher education institutions. Subsequently, an evaluation of assessment systems on teaching and learning will be carried out in late 1996. Such assessments are unprecedented in the Hong Kong system, but have become an issue only as the system has expanded to provide access to practically everybody who aspires to and who is capable of higher education. The assessment exercises have substantially changed the lifestyles in higher education institutions, carrying with them both favourable and adverse implications. This chapter analyses how the assessment exercises emerged, why they have come on to the policy agenda, what actually happened during the exercises and what such exercises have caused. In so doing, the research assessment exercise, which has already taken place, will be discussed in more detail.

The expansion

The first research assessment exercise (RAE) took place in Hong Kong when the system of higher education was witnessing unprecedented expansion. It was initiated by the University and Polytechnic Grants Council (now the University Grants Committee) with features unique to Hong Kong. The RAE occurred when assessments of this kind were seen by the UPGC as an essential element in international trends.

Before the mid-1980s, Hong Kong had always maintained a small higher education sector. The 1978 education White Paper (Development, 1978), as a result of manpower calculations recommended an annual increase of 3 per cent in enrolment in higher education. This was at a time when the net enrolment at the first degree level was around 10,000 students or slightly above 2 per cent of the age group. At that time, any shortfall in manpower demand was largely met by supply from overseas.

It was only in the mid-1980s that the Hong Kong government decided to expand higher education. This had become inevitable because of the introduction of nine-year compulsory education in 1978 and the subsequent natural growth of the post-compulsory sectors. The expansion was further accelerated in policy announcements made in 1988 and 1989, believed to be attributable to the flux of emigration on the one hand and the preparation for democracy on the other, both related to the 1997 takeover. The enrolment in the mid-1990s has become 18 per cent for first degree programmes and another 7 per cent for non-degree studies. Enrolment was of the order of 45,000 students. Higher education institutions have increased from two universities and one polytechnic in 1978 to six universities in 1995, with two others about to join the family.

The expansion has made higher education into a system, rather than just one or two universities, and this entices planners to plan and administrators to control. When the local institutions of higher education offered opportunities to only 2 per cent of the age group, university education was highly selective. The few young people who were admitted to universities were the cream of the cream. They were educated in secondary schools of long tradition which prepared elites. They entered universities with a high level of self-confidence. Academic achievement was never a problem for this breed of university students. Indeed, most of them were all-rounders with good records in sports, music, social skills, organizational abilities and so forth. University life was no more than allowing these persons to nurture themselves to become leaders of the community. Indeed, the scarcity of local graduates, and their prestige in the local society, has also provided an essential incentive for these young people to perform and behave according to social expectations. The quality of higher education was never a real concern. On the one hand, failures among students were extremely rare; on the other hand, it did not matter whether academic staff were good or poor teachers, good or poor researchers.

The expansion of the education system has changed this picture. Developments in two directions have converged to the same effect: a decline in the quality of university students. First, compulsory education was introduced according to the planners' blueprint: there was little preparation or change in pedagogy. When education was meant for the select few, failures dropped out of the system and disappeared. There was a much more prominent function of sifting and sorting by the school system. Students had to adapt themselves to the school system. Coupled to this was the Chinese tradition which stressed individual effort rather than genetic abilities, and hence the consequent cult of adaptability, competition and hard work. The introduction of compulsory education undermined this tradition. Each student is guaranteed a place and schools are responsible for pushing them through the system. Aptitude-based allocations of students have replaced meritocratic examinations and selections. Traditions which place high reliance on student efforts have given way to egalitarian policies of positive discrimination. The net effects of these changes are increasingly less-motivated students, declining student achievement, the growth of student behavioural problems, and all the symptoms that prevail in other educational systems in the West.

The decline in the quality of school education has also affected universities and institutions of higher education. Teachers in higher education have to worry about the standard of students. Supplementary examinations and dropping out, which used to be a rather rare disgrace when they occurred, have now become commonplace in higher education. Some sectors of the universities, the professional sectors in particular, may have to fail a substantial percentage of their students in order to maintain the professional standard of the graduates.

It is a losing battle. The graduates are not comparable in standard with those who graduated 15 or 20 years ago. The employers feel dissatisfied with the output of higher education. Many employers have turned to alternatives such as expatriates who are English-speaking natives from countries with difficult employment situations. Some of the major employers are attracted to graduates from the Chinese mainland, who ironically often possess higher standards, even in the English language. The declining standard of the graduates has also affected secondary schools where these graduates teach. A vicious circle has been formed.

A very significant indication of the decline in quality is that parents and students have lost confidence in the local education system. Until the mid-1980s, secondary school graduates still regarded local universities as their top priority for further education. Although government estimates pointed to as many students studying overseas as those in Hong Kong, overseas study was very much a reluctant alternative to the highly selective local system. Thereafter, and this is the case in the 1990s, the best students from the most prestigious secondary schools opted for overseas institutions. Many of these schools may lose as many as half of their sixth form students to overseas studies before graduation. Parents who are professionals or who can afford to, prefer to send their children to overseas institutions. Entrance to local institutions has now become a reluctant second-best choice. It is perhaps not exaggerating to assert that the top 2 per cent of those who used to fill local higher education places are attracted to doing higher education overseas.

It is in this context that quality of higher education has become a concern. The local higher education institutions are no longer seen as reliable as they used to be. Under these circumstances, the employers and the community at large are reminded of their consumer role and would like to see some kind of quality assurance.

The University Grants Committee

The University Grants Committee was initially a device for resource allocation and was established in 1965 when the second university, The Chinese University of Hong Kong, came into being alongside the traditional University of Hong Kong. The UGC was established very much on the old British model which tried to maintain a balance between financial accountability and academic autonomy. Afterwards, the UGC was asked to include in its auspices all the other higher education institutions under public funding. As a deviation from the British model, the Hong Kong UGC was also in charge of the polytechnics and other non-universities, and was therefore once known as the University and Polytechnic Grants Committee (UPGC) (Griffiths, 1984). Since 1981, the UGC (then the UPGC) has been charged with the mission of advising the Governor on overall policies for higher education. Since *de jure*, the Governor of Hong Kong is the only decision-maker in policies, the UGC is virtually the highest level policy adviser to the Governor.

Ever since its inception, the UGC has also differed significantly from the British model in that half of its membership has come from overseas. In its early years, the overseas members were exclusively from the UK. At one time, the overseas members included prominent academics from the UK, such as Lord Briggs of Lewis, Sir John Butterfield and Sir Edward Parkes. Since the early 1980s, non-British academics were also appointed, but were at first restricted to those from the Commonwealth. The UGC now includes members from US institutions such as Harvard and Stanford. It was only in the mid-1980s that local academics were appointed to the UGC. In 1995, eight of the 15 UGC members are from overseas; only three are from local institutions.

The exact rationale for the inclusion of an overwhelming proportion of overseas membership was unclear, but the net effect is a strengthening of the academic legitimacy of the UGC. As I have argued elsewhere (Cheng, 1994), internationalization has been the major approach in Hong Kong to legitimate higher education policy-making. In a polity where the colonial government derives its power from the Queen of Great Britain and in the absence of democratic elections, the Hong Kong government was very conscious about building its legitimacy through technical and impartial deliberation on the one hand and extensive consultations on the other (Cheng, 1987). The UGC as a way of third-party consultation possesses a double advantage. It is impartial and neutral. The members are appointed personally by the Governor. The UGC reports to the Governor alone and does not work under any other government agency. As internationally renowned academics, the overseas academics are not supposed to submit to pressures from the local government nor from local politicians. This is rational in two senses: UGC members represent the most prestigious academics in the international community; and the overseas members are supposed to bring to Hong Kong the trends and standards of higher education which prevail internationally. The UGC is a typical demonstration of how the Hong Kong government was ready to sacrifice its power in the nitty-gritty of higher education policies in return for legitimacy and credibility among the citizens. Although there are signs that the government is withdrawing from such a tactic, because long-term investment in its legitimacy is no longer a concern, there is no significant change in the general orientation in higher education policy-making.

The international composition of the UGC has also given Hong Kong convenient benchmarks for quality in higher education. Otherwise, the Hong Kong system could have remained very local and parochial, and needed much reform before becoming acceptable by the international community of scholars. There are other measures such as those in staffing and external examinations which have strengthened local institutions, but the international flavour of the UGC is crucial in placing Hong Kong's higher education against international benchmarks of quality and standards. It is in this context that the UGC introduces quality measures to the Hong Kong system.

The general concern for quality in higher education is an unmistakable trend in the international scene (World Bank, 1994). This has inevitably led the UGC to make decisions about Hong Kong within the same framework. It is also inevitable that trends elsewhere are thought to be *the* trend and hence are more 'advanced', and are therefore what Hong Kong has to keep pace with. Such considerations may tend to neglect the local contexts in which the quality movements emerge elsewhere and tend to over-generalize the trend as something which is context-free. Nonetheless, research assessments and forthcoming measures related to teaching assessments are being introduced by the UGC. Although the actual implementation involves the extensive participation of local academics, the decision to introduce such measures is hardly a contribution from local academics. Therefore, apart from the few who are on the UGC, most local academics see such quality measures as foreign, although not all of them feel alienated or indifferent.

It has also to be noticed that the 'international' trends, as they are introduced to Hong Kong, still often have a heavy British bias (or an English bias, if we distinguish what is happening in Scotland from the rest of Britain). Until recently, one or two members, incidentally from Britain, who were the longest-serving members of the UGC, were more influential than other members. Some of these members have served the UGC almost since its establishment. They were extremely familiar with the local system, were able to follow the development of the system, were able to detect the crucial problems at each juncture and often provide helpful solutions to such problems. The suggestions from these members, however, sometimes inevitably carried an inclination which was appropriate to the British system. The same rationales which were adopted by the British authorities were used to justify policies in Hong Kong, albeit there are controversies about such policies in Britain.

Even with the retirement of some of these members, the general British influence — though not in a political sense — is still strong, and this is reinforced by the views of members from other Commonwealth countries (eg, Australia) which are alert to developments in Britain. The conversion of the polytechnics to universities in 1994 was a typical example. Although similar conversions in Britain are not always judged favourably by international agencies (World Bank, 1994:33), such policies were adopted in Australia and New Zealand and are not unwelcomed by scholars from America where institutions are classified only by the market. Therefore, as will be seen later in this chapter, the RAE in Hong Kong is similar in philosophy to the British RAE.

The scene before 1993

Before the first RAE was introduced in 1993, there were seven institutions which were funded through the UGC: three universities, two polytechnics and two colleges.

The universities were fully autonomous and were entrusted with the crucial authority to accredit their own courses and confer degrees. This self-accreditation was typically done through external examination systems. In most cases, external examiners were appointed from overseas institutions. They were appointed either on a department basis or on a curriculum basis. The external examiners were requested to examine and comment on the curriculum, to monitor examinations and to review examination results. External examiners were also asked to pay regular short visits of one or two weeks to the relevant departments. During the visit, the external examiners interacted with the teachers and students and often observed classes. The external examiners were also often asked to present seminars in areas of their specialization and to conduct a working session at the conclusion of the visit.

The polytechnics and colleges elected courses through accreditation by an external agent. Before 1990, such accreditation was typically done through the British CNAA. Teams were sent from the UK and visits were paid to the relevant institutions. Later the Hong Kong Council for Academic Accreditation (HKCAA) was established to replace the role of CNAA (Sensicle, 1992). The accreditation teams work more or less as external examiners, except that they bear the more serious responsibility of deciding on the fate of the course under examination.

Apart from all these, there was little formal and systematic evaluation before 1993. There are all kinds of curriculum committees in various institutions, but the primary function of such committees is often curriculum planning. Evaluation was done as a matter of academic conscience. Practically nothing was done to evaluate research. Given the heavy government subsidy in terms of funding and the sufficiency in funding, there were hardly any motives to attract research funds. Hence, research was also done basically as a matter of academic conscience.

The only exceptions which are evaluative in nature were student evaluations of courses. Student evaluations existed in most institutions long before the UGC introduced its assessment exercises. In some institutions, it is a requirement for all courses taught. In most cases, results of such student evaluations are employed as feedback in order to improve teaching. Their usefulness is therefore dependent on individual teachers. Student evaluations were seldom used for administrative purposes such as contract confirmation, contract renewal or promotion. Hence, student evaluations are often used as a tool for staff development.

The only 'consumer-oriented' evaluations were 'the best teacher' and 'the worst teacher' elections organized occasionally by some of the student unions. The results were published and often attracted much publicity in the media. The impact was sometimes quite significant, although the elections were often flawed by their poor design and poor participation.

The research assessment exercise

The first RAE was introduced to Hong Kong in November, 1993. It was applied across all the seven UGC institutions. Basically, the exercise evaluated each member of the institutions by assessing his/her 'research output', used that as an indicator for the research performance of that institution, and allocated funds accordingly. It is yet to be decided when the second exercise will be conducted, but the 1993 exercise serves the purpose of fund allocation for the triennium which lasts until 1998. However, most institutions have continued the exercise as an internal practice.

The RAE started by asking each individual member of the institutions to submit three items which he or she regarded as their best research output in the past four years. Research outputs were defined in the categories, as shown in the Annex.

All the submissions were then divided into cost centres, also shown in the Annex. The actual assessments were done through six specialist panels: Arts and Humanities, Social Sciences and Education, Medical and Biological Sciences, Law and Business Studies, Engineering, and Physical Sciences. Each of the panels comprized several local members plus one overseas member. The local membership largely guaranteed fair representation from all local institutions relavant to the specific disciplines. The overseas members were invited on the criterion of their experience and involvement in similar exercises in the UK. The overseas members were defined as process consultants who would not contribute in the specific assessment of individual cases.

The assessors arrived at some consensus about the general approach to the exercise during a general meeting of assessors from all panels. It was decided that the exercise should be a 'threshold' rather than a 'rating' exercise, that is, the objective was only to detect whether or not a person was active in research. There would be no intention to rate the level of activities or the standard of the research. In other words, there would be no 'half researchers' or 'fractional' researchers. It was also understood that the different panels might arrive at different specific measures appropriate to the respective disciplines. Overall, although the whole idea of an RAE was imported and the general framework was preset very much on a British model, the actual procedures were shaped by local researchers. Some local ownership was created by local participation in such a process, but the local academics did not create the intent to launch such an exercise.

During the assessment, the panels were required to judge each individual to see if they qualified as an active researcher. The judgements were based on whether or not the submitted items are above the 'threshold'. In practical terms, only books, refereed journal articles and refereed book chapters were seen as above the threshold. The panel members debated controversial items. Controversies arose most often in the humanities and social sciences where judgements on local publications could not be based on international lists or indexes.

The criteria adopted by different panels vary slightly. In the natural science panels, for example, a member was regarded an active researcher only when all the three items were above threshold. In the social science panels, mostly two items above the threshold would warrant the term active researcher. In this latter case, the idea was to leave room for items which are valuable but may not fall into strict categories of threshold 'research output'. Allowance was made for 'junior researchers' who have just joined academia. Teachers who were working on their own doctorates, or have just finished, were also given special allowance in recognition of their research efforts during doctoral study. In exceptional cases, one distinguished publication may warrant for the individual the status of an active researcher. Overall, the process of assessment was shaped by local academics.

The panels' assessment decisions were collated by the UGC. The objective was to calculate for each cost centre and subsequently each institution the relative quantity of active researchers as a percentage of total academic members. Hence, a department of 2,000 members would obtain an index of 0.75 if 1,500 of them were assessed as active researchers. This was done at the beginning of 1994 when the UGC was preparing the triennial allocation for 1995–98. The UGC top-sliced the total pool of funds, and allocated this top-slice to the institutions according to their respective strengths in terms of the relative number of active researchers. The size of this top-slice was kept confidential, but speculations hinted at 25 per cent.

Controversies surrounding the RAE

The entire RAE was controversial. The controversy emerged partly because of the looseness in the design which was inevitable in such an initial operation, and partly because of conflicts between a foreign framework and local conventions. It would be premature to appraise the RAE, but a discussion of the controversies may help in an understanding of the operation of the exercise.

The exercise started with self-reporting with only vague definitions. This caused little problem in terms of honesty, and anyway it was a small community of academics and mutual familiarity helped very much. However, differences in understanding caused problems of fairness. There were different views, for example, among departments and institutions, about who should be included in the assessment. It was not clear how the assessment results would be used, hence some departments, for example, presented only those who were most active in research. Such departments created disadvantages for their institutions because of their apparently low rate of active researchers. It was not clear, either, what was meant by the 'best' output. The 'threshold' was defined only after the panels met, and therefore the submissions were based on the researchers' own evaluation. There were members whose views on research output and quality were obviously different from those which the panels eventually defined, and hence did not score as highly as they deserved.

Such discrepancies are understandable in an exercise which was the first of its kind, but they have caused much dissatisfaction because there was no indication at the beginning about how the results would be used. The assessment results were eventually used for allocation purposes, and the decision to use the results in that way and to such an extent was apparently determined after the assessments were made.

There were, as might be expected, debates about what constitutes the 'threshold'. Apparently, although members were asked to submit three items, it was not until the panels met that the use of these items was decided. At one level, the debate was about what kind of item should be considered acceptable. There was little debate about internationally well-known refereed academic journals. There was little debate, either, about books published by known publishers. Debates occurred in almost all areas but this was especially true in the humanities and social sciences. There were cases, for example, of rather influential monographs which were published by local publishers and which were not refereed. Should the basis of judgement be the process of production or on the impact made by the monograph? There were also cases of locally developed, relatively young, journals. Whether or not they used a referee system, their standard was by no means comparable to established journals. However, a denial of these journals would immediately discourage writing for these journals and would cause serious damage to such journals. There was the further case of articles published in journals on the Chinese mainland. Peer refereeing is not yet a convention in most of these journals, but publishing in them would serve that very essential function of communicating with scholars on the mainland. Still other cases of debate were related to textbooks written either for higher education or for schools. Tremendous efforts were put into these publications, but should they be accepted as research output in the narrow sense of the term?

There was no simple conclusion to all these debates and dilemmas. Most of these controversial cases were settled by consensus among panel members, according to specific situations. In the end, despite the consistency among similar cases, the measures and criteria were quite different from discipline to discipline, even within the same panel. In the social sciences, for example, the requirements for economics was tighter than, for example, those for social work. The former has a well-established literature and academics normally are very familiar with the conventions and standards in such literature. The latter, on the other hand, often concentrates on local issues with a practical orientation, and academics and teachers in this field of study are reluctant to publish in overseas journals just for the sake of publishing.

The most controversial issue is whether or not it was legitimate for the UGC to use the RAE results as a basis for resource allocation, given that the system was still in a developing stage and the methods and procedures were still immature. This would not have been such a controversy had the UGC applied the results to a smaller portion of the resources. Since there were differences in understanding when the returns were submitted, and the ways and standards of assessment were not know at the time of submission, the results were seen as biased towards a certain ideology about research, against others. Members and institutions might well be victimized not because of their poor performance in research, but rather because of differences in the interpretation of what research is. Such a bias, unfortunately, were not foreseeable when the returns were submitted. Most institutions anticipated the exercise as a trial in itself and that it would not be seriously used until it was modified. The 25 per cent top-slicing has made many institutions feel that they were penalized for their innocence.

Implications of the RAE

The RAE and its subsequent use in resource allocation has major implications for institutions. Such implications infiltrate into departments and, eventually, to individuals.

The RAE has prompted institutions to use similar indicators to measure the research performance of their own departments and to make internal allocations accordingly. The percentage of funds top-sliced for that purpose varies, ranging from 3 to 25 per cent. Some institutions even go into further details in the internal execution of the RAE method. For example, some institutions require individual members to submit their entire profile of research activities rather than a few items of research output.

Such institutional measures have affected the attitudes of administrators at faculty and department levels. Inter-institutional competitions have been translated into intra-institutional competitions. Faculties, and in some cases departments, have to be extremely conscious of the research output of their members, because a percentage of their budget allocation depends on such performance. Department heads have now become very conscious about the composition of their staffs. Members who are less 'productive' in terms of publications have become a matter of concern. A strong track record or a high potential for publishing has to be demonstrated in order for a new member to secure an appointment and for contracts to be renewed. The same has become the necessary and almost sole criterion for the granting of tenure and recommendations for promotion. One can witness a very visible and abrupt change of the currency in personnel matters in institutions of higher education in Hong Kong.

All this has occurred in a matter of months in 1994, immediately after the RAE exercise. The change in personnel orientations had caused changes in the lifestyle of individual academics. The few who have been productive in publications are prompted to produce more. Those who are working on doctorates are prompted, either by self-motivation or by their department heads, to obtain the degree earlier. Those who are less productive, who are not able to produce or who are not prepared to produce, now face high pressure. In some institutions, there have even been attempts to 'weed out' these last categories by, for example, offering early retirement. Some of these attempts are successful given the attractive retirement package and the uncertainties due to the change of government in 1997. 'Publish or perish', a syndrome which was thought to be American, now prevails in Hong Kong's community of higher education.

Changes in institutions have gone beyond the RAE. Research output is of course related to research input which, apart from the personnel factor, is a matter of the amount of research funding and the number of research projects. To some extent, research input is also related to students doing research degrees.

It is noticeable that the RAE worked on personal research output alone. If it is seen as a copy of the British model, then it is a very much simplified version. It did not include, as had once been desired, the counting of research funding. However, the Research Grants Council, which is a sister committee to the UGC and indeed served by the same secretariat, publishes every year the total sum of research grants obtained by members in each institution, and this has great impact on the institutions.

The Research Grants Council handles a total of around US$40 million a year for research funding in the seven UGC institutions. The sum is usually divided into several portions. Apart from funds that are allocated to the institutions for internal distribution and a central pool for large and collaborative projects, a large sum goes to researchers through individual applications. The assessment and selection of research proposals are conducted by panels set up by the Research Grants Council on a competitive basis. Hence, although the research grants reflect individual endeavours, the total each institution obtains tends to be seen as a significant performance indicator of research in that institution.

Postgraduate students doing research degrees have also become a matter of institutional concern; the reasons are twofold. First, the number of research students an institution can attract directly contributes to the measure 'full-time equivalent student' (FTE) which in turn contributes to the overall allocation from the UGC. Second, a large percentage of the research students are given a sizable amount of money, a 'studentship'. Studentship holders are required to provide assistance in teaching or research. The amount of the studentship a department can secure is therefore a substantial input to research. Although there is a set quota for each institution, the number of research students in each institution is used as an indicator for future allocations of income. There is again a tendency toward competition among institutions.

Under all these circumstances, institutions compete to establish special administrative components to take charge of research. Some institutions hire special persons with high administrative authority to oversee research activities in their departments. Some institutions set targets for their sub-units (ie, faculties or departments) for research grants which they should obtain.

Other institutions require a high percentage of their members (as high as 100 per cent) to submit proposals for research grants; some appoint specialists for assistance in proposal writing; still other institutions establish or strengthen special divisions to take care of the research students. As mentioned earlier, there are institutions which centrally screen the staff profiles of their departments and take administrative measures to 'improve' such profiles with a research orientation.

Beyond research

The RAE has significantly tilted the balance between teaching and research. Such a tilt has alerted the UGC, who have initiated a parallel movement in teaching. A 'Teaching and Learning Quality Process Audit' will start in early 1996. Being conscious of the complexity embedded in the issue of teaching quality, the exercise proposes to look at quality assurance mechanisms for teaching rather than teaching *per se*. In other words, the institutions are required to demonstrate that they possess the capacity to conduct quality assurance in teaching.

The institutions have been forewarned of such an exercise well in advance, and institutional organs are already established to deal with the exercise. In most institutions, there are administrative arms to handle or develop quality assurance as well as professional units to conduct research and facilitate staff development in teaching. The latter is generally seen as favourable by teachers. The former, the administrative organ, is controversial. Although funding is promised for the exercise on teaching, the funding is relatively trivial given the anticipation that the teaching exercise will bring as much pressure as the research exercise.

Concerns about the exercise on teaching quality go beyond the exercise itself. There is the worry that attention to the quality assurance mechanism may be diverted to actual teaching in classrooms, which would be judged as 'interference'. There is the other worry that the stated objective of improvement may soon degerate into an objective of policing as is typical with many evaluation exercises elsewhere. The academics have expressed such worries. How much such worries would affect the actual conduct of the forthcoming exercise is uncertain.

There are institutions which have pioneered quality exercises in teaching. One of the most elaborate was to grant awards for 'excellence in teaching'. Teachers were invited to apply for the award through a brief teaching portfolio. Short-listed candidates were requested to submit a detailed teaching portfolio together with whatever would demonstrate excellence in teaching. The detailed teaching portfolio usually included the candidate's teaching philosophy, his/her self-evaluation of perfor-mance in specified aspects, innovations, student evaluation results, and supporting evidence provided by peers and students. Selection was made by a panel who interviewed the candidates. The panel normally includes members external to the institution, with participation by student representatives. The recipient received an honour as well as a token sum as a prize. Such award exercises are not widespread. One of the concerns is the heavy workload involved in preparing the documents. Another concern is the practical difficulty in conducting live classroom observations, without which the selection has to rely heavily upon self-reporting. Those in favour of such an award maintain that quality in teaching can only be enhanced through encouragement and recognition of excellence. Appraisals otherwise can only be useful in maintaining certain standards.

There are further concerns that might not have entered the agenda of the UGC. Teaching and research are undoubtedly essential elements of academic life, but they are not the only elements. Community involvement, for example, may be curtailed because of the high pressure for different kinds of performance by academics within institutions.

In a small community such as Hong Kong, society relies heavily upon academics for policy participation in both a normative and a critical sense. In a normative sense, academics are widely involved in all kinds of policy advisory committees set up by the colonial government as a way of gaining popular support and as a means of effective policy-making. There are over 300 committees covering all policy sectors and few of them are without academics. In a crucial sense, Hong Kong has a very good tradition of public policy debate and the most critical views are often initiated by the academics. Besides, academics are also extensively involved in all kinds of professional communities, non-government organizations, voluntary agencies, political parties and media activities. The intensity of academics' participation in community activities in Hong Kong is rather unusual among East Asian societies, and indeed may compare favourably with many early industrialized societies. The RAE, for example, has already caused some casualties where academics withdrew themselves from public activities in order to survive in a career within the institution. However, given that the RAE was only one year old, it may be premature to judge whether or not such damage is likely to be permanent.

Concluding remarks

Evaluation of higher education institutions, in the fashionable sense of the term, emerged in Hong Kong only very recently. This chapter is an account of recent events and a general interpretation of the context of influences on and of such events. Given the short history of the endeavours, it is premature at this stage to make a full appraisal of the situation. Such an appraisal could be done, with due research, when the longer-term implications of the policy measure are more visible. Nevertheless, some initial thoughts may help illuminate the situation before the serious research is undertaken.

If we concentrate on the RAE which has already happened, then there should be no question that the exercise has greatly increased the intensity of research activities among the institutes of higher education in Hong Kong. Without the RAE, some of the academics might have put less emphasis on their mission of contributing to the body of human knowledge. Good teachers though they were, they might have relied too much upon what they acquired when they were much younger, or relied on research done by others. Active though they were in the communities, they might not be sure whether their views, which had affected policies so much, were based on rational analysis. Even in very pragmatic terms, without such an enhancement of enthusiasm for research, Hong Kong may soon lose its position in the international community. Without an effort to establish a research tradition among institutions, academics in Hong Kong might soon find themselves vulnerable in an environment where politics might override reasoning. In this sense, the RAE has successfully placed Hong Kong on to the international map of academic excellence. There may be still some way to go before Hong Kong can gain a prestigious position when compared with the top institutions elsewhere, but at least it is now on the track which enables it to compete in the international arena.

However, the RAE, as it was, may not be sufficient to allow Hong Kong institutions to achieve excellence as measured by international recognition. First, the use of simple indicators (three publications), while enjoying the elegance of neatness, suffers from over-simplification and may prove antithetical to the ideas of taking a broad view of research and of accommodating a diversity of research activities. Second, using publications as a proxy for research may itself be misleading. The quantity of publications has only a vague relation to the intensity of research activities. It is even more difficult to identify the quality of research through the counting of publications. Third, like all quality assurance measures, the RAE could at best assure that every member is research-active, or paper-productive, but this will not by itself produce quality research and an excellent researcher. The RAE would at best provide extrinsic motivations for individuals to do research, but genuine excellence in research requires real zest in the exploration and creation of knowledge. Such zest is seldom a product of administrative pressure or systemic control.

Hong Kong is perhaps the first among East Asian communities to apply quality measures which are fashionable in the West. While the RAE has created a new type of research culture in higher education institutions (French, 1995), it may also have transformed the organizational culture in such institutions. The kind of 'gentlemanly' relations and traditions of self-discipline which shaped institutions in East Asia have now given way to hard-nosed counting of numbers and dollars, and to severe administrative consequences. Older traditions might not be appropriate in modern times when institutions face public scrutiny and fierce competition, but an academic culture built upon a weak theory is not a helpful substitute.

Even if universities became highly efficient factories of academic papers, and even if the parallel assessments in teaching effectively eliminated all sub-standard teaching, there should still be concern for example that the measures of evaluation, assessment and quality assurance do not cause a withdrawal of academics from the community. Rebuilding the ivory tower is definitely not an objective for today's higher education, but it is, at the time of writing, not completely clear what kind of tower is being built.

Annex

Research output categories and sub-categories

I *Scholarly books and monographs*

1. Research book or mono- graph (author)	Authored work generally arising from an academic research project although contract research
2. Textbook (author)	A full-length authored work used for instruc- tional purposes; include revisions if they involve 'substantial' (say 20 per cent) new material
3. Edited book (editor)	An edited book of essays, readings, research papers or the equivalent, complied for research, teaching or other purposes

II *Journal articles, book chapters, and other published papers*

4. Chapter in an edited book (author)	A paper, essay, or other material authored specifically for inclusion in an edited book; does not include an opening or summary chapter prepared by an editor for inclusion in a work counted in (3)
5. Article for externally refereed journal	A paper in a refereed journal devoted to reporting the results of basic or applied research
6. Article for policy or pro- fessional journal	An article for a policy or professional journal; that is, a refereed or unrefereed journal publishing policy or educational material for a professional audience
7. Article for newspaper or popular journal	An article, column, or other work in a newspaper or popular journal; that is, an unrefereed journal devoted to the dissemina- tion of news and commentary for a broad audience

III *Conference and working papers*

8. Invited conference paper	A paper invited for presentation at an academic or professional meeting; the paper may or may not be published in a conference 'Proceedings', but any such publication should be considered part of this entry and not be counted as a separate item
9. Refereed paper at a con- ference	A paper accepted for presentation at an academic or professional meeting on the basis of a formal peer review process external to the institution; 'Proceedings' should be handled as in (8)

10. Other conference paper   Any other paper presented at an academic or professional conference; 'Proceedings' should be handled as in (8)

11. Working paper   A research paper distributed for comment to academic colleagues inside or outside the institution

IV Works of fiction, consulting reports, case studies, etc

12. Authored play, poem, novel, story   Fictional or similar works published in a form appropriate to the type of work

13. Consulting or contract research report   Report on work performed under an institutional consulting or research contract report counted here generally will be prepared for the client, and they may be proprietary if institutional rules permit

14. Written teaching case study or extensive note   Material prepared for teaching purposes with applicability beyond one's own course needs; short notes and descriptions prepared for immediate class use should not be included

V Review, translations, and other written outputs

15. Review of books or software   Published or widely-disseminated reviews of books or other publications, software, or other similar items, dissemination must extend beyond the institution and its research sponsors (reviews prepared for institutional clients should be counted under 13)

16. Other written outputs   Any substantial written work not mentioned above (except translation, which is counted under 17 below), inclusive of consulting reports for private (non-institutional) clients

17. Translation of another's work   Translation of an item of type (1) through (16) above, written by another; translation of one's own work is considered part of the authoring process and should not be included

VI Editorships and high-level service external to the institution

18. Journal or series editorship   Editor, associate editor, or the equivalent of a journal, book series, or similar on-going publication venture; do not include one-time edited-book projects which are counted under (3), or service on an editorial board with more than six members or on reviewing panels

19. High-level public or professional service   High-level service external to the institution: for example, on a committee such as UPGC, RGC, or VTC, as an officer of a professional body, or as a senior adviser to government or business

VII *All other outputs*

20. Speech or other prestigious public presentation	A public presentation not classified as teaching or falling under the 'conference' headings given above; the presentation may be within the institution or to an external audience; 'prestigious' means 'significantly enhancing the reputation of the individual and his/her institution' as opposed to (say) a routine lecture
21. Performance	Dramatic, musical, and similar performances
22. Painting, sculpture, drawings, photos	Creation of artefacts capable of being reviewed for merit, generally but not exclusively of an artistic nature (excluding categories covered below)
23. Films, videos	Creation of films, videos, multimedia, and similar productions for research, educational, cultural or environmental purposes
24. Participation in exhibits	Participation as an exhibitor of paintings, sculpture, films, videos, or other artefact; the exhibit may be sponsored by the institution or externally; it should attract significant public or professional attention
25. Engineering, architectural, graphic designs	An engineering, architectural, graphic, landscape, or interior design (or the equivalent), whether prepared for a client or in the public domain
26. Computer software or system	Development of a shareable computer software program, computer language, expert system, computer-aided instruction package or the equivalent
27. Patents applied for	A patent for an invention: applied for in the name of the researcher, whether by the institution, the individual, a contract research sponsor, or another party
28. Licence agreements	An agreement to license a process, software product, invention, etc. created or substantially developed by the researcher; generally the licence will be let by the institution, though exceptions are possible
29. Other outputs	Any creative work not listed above, provided the work can be evaluated for merit and an assessment obtained on either a public or confidential basis

Cost centres for academic departments, etc.

1. clinical medicine
2. clinical dentistry
3. clinical vet studies
4. nursing
5. other para-medical
6. biological sciences
7. pre-clinical studies
8. experimental psychology
9. other bio-sciences
10. agriculture
11. physics and astronomy
12. chemistry
13. materials science
14. earth sciences (including oceanography, meteorology)
15. other physical sciences
16. mechanical engineering
17. electrical engineering
18. electronic engineering
19. chemical engineering
20. production engineering*
21. marine engineering
22. biotechnology
23. materials technology
24. textile technology
25. civil engineering
26. other technologies (including nautical studies)
27. architecture
28. building technology
29. planning
30. surveying, land
31. surveying, other
32. mathematics and statistics
33. computer studies/science (inc. IT)
34. law
35. accountancy
36. public administration
37. business studies (including management)
38. catering
39. hotel management
40. economics
41. geography
42. social work
43. other social sciences
44. Chinese language and literature
45. English language and literature
46. Japanese language and literature
47. other languages
48. translation
49. communications and media studies
50. history
51. other arts/humanities
52. art
53. performing arts
54. music
55. other creative arts
56. design
57. education
58. physical education

* including manufacturing and industrial engineering

References

Cheng, K M (1987) The concept of legitimacy in educational policy-making: Alternative explanations of two policy episodes in Hong Kong, PhD thesis, London: University of London Institute of Education.

Cheng, K M (1994) 'Legitimation through internationalization: The case of higher education in Hong Kong', paper prepared for the International Workshop on Training of Higher Education Administrators and Reform of Higher Education Administration, organized by UNDP, May 19–22, Shanghai, forthcoming in proceedings.

Development of Senior Secondary and Tertiary Education (1978) Hong Kong: Government Printer.

French, N J (1995) 'Higher education in Hong Kong: Past achievements – future challenge', speech made at the Industrial Forum on Information Technology: The next industry in Hong Kong, 5 June, Hong Kong.

Griffiths, R C (1984) 'Hong Kong University and Polytechnic Grants Committee', *Higher Education*, 13, 545–52.
Sensicle, A. (1992) 'The Hong Kong initiative', in Craft, A (ed.) *Quality Assurance in Higher education*, London: Falmer.
World Bank (1994) *Higher Education: The Lessons of Experience.* Washington DC: The World Bank.

9. The evaluation of the higher education system in Japan

Masateru Baba

Introduction

Since 1949, Japanese higher education has consisted of universities, graduate schools, junior colleges and, later, colleges of technology. For admission, universities require the completion of upper secondary schooling and offer four-year courses leading to a bachelor's degree. They are divided into several faculties. Universities have also set up graduate schools offering advanced studies in a variety of fields leading to masters and doctoral degrees. The standard length of a masters course is two years and that of a doctoral course is five years. Junior colleges provide upper secondary graduates with two- or three-year programmes in different fields of study, leading to an associate degree. The majority of the students in these junior colleges are women. Colleges of technology, which have been established since 1962, require for admission the completion of lower secondary schooling, and offer five-year continuous programmes aimed at training practical engineers. The number of students in these colleges is small.

In each prefecture there is at least one national university, that is, a university which is government-supported, in order to afford educational opportunities to all citizens even in remote regions. Private universities, non-profit educational organizations, are legally bound by the Private School Laws and are financially subsidized by grants from the national government to help them develop side-by-side with national universities.

Since 1960, Japanese higher education institutions have concentrated on quantitative development. In fact, the quantitative development of these institutions was spectacular. In the last three decades the number of universities and colleges has more than doubled: there were 492 institutions in 1955 and in 1990 there were 1,100. Enrolment was also explosive: there were 580,000 students enrolled in higher education institutions in 1955 and this has since increased to 2,462,000 in 1990.

More recent trends in enrolment are shown in Table 9.1. Currently more than 500,000 students attend university; more than 240,000

Table 9.1 *Recent trends in enrolment in higher education (%)*

Year	Universities	Junior Colleges	Total
1989	24.6	11.7	36.3
1990	24.6	11.7	36.3
1991	25.5	12.2	37.7
1992	26.4	12.4	38.8
1993	28.0	12.9	40.9
1994	30.1	13.2	43.3

(Source: Ministry of Education, *Statistical Abstract of Education, Science and Culture*, 1995, p. 30, Tokyo: Ministry of Education.)

students attend junior colleges; and more than 400,000 students attend special training institutes (college courses) after secondary school. The percentage of students going to university or junior college has already exceeded 43 per cent of the population of the appropriate age group.

How did this expansion happen? This can be attributed to two major factors. First, there was an increase in demand for higher education as the national economy developed during that period. Second, the income level of households increased and higher education became more affordable.

How did universities accommodate this expansion? The private sector was the primary contributor to the expansion of the universities. Private institutions comprise three-quarters of the total enrolment of students now. The government responded by providing assistance only in developing the fields of science and engineering in order to meet the economic growth needs of Japan.

How was quality maintained at the universities during this expansion? Was there a serious attempt to evaluate them? The answers to these questions are unfortunately negative. There was no really national, systematic and formal evaluation system. There are 552 universities (including the University of the Air) in Japan and the academic standards of each university vary considerably. It is widely acknowledged in Japan that only 5 per cent of these universities maintain the highest academic standards, comparable to those of highly ranked universities worldwide. These institutions were once called Imperial Universities and were founded by the Meiji government before and after 1900 for the purpose of producing national leaders. There are also several national and private universities which have developed quite remarkably since 1960 and have succeeded in reaching the highest academic standards in a short period despite the competition from a host of other universities. Today, these prestigious universities maintain high admission standards and provide a broad range of graduate programmes. However, the majority of Japanese universities and colleges maintain relatively mediocre academic standards and offer limited graduate programmes. Their methods of evaluation are also skewed. University evaluation is synonymous with entrance examinations; in other words, university evaluation is made by students based solely on how difficult it is to gain admission to the university. The more difficult the entrance examination, the higher the *de facto* evaluation the university receives.

As a result, people have begun to question the quality of higher education, in particular the quality of average, ordinary universities. Methods of university evaluation have become the focus of academic study as well as a practical argument and a call for a new evaluation system has been voiced. This new system is called 'university self-monitoring and self-evaluation'. The purpose of this new concept is to move the Japanese higher education system from quantitative to qualitative development, thereby improving the quality of teaching, learning and research at universities.

Factors affecting the emergence of the new university self-monitoring and self-evaluation system

The following five factors have been and are significant in the emergence of self-monitoring and self evaluation:

Declining enrolment – in 1992, the population of 18-year-olds decreased and will continue to do so. It is estimated that it will decrease to 1,300,000 in 15 years. Therefore, the population of students seeking higher education is also expected to decrease. This has made most universities realize the need to improve the quality of their education in order to attract more and better students.

Deregulation by the Ministry of Education – Japanese universities have been largely controlled by legal and administrative branches of the Ministry of Education, Science and Culture since 1945. However, recently criticism of regulation has been widespread among universities, and the Ministry of Education, Science and Culture has relaxed its supervision somewhat. A deregulation movement in curriculum and self-governing procedures has given universities room for self-evaluation.

Financial funding problem – the government's budget for funding universities is limited and a system of selective and effective distribution of grants to these universities has become necessary. Therefore universities must conduct self-monitoring and self-evaluation to improve their chances of receiving these grants.

Student dissatisfaction – students are not satisfied with the quality of the professors' lectures and the pedagogic style of mass teaching, which frequently takes the form of large classroom lectures. Mass higher education not only affected the total number of students; it has also affected the quality of lectures by professors. For example, mass higher education has produced some professors who are not interested in doing research, nor are they eager to teach. As a result, students are increasingly dissatisfied. Students claim that their voices must be heard through evaluation.

Influence of European and American universities – Japanese universities have recently become interested in the system of maintaining high academic standards used in European and American universities. American and European universities are highly regarded and provide Japan with a role model for accountability to students, society and government and for the Japanese higher education system in general. In such a perspective, all accountability begins with self-monitoring and self-evaluation.

The development of university self-monitoring and self-evaluation

It was against this background of influences and problems that evaluation was inserted into the policy arena. In 1984, a National Council on Educational Reform was established as an ad hoc advisory committee reporting to the Prime Minister to discuss across-the-board educational reform. University evaluation is discussed in the Second Report of the Committee:

> The university should recognise its duties and responsibilities. Information about teaching and research must be made public by the university at both domestic and foreign institutions. To do that, university evaluation should be carried out and self-monitoring of activities such as teaching, research performance, and social service should be done regularly (ch. I, section 4).

Based on the report of this National Council on Educational Reform (1986), the University Council was established in 1987 to discuss basic matters of higher education. In 1992, as a part of the project of reforming university education, the University Council proposed the following (University Council, 1992, ch. I, section 3, item [2]):

(a) making universities responsible for the adoption of self-monitoring and self-evaluation to reform teaching and research,
(b) basing evaluation on self-monitoring and self-evaluation and
(c) establishing a mutual evaluation system among universities in the future. Evaluation is considered to be a means for improving the quality of higher education.

In the same year, the Ministry of Education required universities to make every effort to establish self-monitoring and self-evaluation:

> The university has to attempt voluntarily to have self-monitoring and self-evaluation for teaching and research activities to improve the standard of the teaching and research, and to achieve its

purpose and duties for the society (Standards for Establishment of Universities, article 2).

Definition of self-monitoring and self-evaluation

The goals of self-evaluation are thus clear: self-monitoring and self-evaluation are attempts to plan and assess the quality of teaching and research by university professors in order to make them accountable to the students, the universities and society at large. However, the current model of self-monitoring and self-evaluation conducted by Japanese professors for their research activities differs from the US and European systems in that it does not involve any external third parties. Professors evaluate themselves within their own departments, seminars and research circles. The Japanese self-monitoring and self-evaluation is considered a preparatory stage on the way to achieving a real evaluation system which involves a third party.

The current model, initiated by the Ministry of Education, is activated once every three years at least. Each professor submits a list of his/her research performance and activities. For non-research work, he/she submits records of both on-and-off campus activities. However, it is not clear exactly how the professor should define and measure his or her educational activities (lectures and examinations) for purposes of evaluation. Although some professors let their students write their impressions of the lecture at end of the term as a part of the evaluation, this is far from an objective evaluation. In Japanese higher education institutions, the autonomy of professors is highly respected and evaluation of professors has not been a tradition at universities. In practice, the content of an instructor's lectures and examinations is seldom seen by other faculty members.

The role of JUAA in evaluation

University evaluation through self-monitoring started with teaching and research and has made significant progress in its scope and depth in recent years. However, evaluating teaching and research is only a part of university evaluation: it is limited and lacks effectiveness without overall support from the university. There is a definite need to improve and restructure other domains in universities such as curriculum, admission policies, student life, etc. These areas also need to be scrutinized by a neutral third party. In this regard, the role of the Japanese University Accreditation Association (JUAA) is very important.

In 1992, the JUAA, a volunteer group made up of national and private universities which set up a university standard for self-monitoring and self-evaluation, published *A Handbook of Self-monitoring and Self-evaluation* to be used as a leading guideline for university evaluation.

Table 9.2 *Number of universities implementing self-evaluation in 1994*

	A	B
National	98	87
Local	30	11
Private	274	32
Total	402	130

A: Has adapted for self-monitoring and self-evaluation by JUAA
B: Has published self-monitoring and self-evaluation reports.
(Source: Ministry of Education, *Universities and Students*, August 1994, p. 38, Tokyo: Ministry of Education.)

Each university is required to evaluate itself according to this Handbook with some input from its own ideas. The intention of the UAA is to establish a more neutral standard which includes external party evaluations by 1995. The number of universities currently implementing self-monitoring and self-evaluation is shown in Table 9.2.

The JUAA *University Evaluation Manual*, published in January 1995, spelled out the following three-stage approach:

1. First stage: Each university must submit its self-evaluation report, in line with JUAA specifications and format, to make sure that the university meets the minimum requirements set by the JUAA.
2. Second stage: The JUAA Committee consists of specialists in various fields who extensively evaluate the report submitted by universities. The committee then makes a report on their assessment of the university.
3. Third stage: Upon receiving the University Report and the Committee Report, the JUAA issues recommendations and suggestions to the university. Their assessment is directed to the university as a whole and not to specific departments or seminar groups (pp. 49, 65).

Upon receiving the JUAA recommendations, each university is required to submit its implementation plan which must include a target date for completion. The JUAA's evaluation is primarily carried out on the basis of data and documents. However, when a question arises, they may make a field trip to the university to verify the data. The university may or may not publicize the results of their evaluation; this decision is at the university's discretion. The university must bear the cost of the JUAA evaluation. It is to be conducted once every ten years. The scheme will start in September 1996.

The following are the areas of evaluation used by the JUAA:

Philosophy and objectives
Organization

Admission policies
Curriculum
Research activities
Teaching
Facilities and equipment
Library and resources
Student life
Administrative procedures
Specific organizational structure for monitoring.

A budget is also required as an independent entity and has to be attached to the package of evaluation materials.

Table 9.3 shows the areas in which universities would like to do self-evaluation, based upon the JUAA's Handbook and their own ideas.

Over 75 per cent of the universities responded in the areas of research, curriculum and admissions. When one compares government-supported universities and private universities, there is a difference in their emphasis on which areas to evaluate. Private universities emphasize research, curriculum, admissions and objectives and philosophies in order to attract more students of diversified backgrounds. National universities emphasize research and admissions, and place relatively less emphasis on objectives and philosophies.

There is one problem with their reports. The validity of the reports is somewhat questionable because they are generally descriptive and detail-oriented, not analytical nor objective in evaluation.

Table 9.4 classifies the types of reports into four different categories. One category is the White Paper format which is detail-oriented. Category two is the teaching-oriented report; three is the research-oriented report. The fourth category is classified as 'others' and deals with admission examinations, curriculum and the universities' affiliation to the society. The comparison is made between national, local and private institutions.

Table 9.3 *Preferred items for self-monitoring and self-evaluation of reports*

	National	Local	Private	Total
Philosophy and objectives	41	7	20	68
Admission policies	52	7	20	79
Curriculum	48	7	24	79
Teaching	31	2	14	47
Research activities	66	7	24	97
Student life	42	8	15	65
Administration procedures	29	5	12	46
Number of institutions	68	8	26	102

(Source: Ministry of Education, *Universities and Students*, August 1994, p. 39, Tokyo: Ministry of Education.)

Table 9.4 *Types of reports*

	National	Local	Private	Total
White Paper	30	5	8	43
Teaching	8	0	1	9
Research	44	1	5	50
Others	18	2	18	38

(Source: Ministry of Education, *Universities and Students*, August 1994, p. 39, Tokyo: Ministry of Education.)

The most popular report is the research type; the White Paper approach is the next most popular. The reason the research approach is widely used for evaluation is that it is easy to identify and relatively simple to evaluate the pursuit and quality of research activity on the part of professors. However, the problem remains that the real research evaluation is not analysed and evaluated objectively.

Self-monitoring and self-evaluation by third party involvement

There are two problems facing research evaluation. One is the lack of uniformity between departments and universities, the other is the lack of objectivity in their evaluation. In order to overcome these problems, there have been some objective evaluations conducted by a few Japanese higher education institutions.

For example, in 1993, the University of Tokyo's Physical Laboratory made such an attempt. They established a ten-member evaluation committee which consisted of a Nobel Prize-winning scholar and other nationally recognized scholars. These ten members evaluated the research output of scholars outside their own departments and seminars in terms of number and quality of articles written. Following this example, many departments and other universities are having their research evaluated by other departments as well as other universities.

Another noted example was established by the University of Tokyo's Faculty of Letters Seminar on the Study of Japan. Its evaluation committee consists of seven members, three of them being foreign scholars: one from Korea, one from America and one from France. The committee members make a personal visit to a Japanese literature, linguistics or history classroom and speak with the professor and students directly to evaluate the professor's performance and total quality of the department. The result of the evaluation covers the following areas:

The common problems of the department and seminars.
Special issues in each classroom, seminar and department.

International exchange programmes.
Personal evaluation.

After careful and extensive consultation with the professors and their students, the committee makes recommendations in the areas found to be deficient.

Research evaluation and funding

Do the results of the research evaluation determine the amount of a scholar's research funding? The answer is no. In Japan, research fund allocation does not depend upon the performance and scope of research but on the academic field or department in which the research is based. Furthermore, whether the university is a liberal arts college or a natural science college is another important factor affecting the receipt of funds. Yet another factor is whether or not the university offers graduate courses. However, the allotment of funds does not consider whether the entire faculty engages in research activities or not. In other words, the Japanese research allocation system is mechanical and quantitative, not qualitative.

In recent years, the selective distribution of research money has become urgent due to limited budgets. The main concern is to formulate a system that determines the amount of research funds based upon the scope, subject and performance of the research activities. This method has to involve some experts in each academic field and it should be standardized. The question remains how to implement this method.

Regarding research activities, there is already a subsidy system which distributes the research allowance based on requests from the scholar or the group. This is called the grant-in-aid system for scientific research. The system determines the amount of the research allotment which depends on the originality of the individual's or the group's theme and the prior research performance. The evaluation is done by selected experts in each academic field.

Students' evaluation of lectures

Students' evaluation of lectures is still in its infancy in Japanese higher education institutions. Statistics in 1993 show that less than 10 per cent of universities conduct lecture evaluations as part of self-monitoring and self-evaluation. Furthermore, the distribution of a syllabus was done in 1994 at only 18 per cent of universities, even though such a process helps students to understand the lectures and adjust to the course at the beginning of term.

The students' evaluation of lectures is regarded as one of the important elements for revitalizing Japanese higher education. Many professors welcome student evaluations as a way to improve their teaching. However, some doubts remain among professors who fear that student evaluations could undermine their autonomy, authority, or status.

Universities recognize the need for lecture evaluation but there are difficulties in the implementation of this procedure. These difficulties include how to use the evaluation, which subjects to evaluate, and who is responsible for making the evaluation. Once the concept of student evaluation is accepted in universities, it will certainly improve the quality of teaching.

The impact of university self-monitoring and self-evaluation

The Japanese university evaluation system has just started and it only covers teaching and research performance through self-monitoring and self-evaluation by the faculty members themselves. It does not include evaluation by a third party to compare an institution with other universities by means of some standardized criteria. Although self-monitoring and self-evaluation have limitations, the positive impact is three-fold.

First is the change in the attitude of professors toward lectures. The professors become more sensitive to the needs of the students as well as society. Second, some 'characterization' (ie, differentiation of universities) would begin to emerge. One category of university could focus on graduate programmes; a second category might focus on undergraduate programmes; and a third category might focus on occupational training at both graduate and undergraduate levels.

Third, university evaluation is likely to promote differentiation of professional roles, according to whether he/she does research or not. As a consequence, it may produce a separation of the teaching staff from the research staff. Furthermore, it may delineate the difference between graduate and undergraduate programmes more clearly. For example, a professor whose focus is on research may teach more on the graduate programme than on the undergraduate programme. Conversely, a professor whose focus is on teaching may contribute more to the undergraduate programme than to the graduate programme.

Conclusion

The Japanese university evaluation system has focused on how and what areas to evaluate in order to improve the quality of teaching and research which are the main functions of the university. However, there is no perfect evaluation method established anywhere that can withstand real scientific scrutiny. In my opinion, it is impossible to formulate such a system because of the complexity of university functions. However, I do believe that recent Japanese efforts to formulate a legitimate evaluation system certainly enhance the awareness of the quality of teaching and research in higher education institutions. In many cases, the process has already contributed to the improvement of teaching and brought benefits to the students, university and society. There are a number of problems facing Japanese higher institutions and it is wise to focus attention on teaching and research because it is these areas that can be most improved by self-evaluation.

My best advice to improve the evaluation system is for universities to continue to modify the current self-monitoring and self-evaluation system in order to earn broader support and approval from society. It would also be beneficial for Japanese universities to turn their attention to American universities and their accreditation system as well as the JUAA's experience. The ultimate goal for Japanese universities is to formulate a system that is both effective and suitable for their environment.

References (published in Japanese)

Japanese University Accreditation Association (1992) *A Handbook of Self-monitoring and Self-evaluation*, Tokyo: JUAA.

Japanese University Accreditation Association (1995) *University Evaluation Manual*, Tokyo: JUAA.

Ministry of Education (1994) *Universities and Students*, August, pp. 37–44, Tokyo: Ministry of Education.

National Council on Education Reform (1986) *Second Report*, Tokyo: Prime Minister's Office.

University Council (1992) *The Report of the University Council*, Tokyo: Ministry of Education.

10. The Evaluation of the Higher Education System in the Republic of Korea

Terri Kim

Introduction

This chapter concentrates on the evaluation of the higher education system in the Republic of Korea during the last 30 years. The first section sketches foreign influences on Korean higher education and political and economic problems, as the context of subsequent evaluation systems. The second section will deal with emerging patterns of the higher education evaluation system in the 1970s and 1980s, before evaluation reforms moved to centre-stage. The second section also discusses the higher education evaluation system in the 1990s, and comments on the short-term and longer-term effects on higher education of the present style of evaluation. The third section is a conclusion.

The chapter suggests that the particular politico-economic milieu in the Republic of Korea has been a central influence on how the higher education system was viewed, controlled and evaluated by the state in four phases: the period of control in the 1960s; the pilot evaluation in the 1970s; the third phase of fuller intervention and formalized evaluation after 1982; and the fourth contemporary phase of the new accreditation and evaluation system after 1992.

The context of Korean higher education: foreign influences, politics and economics

Korean higher education in its modern form began to develop in the late nineteenth century. Systematic governmental control over higher education was established under the Japanese colonial regime (1910–45). The Japanese colonial government set up a highly centralized educational administration structure in Korea, similar to that of the Japanese education system of that time. After Korea achieved independence but with national partition in 1945, higher education in South Korea was under the US military government as part of the three-

113

year postwar Trusteeship. During this period (1945–48), American educational ideas (eg, an egalitarian educational ideology, educational pragmatism and behavioral sciences) were influences on the South Korean education system. Since then, the South Korean higher education system has developed, following the structure of the American model of higher education, but with continuing Japanese cultural influence on, for example, pedagogy and examinations, both within a context of centralized control.

Geopolitically surrounded by powerful nations such as the People's Republic of China, Japan, the former Soviet Union, and the United States, the Republic of Korea has been, politically and militarily, sharply aware of the socialist regime in the Democratic People's Republic of Korea (North Korea) since 1945. The South Korean political milieu has always promoted the idea of 'the nation at risk' before that phrase became fashionable. Economically, South Korea has urgently industrialized from a base as one of the poorest economies in the Third World after the Korean War in 1953. This rapid economic development was directed by a series of authoritarian governments (1961–88) strongly influenced by the military until the incumbent civil government came into being in February 1993. The principal goals of the nation have been focused on economic development and national reunification. These two politico-economic targets have legitimized governmental control over most facets of civil society. The unique politico-economic conditions of national development have formed the particular pattern of the higher education system in South Korea.

In this context, institutional autonomy of higher education has not really existed. The government has controlled the higher education system to restrain the growth of the political potential of the university. After the military *coup d'etat* in 1961, the government started to make a series of radical reforms to put the higher education system under its strict control. The so-called 1961 'rearrangement plans' cut back the scale of the four-year colleges and universities from 71 institutions, 686 departments and 91,540 student places to only 44 institutions, 584 departments and 55,410 student places (Kim, Chong-ch'ol, 1985: 193). On the other hand the rearrangements resulted in a drastic increase of the two-year junior colleges from the previous number of 12 institutions with 3,208 student places to 27 institutions with 10,509 students in 1962 (ibid). In addition, ten other junior colleges were newly established in 1962, being reorganized from the existing normal secondary schools (ibid).

As one can see from the results of the 1961 rearrangement plans for higher education, the government did not permit expansion of the top prestigious universities which offered some political threat to the military governing power (Kim, In Whoe, 1993). As the Ministry of Education had discretion over the number of students which each university was permitted to admit, the first priority was given to the politically less dangerous universities which, in general, occupy the lower stratum of the university hierarchy in Korea. Although it had to increase moderately the enrolment quotas in higher education institutions after severe criticisms of the 1961 rearrangement plans, the government continued to strengthen its control over the higher education system through the Private School Law in 1964 and the Presidential Decree on College and University Student Quotas in 1965 (Korean Council for University Education, 1990: 42). Under the Education Law, all higher education institutions whether public or private have been under the direct and indirect supervision of the government (ibid).

The role of higher education in South Korea has also been defined by the state in relation to economic development. Higher education was linked to governmental manpower planning in the 1960s, when human capital theory was gaining prevalence, in correlating educational input and output with economic growth. The military governments sought immediate economic solutions based on short-term, five-year-economic plans. From the early 1960s until the mid-1970s, during the period of rapid economic development, industrial development was led by export-oriented manufacturing activities.

At this stage of South Korean industrialization, the manpower demanded in the industrial sector was middle-level rather than university graduate level. Therefore, the contribution of higher education to the rapid industrialization of the 1960s and 1970s in South Korea was relatively small. The World Bank Report shows that South Korea's economic growth during the last three decades beginning in the mid-1960s owes much to efforts concentrated on basic education rather than higher education. For instance, South Korea allocated 83.9 per cent of its total education budget to basic education, ie, primary and secondary education, and only 10.3 per cent to higher education (The World Bank, 1993).

Nevertheless, higher education expanded dramatically. The university population in South Korea doubled during the 1970s, mainly due to the expansion of the institutions in the lower stratum of the university hierarchy. This expansion was financed mainly by student fees in the private sector. The highest proportion of the revenue of private universities and colleges is from tuition, which was 80.18 per cent of the total in 1981 (Korean Council for University Education, 1986:76). In particular, science and engineering departments were rapidly increased without proper financial investment in those fields, in low-quality higher education institutions. As a consequence, the overall quality of university education deteriorated.

In this context and time, the emergent style of the evaluation of the Korean higher education system was determined by two features of government education policy: i) government 'control' over the higher education system to ensure political stability from the 1960s and ii) government 'intervention' in the higher education system to ensure economic development from the 1970s. Both principles led to control; evaluation was indirect.

In fact, higher education in South Korea is highly centralized. The administration of all higher educational institutions is under the same laws and regulations. Until 1988 the presidents of national universities and colleges were appointed by the President of the Republic of Korea on the recommendation of the Ministry of Education. The Minister of Education still directs and supervises the establishment of new higher education institutions and departments, facility standards, enrolment quotas, appointment of the faculty, curriculum, and academic credits and degrees.

In this centralized higher education system, efforts were made to produce a standardization of the system, including selection for higher education. The uniform criteria established under governmental super-vision include the College Entrance Examination, qualifications of university teaching staff, curriculum and degree requirements, college and university military training, faculty standards for universities and colleges, regulations for the establishment and closure of institutions, fiscal review, inspection of facilities, and the establishment of an overall official quota of students for each higher education institution (MOE, 1990). These criteria are all under the control of the Ministry of Education. In 1969, the government started to take the initiative in controlling the university entrance examination (MOE, 1990: 32). The examination for entrance to colleges and universities in Korea is regarded as one of the most crucial issues in terms of its impact on the content and method of education in secondary school and the complexity of the problems connected with it.

The results of the College Entrance Examination have been used as the major means of evaluation informally, by the parents and students. This has defined a single vertical hierarchical order of higher education institutions. According to this form of evaluation, the top five universities in South Korea, except Seoul National University, are all private universities.

Phases in the emergence of evaluation systems in Korean higher education

The period of control in the 1960s

Until the 1960s, the evaluation of the higher education system in Korea was performed indirectly by parents and students and directly by the standardization measures of the Ministry of Education (Korean Council for University Education, 1990: 105). The entrance selection system was further used as an instrument for government control of mass participation in higher education.

The priority of the government was a definition of the selection process rather than the creation of a national system for the evaluation of the quality of higher education itself. Until recently the 'evaluation' of higher education in South Korea has not been associated with objective, systematic measures and the direct assessment of higher education as a national system. Rather there has been a conventional acceptance of quality by traditional and reputational judgements on universities. Thus, governmental control and standardization (of curriculum, entrance examinations and so on) were a substitute for systematic evaluation of higher education.

Therefore, the qualitative evaluation of higher education has been relatively neglected, partly due to the lack of governmental investment in higher education during the past 30 years. It is something of a contradiction that the government has not funded higher education institutions sufficiently, despite the urgent needs for high-level manpower in the advanced industries. These needs were partly met by a considerable contribution of the private sector to the output of higher education in South Korea. The governmental strategy seems to have been mainly focused on cost-effectiveness in higher education. Thus, the government indirectly increased the supply of trained manpower without much investment in higher education. There is a widespread judgement among Korean academics that the quality of higher education suffered as a consequence of this cost-conscious expansion. The evaluation system of higher education in this period was not consistently formalized but rather oriented to the solution of problems as they occurred.

In many ways this is very understandable. Korea as a whole has experienced in this century Japanese colonialism, wars, political instability, rapid changes in governments, and experiments in political style. Recovery from the Korean War has been difficult for both parts of Korea. In South Korea, the government had also set itself ambitious aims: not merely political stability and economic growth, but also the need to construct a 'modern' educational system including a rapidly expanded higher education system. The very high proportion of private institutions within the higher education sector also led to problems of definition: how many such institutions should be encouraged; in which academic areas should they be encouraged to specialize, if any; how should they relate to national, state-run universities; what should the shape of the system be and become? How tightly should the system be made to articulate with the labour market, and in which speedy ways might South Korea 'catch up' with the strong 1960s Western economies and the emerging strength of the Japanese economy?

In this context, that the South Korean government, using the tradition of central control inherited from the Japanese colonial period, emphasized standardization of inputs (the examination of students at point of entry, centralized curricula and so on) is not surprising. It has been a way to give minimal coherence to the national higher education system. But the very success of these measures of standardization and control produced consequences, of which one of the most important was the quality of outputs of the system. These issues of quality — and efforts to evaluate the quality of higher education as a national system — began to surface in the 1970s.

Pilot evaluation in the 1970s

In the 1970s, the government manpower planning approach geared the evaluation of the higher education system to the supply of industrial needs. In consequence, the government adopted a human resource development policy, with particular emphasis on the natural sciences and engineering fields.

From that perspective, the 'University experimentation programme' was devised to provide external criteria:

> to judge the quality of higher education and to support selectively those pilot institutions which met the external criteria, by either providing subsidies or allowing them more autonomy (Korean Council for University Education, 1990: 38).

The pilot institutions participated in the following programmes: selection of students by certain fields and colleges rather than by departmental divisions; new credit requirements for graduation from 160 credits to 140 credits (similar to the semester-credit system in the United States); and the introduction of a minor and double-major system to extend the knowledge background of students to increase prospects of future employment (Korean Council for University Education, 1990: 38).

In this evaluation process, an initial coalition between the government and each university was made. The Ministry of Education started to perform evaluation through Evaluation Committees composed of relevant professors in each field of study. The government wished to extend the scheme.

In order to undertake a more systematic evaluation, the government established the Korean Council for University Education in 1982. This is composed of the Presidents of all four-year colleges and universities. The objectives of this organization officially include 'enhancing autonomy and accountability in the management of colleges and universities' (Korean Council for University Education, 1986: 107).

The difficulty with this double proposition — autonomy *and* accountability — is that while the tradition of accountability in South Korean higher education has been strong, and been strengthened since 1945, 'autonomy' has been less clearly defined in South Korean higher education culture. Among the foreign influences on South Korean higher education only the American (and by extension the German) tradition has taken autonomy of higher education institutions seriously. Two other foreign models influencing Korean higher education — the Chinese and the Japanese — did not emphasize autonomy. Even before Japanese colonialization, the long historic Chinese tradition of the role of the scholar-bureaucrat found reverberation in Korean higher education. The Korean tradition of *Yangban* also stressed the service of the scholar to the state. The Japanese colonial period included policies to break, culturally, the formation of a Korean identity, and especially to break the tradition of the cultivation of a national (Korean) elite. Advanced education in Korea was closed down, deliberately, and a much smaller Korean elite was trained, especially in vocational or professional disciplines, in Japan itself.

The consequence, currently and in practice, is that the reform movement in Korean higher education from the late 1970s and into the 1990s, has tended to stress less the theme of autonomy and more the theme of accountability; and accountability to the state rather than to civil society or even 'the consumer' of higher education.

Formalized evaluation: after 1982

The official role, then, of the Korean Council for University Education includes evaluating the higher education system in South Korea: devising evaluation plans, selecting evaluation committee members, preparing evaluation standards, performing actual evaluation, and reporting and publicizing the evaluations. Since 1984, the Korean Council for University Education has conducted the evaluation of universities and colleges at both institutional and programme level. Institutional evaluation has been carried out in five-year cycles, and various evaluations were made annually (Lee, Wha-Kuk, 1994: 75). However, the evaluation results were not made public and thus did not provide incentives to public competition among universities and colleges. Such incentives were provided by the evaluation of universities and colleges by many other organizations such as *The Joong-ang Daily News*, *Weekly Newsmagazine*, and also the self-evaluation of some leading universities in 1994. However, the consumer-oriented concepts of accountability and efficiency in higher education did not emerge, at this point, although there was already some external pressure to invite foreign competition in the education field. This was part of a broader notion of competition.

The new accreditation and evaluation system after 1992

After 1992, the government started to emphasize far more highly the importance of the international competitiveness of the nation. Managing and enhancing the quality of higher education became an important issue in the present government's 'internationalization' policy. New steps toward the construction of a full evaluation system were undertaken.

In 1991, the Council for Higher Education recommended the implementation of an accreditation system in Korea. The accreditation of departments of physics and electronics was undertaken first, from January to June 1992, and the result was analysed by the Korean Council for University Education and announced in March 1993 (Lee, Wha-kuk, 1994: 76). The evaluation was conducted through two procedures: institutional self-assessment and then external scrutiny by on-site visits (Korean Council for University Education, 1986: 114). The evaluation system at the national level started in 1994 and institutional accreditation will happen in 1996 (Lee, Wha-kuk, 1994: 76).

The national evaluation and accreditation system has a network linked to the evaluation committee of each university cluster. The Central Accreditation Commission is attached to the Inter-university Coordination Committee. From the viewpoint of raising the academic standards and quality of higher education, the evaluation criteria are the three major functions of a university: teaching, research and service (ibid). There are six major categories of evaluation: objectives, curriculum, students, faculty, facilities and administration and finance (Lee, Wha-kuk, 1994: 77). In each category, there are 50–60 sub-categories for evaluation questions. Within each evaluation item, there are three levels which may be identified: good (A), moderate (B), and poor (C) (ibid).

The results of the governmental evaluation of seven universities were released on 28 February 1995 (*The Korean Academic Newspaper*, 16 March 1995, p. 3). The overall result of the evaluation was that the scores of undergraduate education of those seven universities ranged from 399.11 to 474.25 out of 500 points. The average score of postgraduate education was 84.4 out of 100 points in this evaluation.

Those seven universities were all considered to be accredited as a result of the evaluation. However, the Korean Council for University Education which conducted the evaluation decided not to publish the entire results of the evaluation but only to name the top ranking university in each category, taking into account the probable immediate impact of the evaluation on the universities and public reaction. The full results of evaluation will not be published until 1999 when the experimental evaluation period is over. However, the process continues. In 1995, there are 19 universities under evaluation. After the results of the evaluation of these seven universities in South Korea came out last year, five universities among these 19 postponed the time for evaluation (*The Korean Academic Newspaper*, 1 June 1995, p. 2). Those universities are in the process of self-evaluation and systematic development planning.

Apart from the government-led evaluation and accreditation system in 1994, the evaluation of 131 universities and colleges was also conducted by many other organizations, such as *The Joong-ang Daily News*, and *Weekly Newsmagazine*, and there was self-assessment by some universities, as mentioned earlier.

The boom in evaluation of the higher education system in 1994 and 1995 was because of an emerging perception among education consumers of their right to claim quality in higher education and because of internal and external pressure on higher educational institutions, which are facing the creation of an education market in the near future: from 1996, the private education sector will be open for foreign investment. However, there is contradiction between the evaluation systems. The results of the evaluation of higher education institutions by the press are not consistent with the conventional evaluation of higher education institutions as shown by the public recognition of prestigious universities. Especially, some prestigious universities in Seoul did not reach a satisfactory level, according to the official evaluation results. Instead, some regional universities showed strength in certain academic fields and in amenities as well. That is a different trend from the past, when many private colleges tried to establish or expand their departments of science and engineering to upgrade their status to the university level without the necessary proper physical and financial conditions.

Government control over the enrolment quota has continued, even after the evaluation and accreditation system had been introduced. Autonomy in enrolment quotas and financial aid is supposed to be given on the basis of the results of the evaluation of the quality of individual higher education institutions. In reality, however, the proportion of government financial support in the budget of private higher education institutions is less than 1.5 per cent (1.39 per cent in 1992) even though those private institutions are, in number, 70 per cent of all higher education institutions (Korean Council for University Education, 1992: 155).

Here, then, the purpose of accreditation and evaluation of the higher education system can be critically questioned at two levels: immediate practical problems; and strategically: what is the expected benefit of the government-led evaluation and accreditation system? Who is this evaluation system for?

The emerging practical problems are likely to be, first, that the accreditation system and the results of the evaluation system lack incentive, and motive power, to induce qualitative improvement of universities under evaluation. For instance, the standard of accreditation to be achieved fails to induce competition among universities in a real sense, because the system will permit accreditation if the university reaches the average score. A sharper system would provide direct financial support for the universities that achieved a high score among the accredited institutions which could be a very practical incentive once the minimum goal of accreditation was achieved.

Second, the standard of evaluation was set for the university system as a whole; therefore, it could be unsuitable for the evaluation of some specialized institutions such as Pohang Technical Institute and Korean Teachers' College. For instance, Pohang Institute received a lower score in the evaluation of general education last year perhaps because it is highly specialized in the technology and engineering fields from the undergraduate level.

Third, the size and the level of expertise of the evaluation committee, which was composed of 22 members in 1994, may need expansion considering the increasing number of institutions to be evaluated in the coming years. To evaluate 19 institutions in 1995, it was suggested that there should be at least 50 committee members. For the evaluation process, the members of the evaluation committee may need to acquire professional expertise in evaluation in each speciality.

Certainly the new evaluation system is intended strategically to meet the new domestic and international demands on higher education, which emphasize accountability, efficiency and consumer rights, within a market. However, in the existing single-ladder hierarchy of universities and colleges, the nature of the Korean Council for University Education itself is an example of conformity in Korean higher education. Without fundamental reforms in the infrastructure of higher education in South Korea, eg, differentiation and individualization of the status, function and character of universities and colleges, the newly devised evaluation and accreditation system imitating the US model seems likely to continue the status quo. To confirm a linear hierarchy of universities and colleges through the formal accreditation and evaluation system would be meaningless in terms of the qualitative and efficient reform of education. Educational changes may need to be initiated by individual institutions through open and diversified competition, not through the uniform standardization measurements imposed by the government-led evaluation and accreditation system. In order to develop long-term strategies for efficiency, excellence and productivity in higher education, meeting average standards may not be enough. In that sense, the accrediting organization, the Council for University Accreditation, which is managed by the Ministry of Education and Korean Council for University Education, has a limitation in its nature: it conditions competition among universities and colleges within a single-ladder hierarchy of the higher education system. This is likely to check the development of new and different visions of excellence in higher education.

Such new visions would certainly address the question of basic research. The character of Korean university education and research has been distant from pure basic research work; it has been mostly pragmatic, emphasizing the immediate use of knowledge. It has been argued in this chapter that the function of the university to serve the state has developed ever since the colonial period. It is the state's responsibility to safeguard basic research, whose future use cannot be defined right from the start. This particularly applies to university research.

Nevertheless, progress has been made. New conditions for the recruitment and evaluation of the professorate in 1995 show an effort to redress existing problems such as nepotism and lack of competitiveness in the domestic academic environment. Many prestigious universities have taken initiatives in open recruiting on the basis of short-term contracts and employing foreign scholars as well. For instance, academic recruitment on the basis of short-term contracts has been adopted by Seoul National, Yonsei, Korea University and many other universities since Kyunghee University first started the short contract system. Historically, nepotic recruitment and recruitment as academic-reproduction have been major problems in South Korean academic society; a more prestigious university is more likely to recruit academics who possess degrees from the same university (eg, more than 90 per cent of the professorate in Seoul National University in 1991) rather than to stress competitively demonstrated research competence and achievement (*Korean University Newspaper*, 1994, p. 5).

A major advance is made by the new system which evaluates a professor's research and teaching as a means of allocating funds, determining salary, and even retention on the faculty. Sharper control over the standard of the professorate as well as university education in general has emerged in South Korea in conjunction with the new evaluation system of higher education. Since faculty hired after 1994 have no tenure in many universities, they can be dismissed if they are labelled 'redundant' because they are not engaged in efficient teaching and research. These new standards of academic recruitment, initiated by some of the leading universities, are expected to be used by more universities to facilitate improvement of the academic quality and the dynamic circulation of the professorate in academe. Evaluation of the performance of the professorate is obviously progress toward a meritocracy and the short-term contract will obviously increase competition among institutions.

Other ideas to increase competitiveness in higher education are being discussed. Among the most controversial is the idea of a 'donation' admission, which gives an offer of a place to any applicant who donates a very large sum of money to the university. This is regarded as a suggestion to break open competition hitherto confined by government regulations and control. The advantage of the proposed 'donation system' is that it would be a way of broadening and diversifying sources of university finance and thus possibilities to compete. However, the obvious disadvantage is that it is likely to increase the chances of nepotism, again. Clearly the debate, even if confused, is not completed.

On 31 May 1995, an official report of the Education Reform Committee came out with a vision of a new education system for an 'open society for lifelong learning'. According to the report, the government promises to allocate 5 per cent of GNP for the education budget by 1998. However, more immediate financial support would seem to be an essential prerequisite for successful education reform.

At the core of the debate is a term, and a strategic conception, which is itself confused: 'internationalization' (*Kukjewha*). At its simplest the term means in contemporary Korean discourse the opening up of the provision of education, through a change in the law, to competition from foreign suppliers of education. Foreign 'companies' will be permitted to establish higher education institutions and to 'sell' education to Koreans. 'Internationalization' also means at its vaguest the continuing adaptation of Korean civil society and of the higher education system to influences from world culture and the world economic system. The most practical concrete example of this at the policy level is the increasing ease with which foreign scholars can compete for university jobs in South Korea. Unfortunately, however, the concepts of 'internationalization' and 'globalization' have moved with great rapidity — in about four years — to become part of political rhetoric. South Korea will adapt in a range of ways which are still being invented to a set of international forces which are themselves unspecified, though they have been rhetorically named. The consequence is likely to be, amid this conceptual confusion, a continuation of old and trusted mechanisms, especially the traditional practices of central control, standardization by the state and evaluation mechanisms which do not lead to the kind of publicity and public sanction that can be associated with loss of institutional 'face' (*Chemyeon*). Until the concept and rhetoric of internationalization is clarified, it is unlikely that the answer to the question, 'What is evaluation for?' will be crisply and imaginatively answered.

Conclusion

During the last four decades, the government has made remarkable progress in systematizing the evaluation system of higher education in an effort to make higher education useful to national needs. In a difficult geopolitical context, the South Korean government has made serious efforts and has been successful in consolidating rapid economic development and political stability at the same time.

What probably now needs to be addressed is a need for diverse standards in terms of competition among higher education institutions. The history of the status of universities in South Korea is a history of a hierarchical order confirmed each year by applicants' preliminary college entrance examination scores. The government has also frozen this examination and there are no free and diverse ways of competition within this system, which strongly influences the boundaries and form of competition. The system of higher education has also been remarkably uniform, for example in the university administration system, in ages of entry and completion by students, and in curriculum and teaching method. The centralized higher education system in South Korea binds all institutions under the same laws and regulations.

Without fundamental changes in the government-controlled administration structure of higher education, simple borrowing of the US accreditation system is unlikely to work effectively, even though South Korea retains the second highest rate of enrolment (per 10,000 of the population) in colleges and universities in the world, next to the USA

(UNESCO, 1994). What are needed are new visions of diversity and new ways of constructing excellence in higher education.

References

Kim, Chong-ch'ol (1985) *Education and Development: Some Essays and Thoughts on Korean Education*, Seoul: Seoul National University Press.

Kim, In Whoe (1993) *Hankook Kyoyook Yerksa wa Moonje* (History of Korean Education and its Problems), Seoul: Mooneum Sa.

Korean Council for University Education (1986) *A Study on Higher Education in Korea*, Seoul: Korean Council for University Education.

Korean Council for University Education (1990) *Korean Higher Education: Its Development, Aspects and Prospects*, Seoul: Korean Council for University Education.

Korean Council for University Education (1992) *University Education Development Indicators*, Seoul: Korean Council for University Education.

Korean University Newspaper (1994) No. 161, 7 November.

Lee, Wha-Kuk (1994) 'University Accreditation in Korea' in Craft, A (ed.) *International Developments in Assuring Quality in Higher Education*, London: Falmer Press.

Ministry of Education, Republic of Korea (1990) *Education in Korea 1989–1990*, Seoul: Ministry of Education.

The World Bank (1993) *The East Asian Miracle*, Washington DC: The World Bank.

UNESCO (1994) *Statistical Yearbook*, Paris: UNESCO.

11. The evaluation of the higher education system in the United States of America

Susan Douglas Franzosa

Historically, higher education in the United States has been characterized by a principle of institutional autonomy and a tradition of self-regulation. From its beginnings, the system has not been subject to any direct form of centralized governmental control. The result has been an unusually wide diversity of form and function among institutions. There are now over 35,000 colleges and universities in the United States and close to 14,000,000 students; 40 per cent of the 18- to 21-year-old age cohort are enrolled within the system (Kerr, 1994). As Trow (1993: 40) describes it, American post-secondary education is,

> large, untidy, uncoordinated from the center, and without national standards for the admission of students, the appointment of academic staff, or the awarding of degrees.

Within this context, colleges and universities have been free to determine their individual missions and set their own institutional standards. Their formal evaluation has been voluntary, taking the form of internal programme assessments and institutional self-studies and external peer reviews by private accrediting agencies and professional associations. Until quite recently, this decentralized approach has worked to foster both institutional achievement and public confidence (Semrow *et al.*, 1992). However, following a period of unprecedented legislative scrutiny and public criticism during the 1980s, there have been increasing demands for greater accountability in higher education. Pressure has been exerted at both the state and federal levels to move toward a more centralized form of systematic assessment and to link evaluation and accreditation with nationally determined standards for institutional effectiveness. As a result, the established processes of evaluation in higher education are currently about to undergo significant changes that will very likely affect the system's long-established traditions of autonomy and self-regulation.

The governance and framework of evaluation

Under the United States Constitution, primary responsibility for public education in the United States resides not with the federal government but with the individual states and municipal localities. This responsibility is exercised routinely in the elementary and secondary sectors of education through the provision of funds, creation and regulation of standards, professional certification of teachers, and approval of curriculum requirements and guidelines. In the post-secondary sector the influence of the state is less direct. State legislatures approve an institution's initial charter and appropriate funds to subsidize their public universities and colleges. During the expansion of higher education in the 1960s and 1970s, over half of the states also established state-wide governing boards to oversee their higher education systems (Folger and Jones, 1993). However, state governing boards have tended to coordinate rather than direct institutional policies and have exercised their oversight primarily in the areas of institutional size and enrolment management, the setting of tuition fees, and the approval of proposals for new programmes and degrees. Traditionally the states have trusted colleges and universities to determine their own internal standards and manage their own processes of evaluation.

Prior to the 1980s, the federal government extended an equal degree of trust in the traditions of self-regulation in higher education. At the national level, the government's interventions in post-secondary education were confined to legislative actions that provided financial support for system-wide improvement projects (Trow, 1993). The nineteenth century Land Grant Acts supported the establishment of state universities and, during particular periods of national need, subsequent Acts of the United States Congress supported the development of vocational and technical education programmes, war veterans' scholarships, libraries and facilities for scientific research, and student financial aid and loan programmes. Apart from requiring that institutions applying for federal funds comply with federal law, the government exercised no regulatory powers in higher education. Thus, at both state and federal levels, involvement in financing remained the most direct form of government influence in American higher education.

Although there were significant variations between their appropriation levels, in the mid-1980s the states contributed an average of 30 per cent toward the costs of post-secondary education and the federal government supplied approximately 13 per cent in the form of research and development grants and between 15 and 20 per cent in student financial aid (Trow, 1993). Tuition, endowments and grants from private sources supplied the remainder. However, these patterns began to change during the more difficult economic context of the 1980s. Federal assistance, particularly in financial aid to students, was reduced and the states were expected to increase their contributions. While the actual result was a reduction in both state and federal support and an increased reliance on tuition revenues (St John, 1994), the controversies surrounding funding in the 1980s became an important factor in discussions of the regulation of higher education.

While significant changes are now occurring, the evaluation of institutions of higher education in the United States is currently conducted from within a loosely structured network of independent professional associations and non-governmental accrediting agencies organized, sponsored and maintained by higher educational institutions themselves (Semrow *et al.*, 1992). At the national level, most colleges and universities hold memberships in professional higher education associations, institutes and councils that promote their group interests, foster collaboration across institutions and assess the need for system-wide reform and change. Studies by the American Council on Education, the Association of American Universities, or the National Association of State Universities and Land Grant Colleges, for example, provide an influential framework in which individual institutions evaluate their own policies, programmes and achievements, and accrediting agencies design their assessment standards and procedures (Eaton, 1991).

At the local institutional level, colleges and universities determine their own requirements for admission and graduation, criteria for faculty appointments and promotion, and standards for curriculum and programme approval through a faculty and administrative committee structure. Influenced by professional expectations and trends within the larger higher education community and in response to particular institutional circumstances, colleges and universities also engage in a wide spectrum of evaluation activities that range from focused appraisals of specific administrative procedures to much broader reviews of the institution's mission and future direction. The results of these evaluations are used in decision-making processes within academic departments, at the central administrative level, and by college and university governing boards.

While colleges and universities applying for research and development grants are often required to submit to reviews by funding agencies, since the 1950s formal external evaluations of post-secondary institutions have been conducted largely as part of a voluntary accreditation process (Ewell and Lisensky, 1988). The accreditation process as it now exists however should be understood as being 'external' only in the sense that members of visiting evaluation teams, as well as those individuals within agencies that vote on accreditation status, are higher education professionals who are unaffiliated with the institution under review. College and university administrators and faculty constitute the majority of the membership and occupy the administrative offices within accrediting agencies. Thus while accreditation is now on the brink of changes, as presently practised it operates within, rather than outside, the higher education community.

Until the mid-1980s, the prospect of external intervention in the customary institutional evaluation practices seemed remote and the higher education community's control over their management was assumed to be secure. Although there were recurrent discussions about institutional evaluation among professional associations, institutions and accreditors, these discussions were directed primarily at exploring the value of newer techniques and assessment measures, incorporating qualitative as well as quantitative data, and monitoring student achievement and educational outcomes (Astin, 1991). There was also some consideration given to the need to improve the ways in which evaluation findings were communicated to groups outside of the academy (Ewell, 1993). But while the higher education community invited consultation with its external constituencies, there was no perceived need to include them in the actual management of evaluation. The existing patterns of governance and control in higher education did not appear to be in question and voluntary accreditation review, as the only system-wide form of institutional evaluation, remained consistent with those patterns.

Accreditation

Accreditation has traditionally represented an alternative to external government control of institutional and programme evaluation in American higher education and the vast majority of post-secondary institutions have chosen to participate in the process. Conferral of accredited status indicates that an institution or programme has met or exceeded the criteria for educational quality as determined by an accrediting agency acting for the larger professional community (Kells, 1984). Accreditation takes two forms: specialized accreditation and institutional accreditation.

Specialized accreditation focuses on the evaluation of academic programmes and is awarded by 'field-specific' professional associations: that is, it is confined to assessing whether courses of study leading to a particular professional degree or licence meet established standards within particular professional subject fields. Specialized accreditation of post-secondary programmes in teacher education, for example, is carried out by the National Council for the Accreditation of Teacher Education while the American Assembly of Collegiate Schools of Business evaluates programmes in business and administration. Specialized accreditation is not a licensing mechanism. Rather it operates to assure state licensing bodies, or employers in fields which do not have licensing requirements, of the quality of an applicant's professional preparation. Thus specialized accreditation differs from institutional accreditation in that its major reference point is the profession rather than the larger academic community. In practice, it has been more prescriptive in establishing specific standards in curriculum and setting the requirements for students' field work and clinical experiences. Currently, there are over 40 specialized accreditation organizations in the United States (Ewell, 1994). While not all colleges and universities apply for specialized accreditation in all curricular areas, most pursue accreditation in several, resulting in institutions that hold multiple programme accreditations.

The focus of institutional accreditation is the institution as a whole. Since 1949, the process of institutional accreditation has been conducted by six commissions of higher education that function within regional accrediting associations: the Middle States Association of Colleges and Schools, the New England Association of Schools and Colleges, the Northwest Association of Schools and Colleges, the North Central Association of Colleges and Schools, the Southern Association of Colleges and Schools, and the Western Association of Schools and Colleges. To ensure the participation of professional peers in the development of standards for evaluation, each of the regional associations is governed by a board or council composed of representatives elected from the agency's member institutions which are already accredited. Institutional accreditation, by a regional association's commission on higher education, constitutes assurance that a college or university as a whole: (a) has appropriate purposes; (b) has the resources needed to accomplish its purposes; (c) can demonstrate that it is accomplishing its purposes; and (d) gives reason to believe that it will continue to accomplish its purposes. Each institution is evaluated in terms of its stated mission and objectives. 'Quality' is not defined in universal terms, but must be evaluated in relation to the purposes the institution seeks to accomplish (New England Association of Schools and Colleges, 1987: 2–3). This perspective reflects the extent to which accrediting agencies have thus far supported, and attempted to legitimize, the principle of institutional autonomy.

The process of accreditation itself has also been generally consistent with the principle of institutional autonomy. Although the accreditation process involves verifying in quantitative form whether a college or university has adequate resources to carry out its stated mission, since the mid-1950s it has also recognized institutional self-study as a central component (Kells and Kirkwood, 1979). The addition of the self-study was intended as a way of acknowledging the importance of the institution's own judgements of its performance within the larger accreditation process. Self-studies respond to a series of general criteria which normally include the following areas of focus: mission and purposes, evaluation and planning, organization and governance, programmes and instruction, public programmes and community services, faculty qualifications, student services, library and information services, physical facilities, financial resources, publications and advertising, and ethical practice (New England Association of Schools and Colleges, 1987). The self-study results in a written document which is submitted to the accrediting agency for review, prior to an on-site evaluation team visit and the final action of the agency's commission on higher education.

For most colleges and universities, self-study has become a lengthy, time-consuming and costly process (Ewell, 1994). Regional accrediting agencies recommend that preparation begin at least 18 months prior to the evaluation team's visit. Although full accreditation reviews are on a ten-year cycle, institutions, to maintain accreditation, are required to file updates of their self-study documents as well as interim reports at regular intervals (New England Association of Schools and Colleges, 1987). Nevertheless, over 95 per cent of all public institutions and a growing number of private institutions in the United States have voluntarily undergone institutional accreditation.

There are of course significant incentives that contribute to an institution's decision to be evaluated for accreditation. Clearly, the number of institutions participating in the system is a factor and operates as a form of peer pressure. An institution's accreditation status is also listed in college and university catalogues as well as in independently published directories. Accreditation status thus enhances the recruitment of students within an increasingly competitive context for enrolments. Graduates from accredited institutions have significantly higher chances of finding employment, and accreditation is often required for the approval of credit transfer between institutions (Heywood, 1989). The most influential factor in an institution's decision to seek accreditation, however, is that unaccredited institutions are ineligible for federally funded student aid and government research and development grant programmes. It is this connection to government subsidies that has made accreditation in American higher education particularly vulnerable to government intervention (Folger and Jones, 1993; St John, 1994).

During the mid-1980s it became clear that legislative efforts would be directed at regulating evaluation in higher education more carefully. The federal government, as well as state legislators and the general public, found the system's accreditation practices inadequate and largely irrelevant to new concerns about institutional performance and cost-effectiveness.

National trends in higher education in the 1980s

Following a period of unprecedented growth and expansion in the 1960s and 1970s, higher education in the United States was unprepared for the relative stasis of the 1980s. Enrolment and graduation rates stabilized, as did academic programme offerings and institutional governance patterns. Financial support and resources remained static (Gordon, 1993), faculties aged and resumed less active roles in campus political life (Boyer, 1987) and, despite the previous two decades' attention to equality of

educational opportunity, there was little improvement in the participation rates of racial and ethnic minorities (Green, 1989). Noting the
absence of dramatic changes, Kerr (1994: 118) has observed that for
American higher education, 'The 1980s were a nonhistorical decade —
nonhistorical in the sense that so little happened that made history'.

The 1980s however did mark a period of national transition that had
and is continuing to have profound effects on higher education. The
federal government moved away from a liberal consensus concerned
with extending provisions for equality and educational access toward a
more conservative interest in consolidation, cost management, and
improved effectiveness (Eaton, 1991). The prevailing agenda of the
Reagan administration was a 'New Federalism' in which the major
responsibilities for the oversight and support of public education would
be taken up by the individual states. Within this context, President
Reagan proposed abolishing the United States Department of Education
in his first State of the Union Address. Over the course of his presidency,
he continued to support critical appraisals of the effectiveness of higher
education and recommended cut-backs in allocations for research and
development as well as reductions in student loans and direct financial
aid (Gordon, 1993).

The Reagan agenda was only partially realized. The Department of
Education was not dismantled, although its authority was diminished,
and funding to higher education was reduced less drastically than had
been anticipated (Callan, 1993). However, the federal government's
commitment to higher education was weakened and individual state
involvement in higher education grew. During this period, the
performance of the public education system was also increasingly called
into question by federal and state legislators, influential members of the
business community and special task force reports. As criticisms
intensified, the American public seemed to lose confidence in the quality
of its educational institutions (Ewell, 1991). There was a corresponding
change in attitudes about the value of a post-secondary education.
'Strategic investment and demonstrated return' tended to replace 'social
mobility and quality of life' as desired goals (Nedwek and Neal, 1994).
Kerr (1994: 19) suggests that:

> Higher education in the United States is now entering a period of
> mature development after a long period of childhood, youth, and
> young adulthood. The times of great and assured growth are past.

Kerr foresees a period of 'troubled times' characterized by continuing
static enrolments, decreased state and federal support, and greater
competition for scarce resources. At the same time, institutions will be
called upon to expand and strengthen their social and vocational
functions, adjust to shifts in student and faculty demographics, and
respond to the emergence of new areas of knowledge and research.
Within this context, Kerr believes that there will be no diminution of

public expectations for the performance of higher education. In fact, pressures to account for institutional effectiveness from all constituencies will continue to increase.

The accountability trends that Kerr describes had their origin in the 1980s. Throughout the decade, as higher education came under increased scrutiny, there was consistent pressure to evaluate more carefully the standards, practices and outcomes of post-secondary education. The primary source of the pressure was external to higher education institutions. The federal government, state and federal legislators, state departments of education and tax-payers expressed concern over the cost-effectiveness of public higher education. These external constituencies saw formal assessment as a means of obtaining the evidence necessary to make decisions on funding allocations that would lead to greater institutional efficiency.

Pressure to attend to educational evaluation and adopt assessment policies and procedures also originated, however, from within the higher education community. Academics, adjusting to a period of relative stasis within their institutions, engaged in internal reappraisals of the content and scope of undergraduate education (Heywood, 1989). The prospect of shrinking resources caused administrators and faculty members on most campuses to reconsider not only the perennial question of what should be taught, but also how to evaluate the effectiveness of teaching and the impact of the curriculum. Although contested by some faculty, new forms of performance and outcomes assessment were increasingly understood as important components in strategies to improve teaching and to restructure the curriculum (Ewell, 1994).

Responding to the discussions taking place within colleges and universities as well as to the demands of external constituencies, regional and professional accrediting organizations in higher education also supported the implementation of new assessment measures (Astin, 1991; Semrow *et al.*, 1992). Thus, with a general agreement on the desirability of assessment beginning to take shape, the question became not whether new evaluation policies and procedures would be instituted but how they would be designed and controlled. The Task Force Reports that were published during the 1980s were influential in determining how these important questions would begin to be resolved in the early 1990s.

The Reports of the 1980s

Beginning in 1983 with the Report of the National Commission on Excellence in Education, *A Nation at Risk* (USDoE, 1983), a series of national task forces and commissions examined public education in an effort to coordinate the system with newly perceived economic, national defence and technological needs. During the five years following the release of *A Nation at Risk*, over 30 other reports on education, variously sponsored by state and federal agencies, independent research organizations and professional education associations, were published (Cross, 1993). Although the accuracy and rhetorical stance of many of these reports were subject to considerable criticism (Rossides, 1987; Trow, 1987), they nevertheless contoured discussions of evaluation in higher education during the decade and had a significant impact on educational assessment policies and practices (Cross, 1993).

Responding in part to comparative international assessments of student academic performance, A Nation at Risk asserted that the country's 'once unchallenged pre-eminence in commerce, industry, science, and technological innovation is being taken over by competitors throughout the world', and warned that, without improvements in the schools, the nation risked economic and social imperilment (USDoE 1983: 3). A Nation at Risk recommended a more rigorous curriculum, common national standards, higher performance criteria and tightly monitored assessments of student progress and institutional productivity. While these recommendations addressed only the elementary and secondary sectors of public education, they established important parameters for the discussions of higher education that followed.

In 1984 the National Institute of Education's Study Group on Conditions of Excellence in American Higher Education issued Involvement in Learning: Revitalizing the Potential of American Higher Education. Unlike A Nation at Risk, the study group's report did not define educational purposes in narrow economic terms or concentrate on educational failure. Rather, it offered an analysis of the relationships between teaching and learning and the responsibilities of administrators, faculty and students within an educational community.

Addressed to members of the higher education community, the report attempted to acknowledge the difficulties faced by colleges and universities as they adjusted to new social and economic circumstances and it advanced three criteria for the renewal of academic excellence: student involvement, higher expectations for student performance and degree conferral, and regular assessments of student achievement, programmes and instruction. Although Involvement in Learning adopted a more positive tone, its proposals for achieving excellence echoed those found in A Nation at Risk. It recommended that colleges and universities apply more rigorous academic standards and institutionalize quality controls in teaching, learning, curriculum and degree requirements.

What was notable about Involvement in Learning was that its authors recognized the possibility that the externally controlled accountability practices used to regulate public schools could be extended to regulate higher education, and thus threatened traditional institutional autonomy. Significantly, the report did not question the legitimacy of public demands for accountability nor the need for assessment policies in higher education. It made a strong argument for their acceptance. However, Involvement in Learning advocated that institutions themselves manage assessment and retain control over the determination of academic standards and their evaluation. As the National Institute of Education sponsored regional discussions of *Involvement in Learning* in the two years following its publication, administrators and faculty in higher education began to realize more fully the significance of the issues surrounding the management and control of assessment.

Two other prominent reports on higher education in the 1980s evaluated the quality of the undergraduate curriculum and pointed to the need for changes in the ways institutions defined and demonstrated their effectiveness. The National Endowment for the Humanities' *To Reclaim a Legacy: A Report on the Humanities in Higher Education* which was published in 1984 and the Association of American Colleges' *Integrity in the College Curriculum: A Report to the Academic Community*, in 1985, critiqued curricular differentiation and incoherence, emphasized the need for more depth in the major field of study, argued for a required core of general education courses and — consistent with Involvement in Learning — recommended more rigorous standards in teaching and learning. While neither of these reports treated assessment directly, their calls for establishing greater curricular coherence and standardization, as well as agreed-upon norms and expectations for teaching and learning, lent support to the movement to define criteria to assess institutional quality.

Responses *To Reclaim a Legacy* and *Integrity in the College Curriculum* took several forms. In the public and political spheres, the reports provided a vocabulary of critique and popularized the belief that uncontrolled curricular expansion in the 1960s and 1970s had trivialized and weakened undergraduate education (Trow, 1987). Within the academic community, the reports fostered continuing internal evaluations of curriculum content, of the nature of the liberal arts, and of the need to reform general education programmes. Professional associations and accrediting agencies responded to the reports by re-examining their curriculum standards and initiating revisions of their organizations' recommended curriculum guidelines (Astin, 1991). And, within the research community, *Integrity in the College Curriculum* occasioned new studies that sought to monitor, quantify and compare institutional changes in graduation requirements and the results of curriculum reform efforts (Cheney, 1988; Zemsky, 1989). Each of these responses, while differing in focus, indicated a tacit acceptance of accountability and the regulation of standards in higher education.

In 1986 the governors of the individual states joined the national debate on quality and effectiveness in higher education. *Transforming the State Role in Undergraduate Education*, issued by the Education Commission of the States, and *A Time for Results*, from the Task Force on College Quality of the National Governors' Conference, addressed a wider public audience and reiterated the now familiar theme that there was a need for improved institutional performance and increased accountability. The recurrent argument of the governors throughout the 1980s was that if

the individual states, in keeping with the 'new federalism', were to
assume greater responsibility for their colleges and universities, there
must be a corresponding willingness on the part of institutions to
evaluate their progress and report their findings to the public. In this
vein, the authors of *A Time for Results* asserted:

> The public has a right to know and understand the quality of
> undergraduate education that young people receive from publicly
> funded colleges. They have a right to know that their resources are
> being wisely invested and committed. ... We need not just more
> money for education, we need more education for the money
> (National Governor's Conference, 1988: 16).

As a means to increased accountability, *Transforming the State Role in
Undergraduate Education* and *A Time for Results* advocated going beyond
the resource measures routinely used by regional accrediting agencies to
include evaluations of the quality of the curriculum, teaching and student
achievement. To foster educational improvement, they recommended
that institutions define and delineate their individual missions with
greater clarity and devise systematic procedures for the assessments of
student and instructor performance as well as educational outcomes.

Recognizing and fully supporting state involvement in setting
standards for higher education, newly-elected President George Bush
convened an Education Summit of the country's 50 state governors in
1989 and charged them with identifying educational goals for the nation.
The summit meeting was followed by the formation of a National
Education Goals Panel in 1990 and the publication of *Goals 2000* in 1991.

The *Goals 2000* agenda is to define national educational purposes that
can be pursued differently at the individual state level while they are
centrally monitored and assessed at the federal level. Federal funds have
now been appropriated and provided to states agreeing to plan and
develop local educational improvements. All but two states, New
Hampshire and Virginia, have chosen to accept federal funds and
participate in the project. It is too early to predict how the *Goals 2000*
agenda will affect higher education. Yet what seems clear is that its
approach to educational improvement, reliance on nationally defined
criteria and federally monitored assessment indicators, and delegation of
responsibilities for development and implementation to the states will
have significant implications for the way relevant constituencies are
defined, critiques are conceptualized, and proposals for reforms are
framed in higher education within national and state contexts.

As the decade of reports drew to a close, a general consensus seemed
to have taken shape among the groups that are now popularly referred to
as 'stake holders' in higher education. The system was not adequately
supporting the nation's ability to compete in a global economy by
preparing graduates for 'work force capability' (Hutchings and Marchese,
1990) and the solution was to be found in increased state authority and

greater institutional responsibility for accountability and systematic assessment.

Within the higher education community, especially among faculty, there was considerably less agreement about the desirability of assessment. Many supported it as a valuable means to secure educational improvement and reform. Others merely seemed to have accepted its inevitability. In any case, the predictions made first in *Involvement in Learning* were taken seriously: if faculty members did not participate in the creation of newer forms of evaluation, they would lose their authority over the academic integrity of their institutions. A growing number of faculty at the end of the 1980s thus became engaged in articulating criteria for evaluation and designing institutional assessment policies and procedures (Ewell, 1994). At the same time, state governing boards and regional and professional accrediting agencies had begun to develop accountability mechanisms and plan for the assessment of institutional effectiveness (Callan, 1993).

At the end of the decade, the political success of the assessment movement during the 1980s was indisputable. The number of states requiring some form of assessment in higher education grew from four in 1985 to 40 in 1990 (Hutchings and Marchese, 1990) and by 1990 over two-thirds of all colleges and universities in the United States had established institutional assessment policies (Ewell, 1993). What had not been determined was the locus of control that would govern assessment. Further, the changes in relationships between institutions, legislatures and accrediting bodies entailed in the recontouring of accountability in higher education remained unclear.

Reconfigurations of control in the 1990s

Prior to the 1980s the higher education community was complacent about its ability to retain its powers of self-regulation. However, with the intensification of criticisms of higher education, the tradition of institutional autonomy, particularly in the control of evaluation, became more difficult to defend (Ewell, 1994). Reflecting the diversity of institutions in American higher education, internal evaluation practices tended to reflect individual institutional purposes and goals rather than the standardized national norms that had become popular within the national discourse on post-secondary education. Outside of the academy, the customary forms of evaluation were often characterized as archaic or self-serving and were not understood as sufficient guarantees of institutional effectiveness (Hutchings and Marchese, 1990). Institutional accreditation, despite its decentralized and voluntary nature, was nevertheless seen as having some potential for system-wide regulation and the enforcement of national standards. Thus, with the Reauthorization of the Higher Education Act due in Congress in 1992, legislators began to design amendments that would initiate federal control of institutional accreditation (Nedwek and Neal, 1994).

Accreditors were not positioned to resist federal intervention. In fact, the organizational structures governing accreditation and the historic differences between specialized and institutional accreditation agencies only contributed to their vulnerability. From 1949 until 1975 specialized accreditation and institutional accreditation were organized separately in two national associations: the National Commission on Accreditation (ACA) and the Federation of Regional Accrediting Commissions of Higher Education (FRACHE). In order to achieve greater coordination among accreditors and to improve the understanding of accreditation within professional and public constituencies, ACA and FRACHE merged in 1975 to form the Council on Post-secondary Accreditation (COPA) (Semrow et al., 1992). As a way of establishing wider participation in the oversight of accreditation, membership in COPA was then extended to include other non-accrediting national organizations in higher education, such as the Association of American Colleges and the National Association of State Universities and Land Grant Colleges, as well as a limited number of unaffiliated members of the public and representatives from the professions, academic unions, state legislators and institutional governing boards (Kauffman, 1993). Until its demise in 1994, COPA was charged by its members and authorized by the federal government with granting approval of the special jurisdictions of all accrediting agencies.

Despite COPA's efforts to provide a comprehensive framework and enhance collaboration among its members, the alliances created within the association remained uneasy at best. When faced with the critiques of higher education in the 1980s, COPA members disagreed on how to respond. Representatives from outside the higher education community tended to support the public accountability movement and pressed for reforms in assessment and improved data-gathering techniques. Following recommendations by the United States Department of Education in 1988, the larger regional accrediting agencies also acknowledged their support of new forms of assessment and revised their organizational mission statements to include descriptions of the relationship between institutional self-study and effectiveness (Hutchings and Marchese, 1990). Since the major concern of the critics was the quality of the higher education system as a whole and not the quality of individual professional preparation programmes, specialized accrediting agencies remained relatively unaffected. Their response was to distance themselves from the larger and more powerful regional accreditors and continue to pursue refinements of their curriculum guidelines. However some specialized accreditors, notably the National Council for the Accreditation of Teacher Education, recognized the possibility that powers of regulation might be shifted to the states and thus pursued formal partnership agreements with state boards of education or state licensing agencies.

By the end of the 1980s, COPA found it increasingly difficult to address the particular needs and coordinate the differing agendas of its members. The prospects of government intervention in institutional accreditation in the early 1990s exacerbated the traditional divisions between specialized accreditors and regional accrediting agencies and COPA members began to discuss the possibility that they would be better served by separate coordinating associations. In 1993 the governing board of COPA voted to discontinue the organization, effectively re-establishing the structures that had existed in accreditation prior to 1975. The final dissolution of COPA was not only a forceful indication of the tenuous relationships among sectors of the higher education community, it also underscored the absence of a system-wide consensus on the nature and purposes of evaluation in higher education. Without recourse to either structural or conceptual cohesion, it was difficult for those involved in accreditation to advance a convincing rationale for retaining a policy of self-regulation in higher education.

Although regional accreditors had been responsive to recommendations of the United States Department of Education in the late 1980s and had attempted to strengthen public perceptions of their contributions to educational improvement, the legislative debates leading up to the 1992 Reauthorization of the Higher Education Act indicated that their efforts had failed to gain widespread support. Previous reauthorizations had acknowledged the value and reliability of institutional accreditation by requiring it as a condition for student financial aid eligibility. In the first drafts of the 1992 reauthorization that were circulated for comment, institutional accreditation was removed as a requirement for student aid determinations. In keeping with the political agenda of the New Federalism that survived in Congress despite the change in presidential administration, the drafts stipulated that approval of post-secondary institutions would now be delegated to state agencies or state boards of education (Peters, 1994).

Connection to financial aid eligibility had, as noted earlier, provided a major incentive to voluntary accreditation. The early drafts of the reauthorization removed that incentive and shifted authority for institutional evaluation to the states. While this constituted a redistribution of control, delegation to the individual states only increased the prospects of continued decentralization in the evaluation of higher education rather than providing a mechanism for a more centralized system of regulation.

In the final version of the 1992 Reauthorization of the Higher Education Act, institutional accreditation by a recognized regional accrediting agency was restored as a qualification for student aid. However, the reauthorization also included new regulations governing the standards of institutional accreditation (Jaschik, 1994). Agencies are now required to evaluate the effectiveness of post-secondary institutions in 12 standardized categories. Although these categories are similar to those listed earlier in this chapter, the criteria for their evaluation reflect the ideological perspectives of the 1980s reports and thus emphasize economic rather than educational goals. For example, within the traditional standards dealing with students, accreditation reviews must now assess and report the rates of student course completion, graduation and employment, records of student satisfaction and complaints, and how reliably and quickly students repay their federal educational loans.

Following the passage of the reauthorization, the United States Department of Education began to design implementation policies and procedures that will take effect in the fall of 1995. In 1993 extensive draft guidelines were developed that included requirements for specific forms of assessment, outcome measures, appraisals of institutional productivity, and evaluations of cost- effectiveness (Peters, 1994). The draft guidelines also made provisions for setting national standards for institutional performance and establishing a 'baseline' for a national comparison of institutions. Representatives from professional associations and accrediting agencies as well as college and university presidents lobbied strenuously against these initial guidelines, and some revisions were made. However, when the final version was issued in the spring of 1994, most of the original provisions were retained — although they now appeared as 'recommended' rather than required.

The final implementation document also addressed the structure of institutional evaluation. Institutional accreditation would remain the province of the regional institutional accreditation agencies and accreditation status would still be required for awards of student aid. However, institutional accreditation reviews would now be required to include the 12 categories and standards for institutional effectiveness as outlined in the 1992 reauthorization. In the absence of COPA, the United States Department of Education would monitor the regional accrediting agencies' performance and be responsible for the approval of their policies and procedures. (A new national association, the Commission on Recognition of Post-secondary Education, had replaced COPA as the coordinating body for specialized programme accrediting agencies in the spring of 1994.) Each state was required to establish a State Postsecondary Review Entity (SPRE) by September of 1995 that would review the financial aid repayment rates of institutions (Ewell, 1994). In the case of those colleges and universities identified as having poor repayment records, SPREs would

> assess the quality and appropriateness of the curriculum, the quality of faculty and the system used to promote faculty members, and the way in which an institution sets its tuition (Peters, 1994: 18).

Despite the far-reaching nature of the new legislation and the impact it will have on customary evaluation practices in higher education, it has thus far received very little critical scholarly attention (Cross, 1993; Levine, 1993; St John, 1994). Responses to the critics of higher education during the 1980s and challenges to the legislative drafts in the early 1990s came from college and university presidents and leaders within national professional associations (Eaton, 1991; Peters, 1994). In congressional hearings as well as in meetings with the Education Commission of the States and the National Governors' Association, these representatives argued that the problems that existed in higher education had been exaggerated and could be attributed to economic recession, changing student demographics and the reduction of state and federal financial support rather than institutional incompetence and failure. However as Slaughter (1991) and others (Peters, 1994; St John, 1994) have recognized, the defence of higher education and rationales for maintaining the principle of self-regulation were often conceptualized in terms consistent with the rhetoric of the 1980s' reports. The purposes of higher education were equated with national economic goals and thus the central problem for higher education was defined as the cost-effective management of human capital and workforce productivity. This had the effect of legitimating a tacit agreement that evaluation in higher education should measure and monitor institutional productivity through techniques developed in industrial management.

Within American colleges and universities there has been no widespread resistance thus far to the federal government's attempt to reconfigure the control of evaluation. Faculty on most campuses during the late 1980s and early 1990s were more concerned with controversies over the content and ideological perspective of the curriculum than with the prospects of federal intervention in customary evaluation practices (Bloom, 1987; Boyer, 1987; Eaton, 1991; Hirsh, 1987). Faced with shrinking state and federal appropriations to higher education, college and university administrators have tended to accede to the implementation of new forms of institutional accountability as a way of gathering additional evidence to support their budget requests (Kerr, 1994). Thus the development of assessment programmes in higher education proceeded with very little internal debate (AAUP, 1991).

Whether the legislative reframing of evaluation in higher education will succeed in improving or weakening the American system remains an open question. Administrators and faculty who supported the need for greater accountability and advocated newer forms of assessment typically focused on the non-controversial technical problems of application and left more critical questions of institutional governance and structural change unanswered (Ewell, 1993; 1994). A recurrent theme, originally presented in *Involvement in Learning*, was that the accountability movement had made the implementation of assessment measures in higher education inevitable. However, the belief persisted that institutions and their faculties would have the abilities to 'adapt with flexibility', retain the power to 'control their own measures and goals' (Ashworth, 1994), and develop assessment mechanisms that are 'consistent with institutional missions and clientele' (Hutchings and

Marchese, 1990). With the new guidelines for the implementation of the 1992 Reauthorization of the Higher Education Act about to go into effect, it seems unlikely that these hopes can be maintained.

References

American Association of University Professors, Committee C on College and University Teaching, Research, and Publications (1991) 'Mandated Assessment of Educational Outcomes', *Academe*, July/August, 77 (4), pp. 49–56.

Ashworth, K (1994) 'Performance-based Funding in Higher Education', *Change*, 26 (6), pp. 18–22.

Astin, A W (1991) *Assessment for Excellence: The Philosophy and Practice of Assessment and Evaluation in Higher Education*, New York: American Council on Education, Macmillan.

Bloom, A (1987) *The Closing of the American Mind: How Higher Education has Failed Democracy and Impoverished the Souls of Today's Students*, New York: Simon and Schuster.

Boyer, E L (1987) *College: The Undergraduate Experience in America*, New York: Harper and Row.

Callan, P M (1993) 'Government and Higher Education', in Levine, A (ed.) *Higher Learning in America: 1980 – 2000*, Baltimore, MD: The Johns Hopkins University Press, pp. 3–19.

Cheney, L (1988) *Humanities in America: A Report to the President, the Congress, and the American People*, Washington, DC: National Endowment for the Humanities.

Cross, K P (1993) 'Improving the Quality of Instruction', in Levine, A (ed.) *Higher Learning in America: 1980 – 2000*, Baltimore, MD: The Johns Hopkins University Press, pp. 287–308.

Eaton, J (1991) *The Unfinished Agenda: Higher Education in the 1980s*, New York: Macmillan.

Ewell, P T (1991) 'Assessment and Public Accountability: Back to the Future', *Change*, 23(6), pp. 12–17.

Ewell, P T (1993) 'Total Quality: The Idea We've Been Waiting For?', *Change*, 25 (3), pp. 49–55.

Ewell, P T (1994) 'A Matter of Integrity: Accountability and the Future of Self Regulation', *Change*, 26(6), pp. 24–9.

Ewell, P T and Lisensky, R P (1988) *Assessing Institutional Effectiveness: Redirecting the Self-study Process*, Washington, DC: Consortium for the Advancement of Private Higher Education.

Folger, J and Jones, D (1993) *Use of Fiscal Policy to Achieve States' Educational Goals*, Boulder, CO: National Center for Educational Management Systems.

Gordon, M (1993) 'The Economy and Higher Education', in Levine, A (ed.) *Higher Learning in America: 1980 – 2000*, Baltimore, MD: The Johns Hopkins University Press, pp. 20–35.

Green, M F (1989) *Minorities on Campus: A Handbook for Enhancing Diversity*, Washington, DC: American Council on Education.

Heywood, J (1989) *Assessment in Higher Education*, New York: Wiley.

Hirsh, E D (1987) *Cultural Literacy: What Every American Needs to Know*, Boston: Houghton Mifflin.

Hutchings, P and Marchese T (1990) 'Watching Assessment: Questions, Stories, Prospects', *Change*, 22(4), pp. 12–38.

Jaschik, S (1994) 'A Modest Retreat on Accreditation', *The Chronicle of Higher Education*, 4 May, pp. A 31–4.

Kauffman, J F (1993) 'Governing Boards', in Levine, A (ed.) *Higher Learning in America 1980 – 2000*, Baltimore, MD: The Johns Hopkins University Press, pp. 222–42.

Kells, H R (1984) *Self Study Processes: A Guide for Post-secondary Institutions*, Washington, DC: American Council on Education.

Kells, H R and Kirkwood R (1979) 'Institutional Self-Evaluation Processes', *Educational*

Record, Winter 60 (1), pp. 25–45.

Kerr, C (1994) *Troubled Times for American Higher Education: The 1990s and Beyond*, Albany, NY: State University of New York Press.

Levine, A (1993) *Higher Learning in America, 1980–2000*, Baltimore, MD: The Johns Hopkins University Press.

Nedwek, B P and Neal, J E (1994) 'Performance Indicators and Rational Management Tools: A Comparative Assessment of Projects in North America and Europe', *Research in Higher Education*, 35 (1), pp. 75–103.

New England Association of Schools and Colleges (1987) *Accreditation Handbook*, Winchester, MA: NEASC Commission on Institutions of Higher Education.

Peters, R (1994) 'Some Snarks are Boojums: Accountability and the End(s) of Higher Education', *Change*, 26 (6), pp. 16–23.

Rossides, D (1987) 'Knee-Jerk Formalism: The Higher Education Reports', *Journal of Higher Education*, 58 (4), pp. 498–514.

Semrow, J J et al., (1992) *In Search of Quality: The Development, Status, and Forecast of Standards in Post-secondary Accreditation*, New York: Peter Lang Publishers.

Slaughter, S (1991) 'The 'Official' Ideology of Higher Education: Ironies and Inconsistencies', in Tierney, W G, *Culture and Ideology in Higher Education: Advancing a Critical Agenda*, New York: Praeger, pp. 59–85.

St John, E P (1994) *Prices, Productivity, and Investment: Assessing Financial Strategies in Higher Education*, Washington, DC: Association for the Study of Higher Education.

Trow, M (1987) 'The National Reports on Higher Education: A Skeptical View', *Educational Policy*, 1 (4), pp. 411–27.

Trow, M (1993) 'Federalism in American Higher Education', in Levine, A (ed.) *Higher Learning in America: 1980 – 2000*, Baltimore, MD: The Johns Hopkins University Press, pp. 39–66.

US Department of Education, US National Commission on Excellence in Education (1983) *A Nation at Risk: The Imperative for Educational Reform: A Report to the Nation and the Secretary of Education*, Washington, DC: US Government Printing Office.

Zemsky, R (1989) *Structure and Coherence: Measuring the Undergraduate Curriculum*, Washington, DC: Association of American Colleges.

12. The evaluation of the higher education system in the United Kingdom

Ronald Barnett

Introduction: academics in an age of anxiety

There are two stories of the evaluation system for English higher education: one external and one internal. The external story is wrapped up in a wider analysis of governmental policy; the internal story is bound up with an account of changing forms of professionalism within the academic class. Of course, the two stories are intertwined. The external story about the evolution of governmental policy towards evaluation cannot be understood without some recognition of the responses and resistances of the academic community. And the internal story cannot be understood independently of the changing character of governmental policy.

The sub-title of this introduction draws upon Zweig's classic text of the 1950s, *The Student in an Age of Anxiety.* Zweig situated students in an age of anxiety; the story being unfolded here is that anxiety is now being generated by the development of a state apparatus for evaluating higher education. This anxiety is a response to state policy, embodied in new national forms of external accountability. The anxiety is readily understandable as the loss by the academic class of a significant degree of trust in their work as professionals. A H Halsey has recently elevated the point into one about a loss of control over the academics' conditions of work, so bringing about a proletarianization of the academics. This exaggeration is unnecessary; what is significant is that what was private a generation ago is now prised open to external view through the erection of systems for public accountability. The academics are no longer trusted. The resultant anxiety on the part of the academics is less one derived from a loss of control over their means of self-production and more one which derives from a sense of a loss of esteem. This anxiety is one of status, not class.

If the presence of the anxiety is readily explicable, what is less so is whether the anxiety is an intended or an unintended outcome of state policy. I shall come to that question in due course. First, we have to

144

sketch in the changing forms of higher education evaluation in England over the past generation.

The great divide

Not unlike some other countries, from the mid-1960s England possessed two sub-systems of higher education. In 1966, the government of the day indicated its intention to establish 30 polytechnics to form a separate system of higher education alongside the universities. This sector of higher education was to be more 'responsive' to the wider society in a number of senses: its courses were to be more oriented to industry and commerce, they were to be more open to a wider intake, more representative of all social classes; and any research undertaken was to have an applied character (HMSO, 1966). The policy was intended to be progressive: it did not curtail the right of the existing universities to persist with their current offerings but, in establishing a distinct sector of higher education, it sought to widen the range of services and opportunities afforded by higher education.

However, the policy contained an implied rebuke of the universities. The use of the term 'responsive' was a clear signal that the universities were seen by the government of the day to be insufficiently responsive. Yet the very act of establishing the new sector contained something of a contradiction: government intervention was apparently needed in order to bring about greater responsiveness. The required level of responsiveness would not happen by itself: it had to be manufactured. This responsiveness was not, therefore, a real response at all, but was a case of state fiat.

The policy contained another act of note. Since the universities could not be trusted to offer the required level of responsiveness, non-university institutions had to be established. The polytechnics were the result. Since polytechnics, both by definition and by government intent, could not be universities, they were unable to award their own degrees. A device, therefore, was needed to enable graduates of polytechnics to gain degrees in order that they might enjoy parity of esteem with graduates from the established universities. The device chosen was a body called the Council for National Academic Awards (CNAA).

The CNAA in fact pre-dated the introduction of the binary policy by two years. Established in 1964 following a major inquiry into UK higher education chaired by Lionel Robbins which led to the so-called *Robbins Report* of 1963, the CNAA possessed a Royal Charter to confer degree awards. In short, a device which enabled polytechnic students to receive degree awards was already to hand. The timing of the formation of the CNAA is irrelevant to the main point: state policy in relation to higher education in the UK for a generation from the mid-1960s to the late 1980s cannot be understood apart from the CNAA (Pratt, 1983). The

CNAA was integral to the binary policy of higher education in the UK.

The CNAA possessed no students of its own but it scrutinized the work of the polytechnics and other colleges, satisfying itself that the work was at an appropriate standard to warrant the conferment of its awards. Successful students in those institutions, accordingly, were graduates of the CNAA, not of the institutions themselves. The 'appropriate standard' was held to be that of the existing universities: enshrined in its Statutes, the CNAA had to have regard to the contemporary standards in the universities (Silver, 1990: 46). The standards were upheld essentially in four ways:

- a requirement on institutions to articulate in detail their curricula intentions and the ways in which those intentions were to be fulfilled: in practice the documentation for multi-disciplinary courses could run to many volumes;
- a double process of visits to institutions to assess both individual courses and the institutional environment as a whole;
- composing those visiting teams, in the early years at least, with academics drawn from the universities;
- the evolution of formal educational principles, regulations and notes of guidance to inform provision both at course and at institutional levels.

Although too slowly for its critics, each of those four facets of its operation changed over the 25 year lifespan of the CNAA. The course documentation was seen as a valuable means of staff development, in requiring course teams to think through their educational intentions, rather than being reified into a formal description of curriculum content. Visits — which never inspected teaching performance but sought to allow course teams to give an account of themselves — were dialogical rather than confrontational. The visiting teams were increasingly drawn from the staff of the polytechnics and relevant professionals. Finally, the regulations became a framework of good practice rather than a set of binding constraints.

The face-to-face element of the CNAA's operations, and the significance it gave to the worth of academic persons as revealed in their texts (both oral and documentary) meant that it was never narrowly bureaucratic. Yet its continuing insistence on documentation, regulation, and the essential replaceability of individuals, through institution-generated internal systems of quality assurance, were in themselves bureaucratic. Over time, that bureaucracy became more benign, allowing and indeed encouraging in institutions more internal localized control. It was, we might say, a shift from a bureaucracy in which the rules were explicit to a bureaucracy in which the rules were more tacit and embedded in forms of dialogue. In this situation, the key players in institutions were those who understood those tacit rules of operation, negotiation and dialogue and who could decode the texts emanating from the CNAA. Latterly, the really successful institutions were those which had incorporated the new discourse so much into their own self-understanding that they could be trusted to take on increasing measures of delegated responsibility from the CNAA. They had, after all, become micro versions of the CNAA.

Thus this devolution of responsibility can be read as the CNAA allowing institutional managements to take on the role of a proxy for the CNAA. The centralization of curriculum control in a national body was supplanted by centralization of curriculum control in institutional managements. The CNAA, therefore, was instrumental in bringing about the rise of the new managerialism, if only in the non-university sector of UK higher education.

There are two other features of the existence of the CNAA which are worth noting at this juncture. First, the CNAA ushered in a discourse of quality evaluation. Before the advent of the CNAA, the academic community in the UK could content itself with the thought that the evaluation of quality was embedded in the culture of academic life. The claim was that universities were autonomous but self-critical institutions for which quality of provision was central to their self-conception. (No matter that, even at the level of rhetoric, that claim seldom if ever distinguished teaching from research.) A concern with quality was assumed to be part of the internal culture of universities.

In requiring institutions in the non-university sector of higher education to articulate their educational intentions, in forming its own criteria of sound course provision and in producing a text-based system of quality evaluation, the CNAA tested assumptions about quality in the academic community. Quality systems were developed both at the national level and locally within polytechnics. In the process, a new language – built around terms such as validation, approval, course teams, conditions of approval, definitive course documents, critical self-appraisal, staff development, student feedback, general educational aims, and course documents – was developed. That language was the outcome of systematic attention being paid to matters of course design and course delivery. But the new language in its turn heightened an awareness of the issues to which it was directed. This was a discourse centred not around research or teachers as such but around courses and (to a lesser extent) the student experience.

The second feature about the fact and style of the existence of the CNAA is that for the first time part of the UK higher education system was dependent on a non-university body. (In the nineteenth century, the University of London had required the formation of a central body without students; but it was a university body. In the twentieth century, the Open University had been dependent on a political decision, but the Open University was also a university.)

Nevertheless it is doubtful that the CNAA can, because of its new role between the academic community and the State, be understood simply as part of the state apparatus (Althusser, 1969). Its chairman was appointed by the government, as were the members of its council. But the day-to-day operations of the CNAA were in the hands of its officers and its subject boards, the members of which were drawn mainly from the established universities. The internal culture of the CNAA, accordingly, was less one of inspection by agents of the state and more one of the academic community in dialogue with itself. For its institutional members, that dialogue was for too long a one-sided affair, and focused around summative judgements of the validity of courses and insufficiently was one of genuine dialogue between equals, looking to improve those courses. But, for the main part, the CNAA took its major client to be the academic community rather than the government of the day. Messages to institutions, rather than to the government, was its central concern. This imbalance, as seen by the state which had set it up, was later to bring about its downfall. Even so, the CNAA had paved the way for non-university bodies to have a crucial impact on quality evaluations in UK higher education, a development with particular point in the 1990s.

The university response

'The university response' may seem an odd phrase. The establishment of the polytechnics, after all, was a response of a kind to the universities. Even if it is acknowledged that some of the polytechnics had their origins in particular technical colleges formed at the beginning of the twentieth century, historically the universities preceded the polytechnics by several hundred years. In what sense might the universities be felt to have been placed in a situation of responding to the polytechnics?

The CNAA was, as stated earlier, a new kind of body in UK higher education. Its presence and its operations had ushered in a new discourse of quality evaluation and had made public and explicit what had been, at most, private and tacit within universities and in the collective culture of universities. Yet no response was forthcoming for 20 years.

In the mid-1980s, the universities collectively began to consider selected issues of quality in relation to teaching. Under the sponsorship of the Committee of Vice-Chancellors and Principals (CVCP), a group was convened under the chairmanship of Professor Peter Reynolds. The group looked first (CVCP, 1986) at the use of External Examiners (a device in the UK whereby independent assessors appointed by universities in particular subjects are expected to maintain a uniformity of standards across the university system). Subsequently, the group looked at the examining of research degree students, the monitoring of courses and the use of professional bodies. The group's reports were first published in 1986 by the CVCP as a set of notes of guidance on *Academic Standards in Universities*. In turn, universities were requested to review their own operations in the light of the recommendations and notes of guidance and to comment on them. Following evidence and comment received from universities, subsequent commentaries on the topic contained modifications to the notes of guidance.

Over a period of four years through refinements to the booklet on *Academic Standards in Universities*, the CVCP laid down for the first time clear guidance to universities on quality matters. For example, universities were directed that external examiners should not take on responsibility for examining more than two courses at any one time; that each university should have a central committee with responsibility for course review; and that supervisors of research degree students should not also serve as examiners of their own students.

The guidance was issued but there the comparison with the CNAA stopped. Unlike the CNAA, the CVCP lacked the resources to monitor the implementation of its own guidance, because the universities collectively felt no strong impulsion to erect what they would have taken to be intrusive surveillance into autonomous institutions. Instead, each university was left to determine for itself its response to the guidance issued by the CVCP.

That situation was to change quickly and suddenly. Within three years – in 1991 – the CVCP was setting up an Academic Audit Unit to evaluate universities' internal quality assurance arrangements. This initiative was a move on the part of the university community to develop its own machinery to assess publicly the extent to which universities were capable of maintaining the quality of their own work. For the first time in their one thousand year history, UK universities were henceforth to be subject to visiting parties inspecting them as unitary institutions. (Professional bodies and Her Majesty's Inspectorate had for long inspected teaching in particular professional fields.) Now, the universities were to be *systematically* accountable; no longer was their claim to be autonomous self-critical institutions to be taken at face value. That claim was to be tested and was to be subject to public examination, with the Reports of the Audit Unit being placed in the public domain. That the visiting teams were to be composed of academics drawn from the universities themselves did not diminish the significance of this innovation.

At this point in the story, we have to retrace our steps. So far as the universities are concerned, there are three stages in this account of their recent history in relation to quality evaluation of their teaching. First, there was a 20-year period following the inception of the UK binary policy on higher education: from the mid-1960s to the mid-1980s, the polytechnics were required to work to the Council for National Academic Awards but the universities remained independent in relation to quality issues. The second stage, from the mid-1980s to the beginning of the next decade, saw the universities collectively addressing issues of teaching quality but at a distance: universities were given not much more than guidance by the CVCP. The third stage, at the beginning of the 1990s, saw the inauguration of a national unit which visited and evaluated quality arrangements in universities.

This series of successive stages prompts two questions: how was it possible for 20 years for the universities to be without any national quality evaluation mechanism when an exemplar existed for the polytechnics in the shape of the CNAA? Second, how was it possible, against that background of inactivity, for universities to move to establish *for themselves* a national mechanism within the space of five years?

Three points can readily be made, though detailed historical and policy analyses are yet to be conducted. First, the period in question coincides with a particular government espousing a market policy in general (and in relation to public services in particular) while simultaneously being interventionist towards the institutions of the welfare state. Accountability measures were to be imposed on public institutions. Second, and related, that period has also witnessed the rise, in Europe at least, of the evaluative state (Neave, 1990). The welfare state had become problematic: no longer was it taken to be an unconditional good. Its key institutions were now required to demonstrate their 'value-for-money'. Third, professionals in general became mistrusted: a sense emerged that they were often acting in their own interests rather than those of the wider society.

Against this background, the belated and then rapid responses of the universities to develop their own evaluative machinery could be seen as an anticipation of state intervention. The thinking, presumably, was that there was the possibility that the universities could convince the government that state-imposed machinery was unnecessary since the universities' self-propelled system would offer the measures of account-ability, scrutiny, public exposure and information to the market that were being sought by the government.

The moves on the part of the universities, therefore, can be seen as a process of resistance to and negotiation with state powers. The state, faced with such manoeuvring by the universities, was then compelled to make judgements about the likely cost-benefits from a university-driven system as compared with a state-run mechanism. The judgement was not long in coming. In 1992, a new Education Act ended the binary policy allowing polytechnics to take the title 'university' and established a new national agency with major evaluative powers. Funding Councils — one each for England, Scotland and Wales — were required to secure the assessment of the quality of teaching in all institutions of higher education.

The new Education Act produced an immediate policy difficulty for the universities. The CNAA was disestablished: as a degree awarding body for the polytechnics, it was no longer needed with the polytechnics becoming universities and having degree-awarding powers of their own.

The universities, however, had only recently established the Academic Audit Unit, and the Unit was only part-way through its first round of audits of universities. The detailed story of the decision-making and interactions between the existing universities and the polytechnics has yet to be written but the upshot was that a new body was formed under the auspices of the total academic community. This body, the Higher Education Quality Council, had two major functions: to continue and to extend the process of quality audits so as to cover all the institutions of higher education; and to maintain a function of quality enhancement developed by the CNAA in its later years.

What accounts for this response on the part of the universities, now doubled in number (roughly from 50 to 100)? Why should the universities feel it to be worthwhile to continue with and, indeed, to develop their own evaluative machinery seeing that an extensive state evaluative apparatus was being established at the same time? For many, if not most, in the universities, to have one body imposed by the state was bad enough; to compound the possible constraints and public critique by developing a university body seemed perverse. The upshot, after all, is that the UK has seen the arrival of not one but two major national bodies, concerned with the evaluation of higher education. How could this situation have come about?

Three interpretations seem possible, in the absence of existing research literature. First, the Funding Councils were not required to conduct their own evaluations but were required to ensure that those evaluations – the assessment of the quality of courses – were conducted satisfactorily. It is possible, therefore, that the universities were looking to a moment when they might be permitted to conduct those evaluations themselves.

Second, against the background of the CNAA and the AAU, there had developed in both sectors of UK higher education some sense that an institution-wide evaluation had merit. Stronger in the polytechnic sector but even in the universities there was emerging a sense that an evaluation of universities driven by the universities themselves had value. This was a time, after all, of a new managerialism in higher education. The Higher Education Quality Council could be construed as a powerful ally to university vice-chancellors looking to bring the teaching function under managerial control. No longer were departments going to be able to adopt their own practices of quality control if, indeed, they had any. Now, with the written advice of the Higher Education Quality Council in the form of the recommendations in its published reports, a new uniformity in quality control within universities was now possible and *sanctioned*.

Third, the new arrangements were underwritten by the government. The legislation explicitly recognized and looked to the establishment of the Higher Education Quality Council (HMSO, 1991). After all, here was yet another potentially powerful force on hand to the state for bringing universities to public account.

There was, therefore, an unlikely consensus at a particular point in time between the government and the university vice-chancellors for establishing the two sets of bodies with a responsibility for the evaluation of higher education. However, the existence of two powerful bodies immediately gave rise to the further questions: what was to be their relationship? Was this a stable situation or was it merely a temporary arrangement, before a new set of national evaluation instruments were devised? Those questions are current and pressing in the UK at the present moment.

The intrusive state

In the UK, in the evaluation of higher education, the evaluative state has become, to invent a term, 'the intrusive state'. The state does not merely evaluate its institutions: its evaluative instruments amount to a form of penetrating surveillance. The surveillance is both direct and indirect; paradoxically, the indirect form is the more powerful.

The surveillance is direct in that assessors are − in the quality assessment exercise orchestrated by the Funding Councils − penetrating the classroom in universities to observe the actual teaching performance. What was hitherto a private and intimate affair, so intimate that it was barely discussed amongst colleagues teaching on the same course, is now the subject of external assessment. For the most part, the dominant culture has been one which has treated teaching as a private transaction between an individual teacher and his/her students. Teaching was a personal matter, and not one for exposing even to one's colleagues. Now, the act of teaching is a matter of examination and judgement by others whom one may not even know.

The metaphor here of a private and bodily act being suddenly exposed is doubly apt. First, one is secretive in society about that which has low status. Research has high status and is public in its nature, in its legitimation and in its production. Teaching, in contrast, has been relatively marginal, and it has been conducted in a secretive fashion.

Second, the act of teaching is immediately personal. Except for distance learning variants − now growing apace but still limited − teaching has been largely construed as an interpersonal transaction between teacher and taught. Bodies, namely those of teacher and student, need to be present. There is at least a double bodily presence and an interactive one, not typical of most research. The visibility of research lies in its published and valid form; but this is strangely impersonal. The same is hardly true of teaching. The human body is deeply implicated in our conception of teaching; but absent in our deep sense of research.

Quality assessment, as conducted by the Funding Councils, is then directly intrusive into the form of personal functioning known as teaching. On the one hand, the act is private through its possessing a slightly dubious, if not to say shadowy, character. On the other, the teaching act is immediately a matter of personal and, indeed, interpersonal, activity. Yet, this direct intrusiveness by no means exhausts the point. There is an indirect, but even more intrusive form of surveillance at work.

The Funding Council has increasingly developed the specification of what its assessors look for on their visits to institutions. The latest document identifies six aspects of the curriculum which it will be judging (HEFC, 1994). Further, the Funding Council expects that institutions will produce a self-assessment, as the main input to the full assessment, structured around the six elements. In turn, the subsequent reports will also be compiled around the same sub-headings. That this assessment system has to lead to judgements is clear and inevitable. If it was to lead, therefore, to a general judgement about quality and some guidance to institutions under the curricula elements, the Funding Council's approach would probably find general, if grudging, legitimacy among the academic community. However, the judgemental component of the assessment will reach much deeper. The performance of institutions, in each subject area, is to be graded in each of the six curricula elements.

The deep logic of such a system is evident. Through the combined strategy of (i) specifying the structure of a self-assessment; (ii) visits to every institution, including classroom observation; (iii) judgements on specified curricula elements; (iv) public reports, setting out the detailed judgements, the Funding Council is devising a new form of surveillance. In *this* form of surveillance, academics are being required to perform and to assess themselves in advance against the criteria established by the Funding Council, *which will in turn assess those academics against the same criteria*. Academics, in other words, are being required over time to internalize the state's own criteria for judging teaching performance. This is such a deep form of surveillance that the subjects of the surveillance perform the required surveillance *on themselves*. This is an indirect form of surveillance and is all the more powerful for that.

Through *this* form of surveillance, academics come to constitute themselves in just the way required by the state. The assessors do not have to be present. Their visits, their inspections and their subsequent reports can become confirmations that the academics have taken on the stipulated personae and performance styles and are delivering the requisite curricula within the given resourcing envelope.

The fundamental point about this state orchestrated assessment is precisely that it is about surveillance and control. It is not one about quality even though the assessment is termed 'quality assessment'. The rhetoric of quality has to be seen as just that. The tacit purpose of the assessment system is one of deep penetration by the state not merely to observe but to control the academics' activities. The domains of control are several but include those of efficiency and of ideology. As well as producing an acceptable proportion of graduates within the given resources, the assessors look for the fostering of certain kinds of pedagogical identities.

For example, the assessors observe the extent to which 'transferable skills' are being engendered among students. That there has been little debate across the system about the worthwhileness of such a curricula approach, that there is dispute about the presence of such skills, are matters which do not hold up the assessors. The claim from the Funding Council that it operates a process of peer review, suggestive of its being based on consensus in the academic community, has to be repudiated. This process of assessment is orchestrated by the state, it serves the interests of the state, and is intent on interpenetrating the academic sphere to further those ends of the state.

The impact on collegiality

The academic community has long held to the claim that it is able to monitor and evaluate its own activities. Universities, so it is held, are self-critical communities.

Unfortunately, the academics had forgotten to apply the standards of rigorous inquiry to their self-understanding as teachers. Searching evaluation may be the order of the day in scholarship and research in the discrete fields which collectively constitute the academic territory. It cannot be assumed that because academics are comfortable in conducting evaluations of each other's scholarly and research work, that they are equally comfortable in examining the manner in which they work as teachers.

A piece of rhetoric within the academic world in the UK is that research and teaching are closely integrated. As a sociological claim, it bears no serious examination. The forms of interaction within the two domains are entirely different. There is a necessary public character to research whereas teaching, as noted earlier, has long been seen as a private, intimate affair.

Accordingly, the arrival of the surveillance state is not to be to read as the displacement of an internal approach to evaluation, run by and for the academics themselves, by an externally imposed evaluation. Rather, it is more a matter of the state imposing a system in what has been a void in relation to teaching. Universities have seen value in the assessment exercise but the perceived value has resided in the preparations that universities have had to undertake, especially in the compilation of their self-assessments (Barnett et al., 1994). Often, the forthcoming visit of the assessors has prompted academics, supposedly working to offer a single course to students, to talk to each for the first time about their conceptions of the course and the relationship of their various contributions to it. The paradox is evident: a state-sponsored evaluation is engendering dialogue among the supposedly self-critical academics. The paradox reaches further for, as expressed, it implies that a system intended to offer external accountability can also yield self-improvement. In other words, the circle can be squared. We are seeing the arrival at the same time of the intrusive state *and* a greater collegial and self-evaluative professionalism towards teaching among the academics.

The analysis is neat and tempting but some caution is justifiable. The drive for self-evaluation and for self-improvement is distinct from the drive for accountability and judgement. It is not just that one is internal while the other is external. It is that the deep social logics of the two forms of evaluation are fundamentally distinct. This is not to say that the two forms of evaluation cannot be performed at the same time. Some believe to the contrary: that evaluation for accountability and that evaluation for self-enhancement cannot be accomplished in the same moment. Such a proposition should not be accepted uncritically. It *may* be possible for both sets of purposes to be met concurrently. The point here is that, sociologically, we are seeing the domination of evaluation approaches by evaluation for accountability. Evaluation for self-improvement is being marginalized. It has little means of asserting itself.

Evaluation and anxiety

The past 20 years of UK higher education have witnessed fundamental shifts in forms of evaluation. New forms have arisen, displacing older forms. Those shifts can be understood in terms of two axes (see Figure 12.1). First, evaluation can be comprehended in terms of the extent to which it enhances understanding within the academic community or, to the contrary, enhances understanding in external constituencies, especially the state. Second, evaluation can be understood in terms of the extent to which it is dialogical or bureaucratic in character. Placing the two axes against each other yields four characteristic forms of evaluation. These are:

(a) *Internal and dialogical*: the older universities would claim that this form of evaluation was indeed characteristic of their approach to evaluation. The claim is ideological, intended to thwart the development of a formal evaluation system. Its deep purpose is to maintain teaching activities as private transactions. Whether, and the extent to which, academics in the UK are seriously interested in collective self-reflection and self-critique in relation to teaching and students' learning is currently problematic.

(b) *Instrumental and bureaucratic*: the newer universities could point, with justification, to the way in which, under the prompting of the CNAA, they had developed their own internal course review systems. The older universities, now under the prompting of the HEQC, are beginning to develop analagous systems. These systems take different forms, focusing on departments or individual courses, but are internal forms of accountability.

Enhanced understanding

of the university as an academic community

(a)	(b)
?	Managerial systems

Communication   Dialogical   Bureaucratic
structures

(c)	(d)
HEQC	Funding councils

of the state

Figure 12.1   *Forms of quality evaluation in UK higher education*

(c) *Dialogic and external*: over time, the CNAA became more dialogic in its conduct and, while it stressed 'partnership' between itself and its associated institutions, and while formally it was very much a mechanism of peer review and therefore internal to the academic community, it retained significant elements of externality. Its successor, the HEQC, is less dialogic and is becoming more bureaucratic in its operations.

(d) *External and bureaucratic*: the Funding Councils are both external systems and bureaucratic in their approach. Their criteria are specified in advance, and there is virtually no dialogue. Their systems are intended to produce external judgements of a robust kind.

There have been two slides across the grid over the past 20 years. First, there has been a slide from internal to external; and second, there has been a slide from dialogic to bureaucratic. The UK is characterized by more external and bureaucratic systems of evaluation than other advanced countries.

In the process, as has been seen, questions arise about box (a): will academics, in their local units in departments, wish to carve out for themselves forms of evaluation which are dialogic and driven by themselves? The concept of professionalism has bearing here. Is the academic community wishing to develop a sense of professionalism towards the teaching act which bites at the level of individuals? There is little sign that it will. Simply complying with the external demands of national bodies and with the bureaucratic requirements of internal quality assurance systems of their own university seem more than onerous enough.

As a crude generalization, then, what is striking about the contemporary dominant forms of evaluation in the UK is that self-evaluation by academics at the level of the operating unit is largely absent. What self-evaluation there is at that level are forms of responsiveness to external bodies. For all their claims to be self-critical communities, the academics have been slow to evaluate, seriously and collectively, their teaching activities. Issues of pedagogical identities among the students, and pedagogical relationships between teachers and students, of curriculum aims and design, are seldom examined by the academics in and for themselves. Such a vacuum is understandable but has implications which connect with the introduction's sub-title, 'The age of anxiety'.

Is such self-scrutiny, of a searching kind, likely in the present situation? The answer is clear: it is unlikely. Genuine self-evaluation, unconnected with the requirements of external bodies, which academics undertake by themselves because they see intrinsic worth in such an exercise cannot be ruled out; but it is unlikely. It is unlikely not merely because academics are having to spend professional time in responding to the demands of external bodies, nor just because – as observed earlier – it remains problematic whether a single evaluation system can be both judgemental and formative. The key point is that the weight of the work of the external bodies (and, here, we must include the accreditation work of professional bodies) collectively is framing teaching evaluation in an instrumental mode.

Genuine self-reflection is unconstrained and dialogical. It is undertaken by participants in and for themselves, in a communicative structure in which they are relatively equal. Elements of power and external rewards and sanctions have to be absent if such a situation is to be brought about. But it is just such elements of power and externality which characterize current arrangements. External assessors are forming judgements: a compliance culture is the likely result and not one of risk-taking or of pedagogical experiment. To the contrary, the *likely* result of there being external assessors forming detailed judgements which in turn might have impact on one's professional standing is to engender a climate of conformity and anxiety.

The contemporary age, the 'risk society' which modern society has become (Beck, 1992), may be characterized as one of anxiety. Anxiety, in other words, has a rational basis in the unpredictability of our times. The argument of this chapter is that, in higher education in the UK, the excessively judgemental stance of national evaluative bodies has introduced new elements of unpredictability into the system and that unpredictability in turn has heightened the level of anxiety in the system. In turn, too, the likelihood of academics seeing virtue in developing their own self-critical processes in relation to teaching is diminished.

References

Althusser, L (1969) 'Ideology and ideological state apparatus', in Cosin, B (ed.) *School and Society*. London: Routledge and Kegan Paul.

Barnett, R *et al.* (1994) *Assessment of the Quality of Higher Education: A Review and Evaluation*, Bristol: HEFCE.

Beck, U (1992) *Rich Society: Towards a New Modernity*, London: Sage.

CVCP (1986) *Academic Standards in Universities*, London: CVCP.

HEFC (1994) *The Quality Assessment Method from April 1995*, Bristol: HEFCE.

HMSO (1966) *A Plan for Polytechnics and Other Colleges*, Cmnd 3006, London: HMSO.

HMSO (1991) *A New Framework*, Cmnd 1541, London: HMSO.

Neave, G (1990) 'On Preparing for Markets: Trends in Higher Education in Western Europe, 1988–1990', *European Journal of Education*, 25(2) pp.105–22.

Pratt, T (1983) 'The Council for National Academic Awards', in Shattock, M (ed.) *The Structures & Governance of Higher Education*, Guildford: Society for Research into Higher Education, pp.116–132.

Robbins, Lord (1963) *Higher Education: Report of the Committee*, Cmnd 2154, London: HMSO.

Silver, H (1990) *A Higher Education: The Council for National Academic Awards and British Higher Education 1964–1989*, London: Falmer.

13. The evaluation of higher education systems in Latin America

Denise Leite and Maria C M de Figueiredo

Introduction

The relationship between the state and the university in Latin America has been characterized by constant tensions, somewhat like the clashes between 'town' and 'gown' in medieval Europe. Like the medieval scholars, who claimed exemption from public jurisdiction mainly through corporativism, the Latin America universities tried from colonial times to retain a degree of autonomy – as other corporations were unable to do.

The Latin American universities have also always been highly politicized. Early in this century, reform movements developed in the various Latin American countries. The most notable example was the Córdoba Movement in Argentina which advocated revolutionary changes in the university. The *Córdoba Manifiesto* of 1918 was a formidable appeal from the students, to all 'free men' of South America. The movement spread to other countries, gaining popular support and even sympathy from governments. Similar movements, arguing for reforms and university autonomy, appeared and were somewhat successful in other Latin American countries such as Cuba, Mexico, Peru and Uruguay.

These historical tensions between the university and the state in Latin America were not always benign: sometimes they took the form of repression and state intervention. This was the case, for example, in Argentina under José F Uriburu, and later under Perón and subsequent dictatorships; in Brazil under Vargas in the 1930s and 1940s, and the military governments from 1964 until 1985; in Chile under Carlos Ibañez, and after 1973 under Pinochet.

In this century, in particular, universities in Latin America have been affected by the volatility of politics and changes in ruling regimes. However, even within such sharp shifts in government-university relationships, a more subtle version of the symbiosis of politics and the university has been visible. At various moments of 'modernization' in

Latin America, governments have placed particular demands on universities. Brunner (1990a; 1993a) has expressed it well, identifying moments when governments have expected the university sector to contribute centrally in the implementation of national science and technology policies (eg, Brazil after 1964). Even at the same time however, governments may be antagonistic to styles of thought and research themes being conducted in social science areas.

Such oscillations in politics and tensions over the expectations placed on universities have, it is argued here, created inside institutions of higher education, and especially universities, cultures of survival which are characterized by periods of *submission*, when norms and guidelines from the central administration are accepted, or of *reaction*, when the norms and rules are rejected. Institutions may also develop *anticipatory* cultures, when they move ahead of the state, anticipating its intentions and pre-empting the agenda with a clear expression of the interests and intentions of the university (Franco, *et al.*, 1989). The relationships, then, between the universities and the state in Latin America have never been very stable.

It is in this political and cultural context that the contemporary interest in the evaluation of higher educational systems and the rise of the evaluative state (Neave, 1988) should be understood. It is in this context that the 'normal' pressures – of increases in public money and accounting for it in a time of belief in competitive market practices – should be understood. In Latin America now there is also a concern for new competencies and creativities, new forms of knowledge, and new technologies. But these pressures which exist in many societies, and which affect the mission of the university, should be understood in Latin America in terms of this historic context of struggle between the university and the state. At the moment the pressures are very much from the state onto the university, and the pressures have a particular style and logic:

> When the State decides to guide the evaluation of the university it chooses in general the regulating logic which has its own meaning and criteria in the evaluation of results or of product, in the quantitative/qualitative equation, and in comparability. This is the logic favoured by the modern and developed States in which the market with its economic and entrepreneurial metaphors presides over the relationships between the parts. Without questioning the validity of this logic which corresponds to the hegemony of capital regulating socio-economic relations in those States, the adoption of this logic in countries which have not yet reached First World status is contradictory (Leite and Bordas, 1995).

It is these themes – the rise of evaluation systems, the tension between state and university interests, and the reaction of higher education systems in terms of cultures of submission, reaction and anticipation –

that will be explored in the remainder of the chapter, which reviews the higher education systems of Argentina, Brazil, Chile and Mexico.

Evaluation of higher education in Argentina

Antecedents

The Argentinian higher education system has 73 universities. The largest number (36) are located in the private sector, 31 universities are federal, and only six are state universities. Historically the university system has enjoyed a considerable degree of autonomy. However there have been recent changes. Control now comes from the Secretariat for University Policies created by law (Federal Education Law no. 24,195 of 1993) which regulates the whole system of higher education. Control over the public universities is exerted through legislation involving financing and coordination of the system of evaluation for higher education.

The issue of evaluation in Argentina was first raised in meetings called by the National University Council, a body responsible for the coordination of the administration of the public universities (Marquis, 1994). Two other organizations were very supportive: the International University Organization, and the Committee of European Vice-Chancellors. Two national meetings on quality and university evaluation took place: the first one in 1991, in Salta; the second, in 1992, in Rosário. These were followed by a number of other meetings and seminars, including a National Workshop for Writing up Documents for University Evaluation and Planning, in Córdoba in 1993.

The Ministry of Culture and Education and the National University Council, with the support of the World Bank, in 1991 wrote a project called 'Subproject 06; Strengthening University Management and Coordination'. This project had a 'boomerang effect' with its proposal of external evaluation (Mollis, 1994: 120). The universities took the idea of external evaluation as a threat, and as portending a possible loss of autonomy. The Ministry has taken evaluation as a governmental goal with implementation by the Secretariat for University Policies. The main purpose of the Secretariat is to modify the complex relationship between the government and the universities; its working agenda is to promote evaluation with a view to improving the quality of higher education (Marquis, 1994). The Secretariat aims also at obtaining precise indicators of the condition and the performance of the universities so financial resources can be allocated. It has also established specific agreements for evaluating quality in higher education.

Agreements for evaluating quality: The Ministry of Culture and Education (MCyE) and the Secretariat for University Policies (SPU)

The agreements signed between the Ministry and the universities are a pilot experiment in evaluation. The universities, responsible for the implementation of projects dealing with internal evaluation, ought to undertake activities of evaluation, strategic planning and programmes to improve quality in higher education. The Ministry is in charge of the financial expenses incurred by external evaluation.

According to Marquis (1994) the projects must include a minimum set of requirements such as explicit objectives and policies, as these are defined at the level of the units to be analysed. The plans for the improvement of academic quality should cover the short and middle term (one year and three years respectively). Suggestions are also made about how the process should take place: all institutional boards must have their participation guaranteed; the universities should propose the units of analysis and define both the methodology and the procedures for evaluation. The internal evaluation, defined as self-evaluation, is to be carried out by a committee, one for each unit being assessed. The criteria of assessment are also made explicit: staff, research, extension activities, students, infrastructure, resources, teaching and learning, and management. The external evaluation is to be carried out by a committee appointed by the projects' appraisers.

By 1994, seven universities had signed the Agreements. It is interesting to note that the University of Buenos Aires, with one-third of the total enrolments in the country (around 200,000 students), refused to sign.

Comments

A basic characteristic of the Argentinian system of higher education has been its autonomy. It was in Argentina that the first movement for higher education reforms occurred, in 1918. The consequences of this reform movement included, for example, co-government, the creation of 'free chairs', and the improvement of teaching and of staff qualification (Marquis and Portas, 1992). Such autonomy was of course threatened in different historical periods. However, autonomy is, and has been, one the basic concepts in the idea of the university among staff and students, particularly those in the public sector. In tension with that idea is the recent discussion about the privatization of higher education, favouring (a) expansion of private institutions, and (b) pressure on the universities through financial cuts. In this context, the relationship of the state and the university in terms of evaluation is basically centred around suspicion and doubts on both sides. The issue seems to be the contradictory role of the state: it acts both as controller and as an agent in the production of services (Mollis, 1994).

Public and autonomous by tradition, the universities see, in these modernizing trends of the state, intentions and tendencies toward evaluation of a punitive kind. Pragmatic governments which see the universities as enterprises have imposed rather mechanistic evaluation practices. Such an approach has been rejected by staff, students and top administrators (Vice-Chancellors) who have adopted a position that is reactive, radical and critical. As Mollis (1994) suggests, consensus between the universities and the state, on programmes of evaluation as proposed, is very unlikely.

Evaluation of higher education in Brazil

Antecedents

Brazil is among the ten largest economies in the world. With a population of over 153 million people, it has 1,594,668 students enrolled in undergraduate courses, 38,316 students in masters courses, and 18,516 in doctoral programmes. Higher education has a strong sector of public universities. They are 99 universities in the whole country, of which 60 per cent are public and the remainder private. Among the 794 institutions of higher education, only 10 per cent are public; the larger sector, 90 per cent, is private. Universities and institutions of higher education in the public sector are federal, state, or municipal. The private ones are community or denominational institutions. The system of higher education is regulated by the Ministry of Education which controls the authorization of undergraduate courses (via the Federal Council of Education), the accreditation of graduate courses, and finances.

The Brazilian experience of the evaluation of higher education goes further back than any other country in Latin America. Since 1977 graduate education has been evaluated by the *Fundação Coordenação de Aperfeiçoamento de Pessoal de Nível Superior* (CAPES), the Agency for Higher Education Staff Improvement, through annual reports, course accreditation, re-accreditation of courses every two years, and local visits with peer review. The criteria and indicators used by CAPES over the years have been refined. Today the CAPES programme is a model for the system of evaluation, in Brazil and elsewhere. The outcomes of the evaluation system are made public, through the press. Resources are then allocated, and student grants are distributed according to these outcomes.

As far as research is concerned, the performance of researchers and knowledge produced in the universities are constantly evaluated by the National Council for Scientific and Technological Development, CNPq (*Conselho Nacional de Desenvolvimento Científico e Tecnológico*) and regional research foundations such as the State Foundations for Research — for example, FAPERGS in Rio Grande do Sul; FAPEMIG in Minas Gerais; FAPESP in São Paulo; and FUNCAP in Ceará.

What is new in evaluation in Brazil is the style and the intensity of the debate (Neves, 1993). The discussion of what to evaluate and how to evaluate the Brazilian university is as important as the treatment to be given to the results of the process. Such concern, as well as the tension between the state and the university, was already visible in the proposal for a system of evaluation for higher education put forward by the National Association of Higher Education Staff (*Associação Nacional de Docentes dos Ensino Superior* – ANDES) in 1982.

Similarly, the Ministry of Education implemented in 1983 the Programme for the Evaluation of the University Reform (*Programa de Avaliação da Reforma Univeristária* – PARU). This programme lasted only three years; it had no major political impact on the university community. In 1986 the government appointed the Executive Committee for the Reformulation of Higher Education (*Grupo Executivo para a Reformulação do Ensino Superior* – GERES). The Committee members were chosen from among academics, government bureaucrats and entrepreneurs. GERES proposed to the Ministry a programme geared, through evaluation, to ranking higher education institutions by their functions. The academic community, feeling threatened by the proposal, made alternative proposals such as the ANDES project and a proposal for a Council of Vice-Chancellors of the Brazilian Universities (*Conselho de Reitores das Universidades Brasileiras* – CRUB). With these proposals – of a clearly reactive nature – a large-scale national debate on evaluation and the GERES programme started.

The governmental programme was aborted. As a consequence, three positions emerged: the governmental position, advocating an evaluation system with the participation of the community; the ANDES position, with democratic, legitimate and transparent mechanisms for the system of evaluation, taking into account the commitments of the university to society and to standards of quality in the Brazilian university; and the CRUB position, linking autonomy and evaluation, including performance (CRUB, 1987; Oliven, *et al.*, 1987).

Even before the implementation of a system for the evaluation of higher education, the Ministry of Education, from 1988, started an evaluation of costs for the federal institutions of higher education (Regulation 278 – Ministry of Education/Secretariat of Higher Education, 8 June 1988). The following year, the Ministry organized a wide debate on evaluation, with the support of the British Council, through a seminar on 'Institutional Evaluation in Higher Education' in Brasília, in 1989.

Individually, some institutions started to organize their own processes of evaluation: the University of Brasília, 1987; the Federal University of Parana, 1988; the University of São Paulo, 1988, are a few examples. Parallel to these initiatives was a succession of meetings to discuss evaluation, in São Paulo and Botucatu (Evaluation of the university: in search in a democratic alternative, 1988), in Rio (National Seminar on Evaluation, 1988), and in Brasília (Evaluation of Higher Education:

context, experience, and perspectives, 1989). Projects on specific problems in evaluation were carried out in different universities. One example was the project on drop out carried out by the Federal University of Rio Grande do Sul. These different experiences during the 1980s were surveyed by Paul *et al.*, (1992). They divided them up into three groups: diagnostic evaluation, follow-up evaluation, and evaluation through the use of indicators. In the same period, the statistical yearbooks of the universities emerged; these yearbooks made information about academic life publicly available. Well accepted by the academics was the work by Saul (1988) about emancipatory evaluation, ie evaluation intended to be critical and transformative.

By 1990 the ideas about evaluation were coming together, and policy choices began to narrow through the processes and debate described above. The Ministry of Education took the initiative to study the use of quality indicators. A committee was appointed, and a proposal for a basic set of indicators to be used by the universities was presented. Next, the Ministry sponsored the visit to Brasília of a British delegation, of British Council and University Funding Council representatives, who participated in a seminar about higher education evaluation. The most important administrators of the Brazilian universities were invited. Professor Greame Davis, Chief Executive of the University Funding Council, and one of the delegates, held a series of meetings in different states in Brazil, talking to important university administrators. The English system of evaluation, already discussed in Brazil in 1989 and in 1992, was favoured by the Ministry of Education as a possible model for evaluation. The objectives of the previous GERES and the work with quality indicators illustrated the point. Apparently, the expectation from the government was to link evaluation and financing in order to establish discipline in a diversified system of higher education finance.

At this time, Durham (1990), discussing the European systems of evaluation, mentioned the reduction of public resources for higher education, and the external pressures on the university from the government, students, and the productive sector:

> The process of evaluation appears in this context as fundamental instruments, used internally by the management of each institution, and externally by the government in order to encourage innovations and *guide them in specific directions.* (p. 55). (Emphasis added.)

The university system, especially the public sector, became the target of severe criticisms in the media. In the late 1980s and early 1990s national newspapers and magazines like the *Folha de São Paulo* and *Veja* were constantly giving news of problems which Brazilian higher education was facing. Of great impact was for example the publicity around the publication output of the staff from the University of São Paulo (the controversial *'lista dos improdutivos'*).

All these activities and criticisms indicated that the movement for evaluation of the university system was nearly ready. One question, though, became crucial given the level of tensions between the state and the university: who would have the greater power: the 'evaluative state' giving 'guidance in a specific direction' or the university – with an *anticipatory* culture'?

The biggest fear in the early 1990s was of the likely force and impact of the 'evaluative state', whose power had been increased by shifts in the world economy, the effects of which had been increased by the neo-liberal policies adopted in the economy. In Brazil, the academics were mobilized by that fear.

Developments occurred quite rapidly. In January 1993, the Ministry of Education received a proposal from the Forum of Pro-Vice-Chancellors about the creation of the Programme of Support for the Evaluation of Undergraduate Courses (UFPR/Prograd, 1993). Six months later, the Ministry appointed the National Committee for Evaluation, with representatives of Vice-Chancellors of the federal universities, represen-tatives of associations of state, municipal, and private universities, and an Advisory Committee with members representing the government. This National Committee had the responsibility of proposing a Brazilian system of evaluation for higher education.

From July to October 1993, the National Committee for Evaluation, chaired by Hélgio Trindade from the National Association of Heads of Federal Institutions of Higher Education (*Associação Nacional de Dirigentes de Instituições Federais dos Ensino Superior* – ANDIFES) drew up the Proposal for Higher Education Evaluation. As Trindade (1995) pointed out:

> The National Programme for the Evaluation of the Brazilian Universities, resulting from a national and integrated effort, and inspired by the ANDIFES basic document was implemented; it established the basis for a constructive process of evaluation. The theme of evaluation – so far controversial, with great resistance from the university community – was then taken over by the Vice-Chancellors, thus contributing decisively to the institutional culture of the universities.

The national programme for the evaluation of Brazilian universities (PAIUB)

The PAIUB emerged therefore from the academic community itself. The National Association of Deans of the Federal Institutions of Higher Education undertook the task of evaluation, anticipating the action of the state. Its proposal to the Ministry of Education was accepted. The principles of the proposal were: financial resources to be made available; free participation of the universities through project bids; and guiding principles in line with the emancipatory and participative approach.

The programme established three central phases to be developed in each university: internal evaluation, external evaluation, and re-evaluation.

The programme is supposed to last on average two years. It involves *self-evaluation* of the university by its 'constructive segments'; *external evaluation* by experts from different areas of knowledge, and by representatives of unions, professional associations, consumers, and alumni; and *re-evaluation* which puts together and discusses the results from the previous two phases, devising action plans for the improvement of quality. Initially the PAIUB will be concentrating on undergraduate courses only; graduate education and research have been systematically evaluated by the Ministry of Education, CAPES and CNPq.

Control is in the hands of the university whose project must have preliminary approval by peers appointed by the National Committee of Evaluation. The Ministry of Education is responsible for the supervision and the allocation of financial resources. The university has to provide financial and technical reports to the Ministry.

Parallel to the development of projects in the individual universities and institutions of higher education, the Ministry of Education encourages meetings of the various committees studying the definition of common methodologies of evaluation. Presently, formulae to estimate the rate of drop out (definitive, temporary and other forms) are being established. The objective is to reach a common language which will permit diagnosis with a common methodology, known publicly. The PAIUB foresees the use of indicators as being useful for internal and external evaluation. These indicators will lead to rethinking the objectives of the institution, and to guiding the necessary changes.

The unit of analysis of the PAIUB is the undergraduate course, not the department. The undergraduate course is viewed in its relationships with research and graduate education, extension activities and management. In each course, the evaluation is quantitative and qualitative, involving data such as the relevant staff, students, administrative staff, curriculum, facilities, laboratories and libraries. Other data are collected on the relations between each course and the community external to the university, including the professional market.

Comments

At the end of 1995, the first evaluation cycle of the PAIUB will be completed. Thirty-nine universities are participating in the programme which is viewed as part of the regular system of evaluation, though it is a pilot project. As Teichler and Winkler (1994: 5) put it, the PAIUB aims, 'to serve both accountability and institutional improvement — choosing both an indicator approach and a self-study external reviewer approach'.

There are now Ministerial plans to implement a national exam to check the knowledge and abilities of undergraduate students (Provisional Document no. 1018, 08/06/1995). This may be a hint that the relations between the state and university have not yet reached a certain degree of balance as far as evaluation is concerned. It is true that the university community undertook the responsibility for evaluation, expressing itself through an *anticipatory culture*. However, this does not guarantee that the university community will maintain hegemony, and will preserve its autonomy. The state, with the new Ministry, has at least five other projects of evaluation which, one way or another, intend to revitalize the idea of linking the outcomes of evaluation with financial resources (Ristoff, 1995). It is clear, in this, that the regulatory motif of evaluation is likely to override emancipatory concerns.

According to Neiva (1993), any viable governmental policy depends greatly on the administrative continuity of the Ministry. Thus the PAIUB has many chances to escape from the logic of regulation if the universities themselves become strongly engaged in the *culture of evaluation*, independent of government actions.

Evaluation of higher education in Chile

Antecedents

In Chile, unlike most countries in Latin America, higher education is now fee-paying following the 1980 Reform. All the 60 universities, 82 professional colleges, and 156 centres for technical training must provide for some self-financing. All of them are entitled to receive core grants from the government, but all of them receive extra public financial reward for enrolling good students. The state maintains a finance programme of educational loans for the students.

Evaluation is seen as one of the first axes around which relations between the state, the university and society must be structured (Brunner, 1993b). Evaluation and accreditation of courses are included in the context of improvement of quality in education. The Programme for Improving Quality in Education aims at the whole educational system, from pre-school onwards (Zurita, 1992).

In the last 20 years, two educational reforms have taken place. The first one was in 1980. Since then, private initiative in education increased, so reducing the pressure upon the state to create more institutions. The 1980 reform also reduced the institutional power that the Chilean universities traditionally enjoyed (Brunner, 1993c), a loss in autonomy which was gradual. In contrast, in 1973, with the fall of the Allende government and the rise of a military dictatorship, the universities had their autonomy literally taken way.

The second reform, the Constitutional Organic Law of 1990, created a Higher Council of Education responsible for the accreditation of new private universities and of professional colleges. Accreditation takes place once a year, over a six-year period. This is called 'temporary institutional validation'. Alongside the accreditation system there is another system, in force since 1980, for licensing. In general a more experienced university was in charge of analysing the request for a licence from a new institution. Evaluation was done after a contract was signed between the two institutions, with no interference from the government. Once approved, the new institution would become autonomous. Since 1990, accreditation is only granted by the Higher Council of Education which approves the academic project of the new unit (Allard, 1993; Lemaitre, 1993).

Higher education evaluation

The Advisory Committee of the Ministry of Education has put forward a proposal for improving the quality and efficiency of the higher education system. The Committee is supervised by the National Council of Higher Education. The universities may or may not wish to participate in the process of evaluation. However, the institutions engaged in the process will have (a) financial benefits through the Funds for Institutional Development, and (b) preference in the distribution of grants.

The procedures for evaluation include a yearly self-evaluation and external evaluation by peers, with local visits every five years. The results will be disseminated confidentially to the institutions, and a summary of results should be provided to the public (Brunner, 1993a).

Comments

Brunner (1990a; 1990b) analyses the proposal for evaluation explicit in the General Law of Higher Education. He points out that accreditation of new universities involves self-evaluation and evaluation by peers. The evaluative process serves both the universities (it leads to improvement of academic quality) and the state (it makes it easier to distribute resources). The aim is to balance corporative and public procedures in the regulation of the system.

How long the system will stay in balance is unclear. Nor is it clear how strong will be the voice of academics in refining and even reforming the system of evaluation as it develops. In other words, it is not yet clear what price Chile is paying, and may yet have to pay, for the long silence among academics, especially during the dictatorial regime of Pinochet. The strong suspicion must be that a *culture of submission* permeates academic circles.

Evaluation of higher education in Mexico

Antecedents

Autonomous according to the Constitution, the Mexican university system is divided up into three sub-systems: university, technological and pedagogical. Only the first two sub-systems are represented, together with governmental bureaucrats, in the committee which coordinates the whole university system. This coordinating committee, the *Comision Nacional de Evaluacion de la Ensenanza Superior*, CONAEVA, was established in 1989. At that time, a national system of educational planning was just being implemented in Mexico. It was believed that planning needed to be complemented by an evaluative process (Arredondo, 1993; CIEES, 1993). A year later, in 1990, the implementation of a system for the evaluation of higher education was proposed by the National Association of Universities and Institutes of Higher Education (*Asociacion Nacional de Universidades y Institutos de Ensenanza Superior* – ANUIES). Such a system included three stages: self-evaluation, carried out by the institutions themselves; interinstitutional evaluation, carried out by Interinstitutional Evaluation Committees; and global evaluation, carried out by the National Association of Universities and Institutes of Higher Education and other governmental organizations involved in educational technology and research.

Higher education evaluation

The first step in the evaluation programme was a document drawn up by the National Commission for the Evaluation of Higher Education. In this document the diversified nature and 'mission' of the Mexican higher education institutions is made explicit. The principles established in the document meant that the plans for evaluation would be guided by two basic ideas: (a) no uniform treatment should be adopted; and (b) no single paradigm should be applied to all institutions. The parameters suggested in the document were to be understood as illustrative so the individual institutions would be free to define their own parameters. Regional meetings took place to discuss the CONAEVA document. After comments from the higher education institutes about the document, external evaluation would follow (Castãnares, 1993).

In 1990, all the institutions led by the National Association of Universities and Institutes of Higher Education had carried out their self-evaluation. Reports on the evaluation process were sent to the CONAEVA, and the Secretariat of Education received the programmes with recommendations for improvement. However, some of the reports were incomplete, due to the lack of resources, a weak institutional culture to handle evaluation, and time. CONAEVA was in charge of providing feedback for this first phase while preparing the methodology of the second step; and extra financial resources were distributed among those institutions which were developing strategic planning.

The interinstitutional external evaluation, the second stage in the process, was conceptualized as an element of, 'comparison between the existing and alternative models, paradigms or parameters of the expected aims' (CIEES, 1993:4).

In addition, evaluative committees were set up by the Secretariat of Public Education in 1991 and 1993 for the different areas of academic knowledge. Each committee is made up of nine members, all academics, and one expert from the productive or social sector. The committees have to write reports with recommendations to the heads of the higher education institutions.

Comments

As in other countries in Latin America where the 'evaluative culture' has not been firmly established, there was some resistance from the academics. Ibarrola (1992) for example criticized staff appraisal as being too tightly linked, in evaluative processes, with the distribution of financial resources.

However, Mexico is a special situation. Evaluation in Mexico ought to be considered in the context of NAFTA (the North American Free Trade Agreement). Improvements in quality of higher education, teaching and research are a key element in internationalization and cooperation in education. It is important to have compatibility in the way the systems work, in the curriculum, the degrees, and in the certification, given the processes of integration in North America (Espinosa, 1994). In this sense, the Mexican proposal for evaluation is certainly part of a shift in the world economy, and part of the very rapid adaptation needed for regional integration. Possibly the evaluative culture developing among the academics is a mix of the reactive and the anticipatory kind. It is reactive in that decisions made at the central level of administration are accepted and modified. It is anticipatory in that the vice-chancellors of the public universities propose the evaluation process. At the moment, to borrow a phrase from Kent (1993) it may be termed 'a gentle evaluation'.

Conclusion

In Latin America, with the exception of Brazil, systems of higher education were implemented at a very early stage, in colonial times. The concept of autonomy has always been advocated, clashing with state interference in university affairs, especially at times of repressive political regimes. There have been intermittent waves of crisis in the university throughout. Shifts within the internal structures of the university (partial or total loss of autonomy) have always been linked to shifts in domestic political regimes. By and large, consensus between the state and the academic community in Latin America has been seldom reached.

Today the Latin American countries are going through less violent, but still difficult, political and economic transitions. In the late 1980s and the early 1990s, in almost all the Latin American countries, the idea of the 'modernizing' and 'democratic' state has dominated the political and economic scenario. Most countries, within the prevailing neo-liberal policies, have experienced major crises: high inflation, economic stagnation at times, and huge external debts, which, for example, led to the Mexican moratorium in 1982.

These crises are working themselves out – and being worked on – in two new contexts. One is domestic: the perspective of 'the market economy' which has already contributed to an increase in the level of poverty and social exclusion. The other is international: the articulation of economic blocs in the name of economic integration. Thus there are tensions between the role of the market in economics; social development which is still something of a responsibility for the state; and civil society – all within a framework of international interdependence and economic integration. Europe began some 30 years ago; Japan has built up an informal Asian bloc. Recently NAFTA has emerged. The MERCOSUL is an example of partial articulation in South America.

It is within this context of neo-liberalism and the formation of economic blocs that the state has reduced some of its roles and expenditure within social sectors such as education and health. But accountability remains.

'Quality' has therefore become strategically relevant. For the government, a system of evaluation may be used as a mechanism of control. For the academic community, such a system may be beneficial in the definition of a more democratic, emancipatory and critical university.

The evaluative state which comes out of the capitalist reorganization tries to use the logic of the enterprise in the way in which its relations with the universities are established. These relations become tense as the academics see the university as an 'intensive-work' rather than an 'intensive-capital' institution (Santos, 1994). The corollary is the fear which academics have of the indiscriminate usage of the logic of the neo-liberal market in societies with huge social differences. There may be, comparatively, some advantages to the developed countries, in terms of the processes of economic integration via the globalization of the economy under the rhetoric of the interdependence among countries. But these advantages are likely to be displaced by the biggest existing dependency: scientific-technological dependency.

This is probably why academics react against those evaluation programmes which emerge from the political and economic power of the state where the competitive process of evaluation is strong linked, as in the English model, to the distribution of public funds. Within the anticipatory culture, the academics resist proposals. Using their professional associations and the alliance of intellectual and political power, academics put forward new proposals. This has been the case in Brazil and in Mexico where university associations have 'anticipated' the state with proposals of their own (based on the Dutch model). In Chile and in Argentina, however, academics' associations have not been strong enough; they have simply reacted against proposals from the state.

The universities in Latin America ought to consider moving towards the 'anticipatory culture' if they are to influence, or even prevail over, the state in terms of their own definition of mission and of quality. One question still remains: is there an ideal model for evaluation of higher education in Latin America? Certainly some patterns are visible. One of them is de-linking evaluation and the allocation of public funds. That may not be negotiable. The other is the respect toward institutional differences.

References

Allard, R (1993) 'Acreditación y Evaluación Institucional de la Situación en Chile', in *Acreditación Universitaria en America Latina*, Santiago de Chile: CINDA.

Arredondo, V (1993) 'El caso Mexicano', in Vessuri, H (ed.) *La Evaluación Académic. Enfoques y experiencias*, Serie Documento Columbus, vol 2, Cap 3, Paris: CRE/UNESCO, pp. 7–28.

Brunner, J J (1990a) *Educación Superior en America Latina, Cambios y desafios*, Chile: Fondo de Cultura.

Brunner, J J (1990b) 'Educación Superior en Chile: Fundamentos de una propuesta', *Educacion Superior y Sociedad*, 2(2), pp. 94–111.

Brunner, J J (1993a) 'El Caso Chileno', in Vessuri, H (ed.) *La Evaluación Académic. Enfoques y Experiencias*, Serie Documentos Columbus, vol 2, Cap 3, Paris: CRE/UNESCO, pp. 37–49.

Brunner, J J (1993b) 'Evaluación y financiamiento de la Educación Superior en America Latina, Bases para un Nuevo Contracto Social', in *Acreditación Universitaria en America Latina*, Santiago de Chile: CINDA.

Brunner, J J (1993c) 'Chile's Higher Education Between Market and State', *Higher Education*, 25 pp. 35–43.

Castañares, G C (1993) 'Notas sobre el proceso de creación de un sistema de acreditación de las instituciones de educación superior en Mexico', in *Acreditación Universitaria en America Latina. Antecedentes y experiencias*, Santiago de Chile: CINDA, pp. 159–67.

CIEES (1993) 'La evaluación interinstitucional de la educación superior en Mexico', *Série Evaluación Educativa*, 9 (15), Mexico: CIEES/CONAEVA.

CRUB (1987) 'Reforma Universitária. Propostas e Controvérsias', *Estudos e Debates*, 13, Brasília: CRUB, pp. 34–195.

Durham, E (1990) 'Avaliação e relações com o setor produtivo: novas tendências no Ensino Superior europeu', *Educação Brasileira*, 12 (24) pp. 37–64.

Espinosa, E M (1994) 'La integración economica de America del Norte y la integración universitaria: la perspectiva mexicana', in Morosini, M (ed.) *Universidade no Mercosul*, São Paulo: Cortez, pp. 36–42.

Franco, M E, Leite, D and Morosini, M C (1989) *University Culture and State Interferences: a Brazilian case*, 15th International Conference: Improving University Teaching, Vancouver, Canada, Procedings, pp. 723–32.

Ibarrola, M de (1992) 'La evaluación del trabajo académico desde la perspectiva del desarrolo sui generis de la educación superior en Mexico', *Serie Evaluación Educativa*, No. 7, 15 December, Mexico: CIEES/CONAEVA.

Kent, R (1993) 'Higher Education in Mexico: From Unregulated Expansion to Evaluation', *Higher Education*, 25, pp. 73–83.

Leite, D E and Bordas, M (1995) 'Avaliação na UFRGS: A qualidade da diferença e a diferença de qualidade', *Educaciòn Superior y Sociedad*, Venezuela: CRESAL/UNESCO, (Forthcoming).

Lemaitre, M (1993) 'El Sistema de Acreditación y el Consejo Superior de Educación', in *Acreditación Universitaria en America Latina*, Santiago de Chile: CINDA.

Marquis, C and Portas, L (1992) 'Analisis de la situación Universitaria Argentina', in Morosini and Leite (eds) *Universidade e Integração no Cone Sul*, Porto Alegre: UFRGS.

Marquis, C (1994) 'La Situación Argentina, 1993', in Morosini, M C (ed.) *Universidade no Mercosul*, São Paulo: Cortez.

Mollis, M (1994) 'La Evaluación de la Calidad Universitaria en Argentina', in Morosini, M (ed.) *Universidade no Mercosul*, São Paulo: Cortez.

Neave, G (1988) 'On the Cultivation of Quality, Efficiency and Enterprise: an Overview of Recent Trends in Higher Education in Western Europe, 1986–1988', *European Journal of Education Research, Development and Policies*, 223 (1), p. 2.

Neiva, C (1993) 'La Evaluación de la E.S. en Brasil: intentos de formulación de una política en el período 1985–1989', in *Acreditación Universitaria en America Latina*, Santiago de Chile: CINDA.

Neves, C E B (1993) 'Avaliação Acadêmica: instrumentos para a melhoria da qualidade universitária', *Revista do SINPRO/RS*, November, Porto Alegre.

Oliven, A, Leite, D *et al.* (1987) 'Universidade Brasileira. Indústria do conhecimento ou consciência das comunidades?', *Educação Brasileira*, VIII (19), pp. 113–38, Brasília: CRUB.

Paul, J-J, Ribeiro, Z and Pillati, O (1992) 'As iniciativas e as experiências de Avaliação do Ensino Superior: Balanço crítico', in Durham, E and Schwarzmann, S (eds) *Avaliação do Ensino Superior*, S. Paulo: USP.

Ristoff, D I (1995) 'Palestra de abertura' (Keynote Address), Seminário Regional de Diálogo Institucional, Junho, Porto Alegre: Regional RS/ANDES.

Santos, B (1994) *Pela mão de Alice. O social e o politico na pós-modernidade*, Porto, Portugal: Ed. Afrontamento.

Saul, A M (1988) *Avaliação Emancipatória*, S. Paulo: Cortez.

Teichler, U and Winkler, H (1994) *Contributions to the Meeting on Institutional Evaluation of Brazilian Universities*, Rio de Janeiro: Seminário ANUP, pp. 26–8.

Trindade, H (1995) 'O Novo Contexto da Avaliação nas Universidades Federais' (paper presented in a round table), Maio, Campinas: UNICAMP.

UFPR/Prograd (1993) *Programa de Apoio à Avaliação do Ensino de Graduação nas Universidades Brasileiras* (anteprojeto e carta de encaminhamento de Maria Amélia Zainko), Curitiba, 13 January.

Zurita, R (1992) *La Docencia Universitaria y los Ciclos Básicos en Chile*, Santiago de Chile: CPU.

14. Coda: autonomy, the market and evaluation systems and the individual

Robert Cowen

According to the *Shorter Oxford English Dictionary*, a coda is, in music, a passage added after the natural completion of a movement, so as to form a more definitive and satisfactory conclusion. So 'coda' is not really the perfect word here. A conclusion cannot be definitive when the reality on which it comments is changing so rapidly. No conclusion can satisfy all the readers, of many nationalities and professional specialities, who consult the *World Yearbook*. But this is certainly a natural moment, after the reader has looked at the volume, to move away a little from the considerable detail in the individual chapters. It is time to draw together a few themes, to wonder about patterns of principles and practices, and even to express one or two reservations, Cassandra-like, about some of the contemporary developments in the evaluation of higher education systems.

There are a number of simplicities to be reaffirmed. The formal evaluation of higher education, from the national level and by increasing intervention from the state or state agencies, is a contemporary phenomenon. The problems which the reform movement is stated as addressing, in a large number of countries, are those of:

> adjusting to new perceptions of world economic relations and competition improving the relation of higher education systems to the economy; controlling the increasing costs of public services including higher education; systematizing higher education systems which have expanded rapidly; making publicly visible an accountability process for higher education; judging and rewarding successful performance and punishing failure; and guaranteeing, to concerned publics, the quality of higher education systems.

Clearly these simplicities imply causes and consequences, major political contestation, and courage, confidence and optimism on the part of the reformers. The stakes are high, it would seem, on the basis of public arguments about the nature of the crisis. We will continue to live through the reform process and its consequences, as citizens and as workers, for some time. It is probably worthwhile to step back, for a moment, from the more dramatic aspects of the reform movements and ask about some of the intellectual and epistemological assumptions which underpin them, while occasionally noting differences in particular social contexts and historical trajectories. Thus this coda moves through three themes. First, it notes how odd and culturally framed is the new phenomenon of the evaluation of higher educational systems. Second, it identifies one of the major discourses which support a particular and powerful version of how to evaluate higher education systems and shows the complexity of what is involved. Third, it suggests some of the dangers and contradictions in the routinization explicit in most ways of evaluating higher education systems.

The evaluation of higher education systems (that is, the national-level creation of systematic ways to make transparent the academic output of higher education systems), and academics in departmental groups and individually, is now a widespread practice. The creation of very publicly visible evaluation systems for higher education has been taken up by many governments, and claims on resources – of time, personnel and public money – are accepted by many as worthwhile. Indeed, the act of creating such systems of evaluation is seen as virtuous, a demonstration of the responsibility of politicians and governments in the proper conduct of the affairs of the state, and practical political returns are clearly expected to follow in some countries, such as Australia, Canada, England and the United States, from calling major institutions – in this case higher education systems – to account.

But the common sense of this is new and is culturally bounded. The common sense belief in accountability, in the need to control the costs of major public institutions, in the need for an 'evaluative state', is in turn based on the proposition that management itself is a culturally neutral technique. It will work, it will pretty much guarantee productivity, and it will produce expected results, regardless of social context and regardless of the institutions to which it is applied. Thus it can with equal facility (and optimism) be applied in all countries; and can with equal facility be applied to making transparent the productivity of armies, police forces, commercial business, moon-shots, and health and educational services. Management – constructed with clear mission statements and a concern for total quality, with new leadership cadres with the right training – will produce measurable improvements in all institutional systems, including higher education systems, everywhere. Clearly 'management' cannot, and will not, do this.

The easy acceptance of the relevance of systems management is itself culturally and politically limited to particular national political contexts. The nature of the political history of Brazil, especially since the take-over of the Generals in 1964 and the gradual recovery, means that management by the central state is a matter for suspicion. The current political crisis in Algeria is not soluble by management techniques; and the problems of the Algerian university are more pressing than lack of efficient management. The contemporary shifts in the economic and political systems of the People's Republic of China and of Belarus, Georgia, Latvia and Russia make administrative coherence important; but they do not suggest that derivatives of systems of management rooted in the thinking of Bertalanffy or Fordism are among the most urgent of problems, or are an appropriate solution for the problems which do exist.

So evaluation systems for higher education have emerged most powerfully in those countries already accustomed to seeing a combination of systems management and commercial management practice as ways of guaranteeing anticipated product; in those countries not in major political and social crisis; and in those countries which have seen a shift in political elites, from the left or traditional conservative governing elites, to confident right-wing governments in which a new political class, associated with wealth generated in business, has emerged. With this political shift, as in Canada, the United States, Australia and England, has come a shift in perspective about national purposes and national needs (Neave and van Vught, 1991; Salter and Tapper, 1994). In parallel there has emerged a different view about specialist institutions devoted to caring and upbringing, whether these be health or social service systems, or educational systems. Such systems shall become accountable and they shall be defined and managed in non-traditional ways. Thus the evaluative state itself, in the sense of the evaluative state stressing certain kinds of managed efficiency, is a culturally specific phenomenon created in formally stable political contexts, by specific newly powerful groups which have won elite political position, and in places where the legitimation crisis of the state itself is limited. The evaluative state does not exist everywhere, though the 'circles of the mind' – the international activity of transfer and borrowing currently fashionable practices in education – has seen the transfer of some of the techniques of the evaluative state between countries.

The second culturally framed aspect of management occurs at the level of institutions themselves. Management has not been central to the institutional culture of the caring and upbringing agencies of the state for most of this century. Instead institutions have invented a persona to be served (patient, pupil, client) and to that person has been attached an ideology of service in which the attributed needs of human beings (as patient, pupil or client) have defined the nature of what should be done for them. Ideas about the management of resources, and measurement of the efficiency of treatment for those human beings have displaced older ideologies. One of the tasks of the new management is to clarify the new terms on which service will be provided. The intention of the new management and accountability styles is to affect the working cultures of the caring and upbringing agencies, by affecting initially the criteria for the provision of a 'quality' service, and by altering work practices through those criteria, of proper productivity, and their measurement.

The potential separation of research and teaching in 'good' universities is a case in point; not least because research is more easily measurable and, especially if the concept of research is left unexamined, seems more likely than teaching to make a direct contribution to the economy.

What is interesting in higher education is the relative quiescence in which the new reforms have taken place. Of course academics are also citizens, and new governments dealing with new crises normally acquired considerable general legitimation from routine political processes. This makes protest difficult and conditional, especially when control over the rhetoric of defence is lost. And control over the rhetoric of defence has been lost. The vocabulary of the evaluative state is strong: quality, efficiency, accountability, transparency, choice, diversity, and indeed 'management' itself with its associated words such as 'audit' and 'productivity' and 'results' and 'consumer' and 'system' and 'evaluation'. The vocabulary is strong and effective precisely because in certain political and social contexts it draws from business vocabulary. The vocabulary itself is a measure of the extent to which the cult of efficiency in education has displaced the cult of equality in education in a wide range of societies. Nor is there, currently, a major alternative vocabulary available, with the delegitimation of socialist rhetoric following the crisis in the socialist states and in Marxist theory.

This does not mean that there are no alternative vocabularies. There are the vocabularies of the minorities: the vocabularies and counter-vocabularies of discrimination in race, gender, ethnicity and even religion. These set out to rescue cultures. They are political and they pose an alternative vision about how societies should correctly be organized (Yeatman, 1995). These vocabularies are not those of management but of identity and belonging and inclusion. They are non-technocratic: they are axiomatically critical discourses but they are not universally distributed, being muted in a number of societies and places. They do, however, suggest different criteria against which higher educational systems might be evaluated and they oppose the narratives of the efficient state and the discourses of technocratic modernity. They belong within the voice of academe itself, functioning through critique in its professional publications (Halsey, 1995; Kogan, 1993; Salter and Tapper, 1994; Shumar, 1995; Yeatman, 1995) so far, without much effect.

The currently most important form of technocratic modernity, in so far as the evaluation of higher educational systems in concerned, is the vocabulary of the market. It is suggested that the general structural characteristics of market-driven educational systems can be identified. It is also suggested that, in market-driven educational systems, a particular kind of educated individual is being constructed, with consequences that are difficult to anticipate, either in Europe and North America or in Asia. There is considerable evidence from national reports, from OECD reports, and from emergency National Commissions in Australia, Canada, Belgium, Britain, France, Hungary, Poland, the United States and even

Japan, of the perceived need to link economies to education, and to finance schooling and higher education systems in fresh ways. The point is also well taken in the 1993 *World Education Report* by Unesco, with its subtitle 'overcoming the knowledge gap, expanding educational choice, and searching for standards' (World Bank, 1993).

What the direction of these educational reforms signifies is the creation of a new kind of educational system: one which is 'market-driven'. Such systems, it is argued, have a number of common characteristics. A market-driven educational system needs action by the state: the state will create a double market. The state must create an *external* market and an *internal* market. The *external* market in this context means that educational institutions must become dependent on, and responsive to, a range of customers located outside the educational system: businesses, research foundations, citizen groups requiring research services, parents and students, and the demands of the state itself for research and development. The crucial act here is to make the financial basis of the university higher education and school systems unstable. Regular and comfortable supplies of money from central, regional or local government to the education system have to be interrupted and diminished. Educational institutions must be made to earn a significant proportion of their funding from agencies other than the state (Cowen, 1991). The *internal* market in this context means that the state must invent new rules within which educational institutions, especially higher education institutions, must compete with each other and then the results of the competition will be made public. This has involved inventing measures of performance or 'productivity' by which educational institutions will be judged – a considerable technical exercise (Jordan, 1989; Kogan 1989) – and a system of rewards and sanctions must be put in place.

Both processes – the creation of the double market – are well-illustrated by English educational reforms captured in a flurry of educational legislation in the late 1980s. For example, the financial basis of universities was made more unstable: the funding cycle was made shorter, and universities and higher education institutions were no longer able to plan with fixed budgets over a five-year period. In parallel it was made clear that universities would not only be expected to earn money by attracting externally funded research, but also that, through a national formula, the more external money they attracted, the more money would come to them, as a reward, from the central state itself (Cowen, 1991). For both universities and schools, national measures of performance were invented. National testing of pupil achievement was introduced for children at particular ages (the original proposal was on a two-year cycle) and the results of the tests would be published. Again the original conception was of a national 'league table' of schools, so that the consumers (here primarily parents) would (a) have information on the basis of which to make a choice and (b) would choose. Thus, in principle, the better schools would, like better businesses, expand, and the poorer schools, like poorer businesses, would fail.

The universities were similarly organized into an internal market. Following national measures of performance, especially research performance, universities would be given a quality grading. The highest grade (at that time, the number 5) would indicate international levels of excellence in many departments, and national levels of excellence in the other departments. The lowest grade (at that time, a number 1) would indicate that the university (or department) had not achieved even a national level of excellence. The gradings, on a four-year cycle, would be made public, and rewards (more money, greater numbers of student applicants, higher attractiveness to future research clients) were expected to follow. Thus the classic ingredients of Western economists' notions of 'pure competition' are put into place. The consumer is assumed to be maximizing returns and utility, an information-system is created so that choices may be rational, effective demand is produced by locating finance in the hands of many customers, and suppliers (the educational institutions) may in principle go bankrupt if they do not respond to the demand for services in the market place.

Second, the state must create both a macro-ideology and a micro-ideology of the market; of these the second — the micro-ideology — is the more difficult to create, transmit and operationalize. By a 'macro-ideology' I mean propositions about a national emergency, the 'nation at risk', new styles of international competition and the need for educational reform (one pattern of which is to become market-driven). As indicated earlier, we have recently seen the construction of such macro-ideologies in a wide range of countries: Australia, Canada, England, Japan, New Zealand and the United States have all produced either major national reports or major educational legislation setting out the nature of the national economic and educational emergency. Such ideologies are *relatively* easy to construct as they follow shifts in political alliances, or formal changes in the governing party; and agencies for the creation of such ideologies are readily available (eg, a civil service) or can be relatively easily created by perfectly legitimate use of state power (eg, a National Commission).

What is much more difficult to construct is the 'micro-ideology', the specific, national, version of the concept of education-as-a-market-place. A vocabulary is available internationally: words such as 'choice', 'diversity', 'education entitlement', even 'competition' or 'parents' rights'. But what is very difficult to do is to create coherence of this mixture within a specific national context. The entitlement to education in current systems of education up to the mid-1970s was an entitlement as 'citizen'; the entitlement to education in market-driven systems is as a consumer. The right to have education and the duty to provide it in education systems for most of this century was political, and national. The right to have education, and the duty to provide it in market-driven systems is economic and individual. The social contextualization of the older systems was the conception of civil society, even a national community: a *Gemeinschaft* principle. The social contextualization of the market-driven systems is a concept of an economic network, the partial, abstracted, identities of supplier and demander, Adam Smith's rational economic consumer: an extreme *Gesellschaft* principle.

Third, the new educational systems see the growth of a new class of 'managers' in educational institutions. The process is double one: at the centre of the institution, and in its sub-units. Both layers in the institution require new personnel (or old personnel with brand-new attitudes), new positions (Planning Officer, a Chairperson who leads administratively, Deans of External Relations, a Staff Retraining Officer) and much more complex databases, in which computers are increasingly vital. Similarly the time-frame for information retrieval (eg, student numbers, or information on existing, developing and possible external contracts) shortens. Information will need to be retrieved once a month, rather than once a year (Kogan, 1993: 56–57; Smyth, 1995). Educational institutions now possess two cultures: their academic culture – pedagogy, knowledge contents, their vision of a good pupil or student – and their management culture which relates the academic culture to the external world. And it is the management personnel, and the management culture, which has grown the more rapidly and has the duty to subordinate the academic culture: the academic culture is the package of 'educational services' which has to be sold for survival. If the management culture gets the marketing and delivery systems wrong, the educational unit fails to survive in the market place.

Fourth, market-driven educational systems have a problem: the academic culture of the university. The culture of the university is the most central obstacle in the educational system in the change toward market-driven education, and the university is the most difficult educational institution to change. The trouble with universities is that they are, often, old – certainly 'the university tradition' is old – and they are international institutions. Their definition of good knowledge, of the purpose of the scholar, of their own purposes, are deeply embedded in a coherent and now traditional discourse about the importance and the power of 'reason', the logics of the sciences, and the ideology of 'scholarship' and 'research'. With few exceptions among national systems, universities are poorly orientated to market ideas. The second problem with universities is that they are already in an international economy – a very specialized international knowledge economy – which provides them with their domestic definitions of excellence, permits in principle the international mobility of their staff, and which offers an alternative and coherent ideology to which appeals may be made in defence against local (ie, national) philosophies of the market. Equally unfortunately for the state, there is an increasing recognition that the research and development industry is a central part of preparation for competition in the new world economy. So changing the university has become a problem for states almost everywhere. Indeed, in some countries of Eastern Europe almost excessive expectations may be being placed on the university (Mauch and Sabloff, 1995, 183–285; PHARE/ OECD, 1994). In particular the assumption that reforming the university on market lines will reform the economy, a reversal of the Marxist proposition, is almost certainly unwise.

Fifth, the definition of what it is to be educated in market-driven systems of education becomes blurred, while what it is to be qualified becomes standardized. Control is being established over qualification systems, not least by evaluating those institutions which issue qualifications. What is not being discussed is the relation of those qualifications to a conception of education, to coherent visions of what it is to be have been not trained, but educated.

I have argued elsewhere that market-driven systems of education produce 'barbarians' (Cowen, 1994). By this word I mean skilled persons, whose knowledge is useful, specific, certifiable, and saleable. This is a new and severe extension of Max Weber's idea about the production of 'experts' and a shift from the older assumptions about educational systems and their production of identities, the most elite forms of which are easily identifiable: the English essentialist, who knows a small number of subjects well; the French *agregé*, or the French intellectual, with an encyclopedist range of knowledge and a severe training in logical analysis. Bourdieu has written brilliantly about this form of training (Bourdieu, 1971: 161). Of course such conceptions of what it is to be educated are also exported, and emerge in new combinations: the North African French-speaking intellectual, the educated elite of Brazil combining some of the French encyclopedist tradition with an increasingly clear sense of pragmatism (which also exists in its own local formation as *Jeitinho*), or in the well-educated elites of India.

These long-standing traditions of 'cultivated' education become replaced in the market model by forms of 'expert' education: the transmission of skill packets, useful in the market-place, measurable in the examination halls, and certifiable through a licensing system. The epistemological coherence of an educational form, drawn perhaps from John Locke (England), Dewey (the United States), Descartes (France), von Humboldt (Germany) or, for example from Paulo Freire, contemporaneously, is lost. What is lost is not merely a culturally-specific style of knowledge, but a social morality. Humbolt or Locke or Freire for example, as well as proposing models of knowledge to be acquired in education, also offer a view of the correct relations of society and people, people in societies, and of the social responsibilities of the education system.

The 'market', and its philosophy of knowledge – secular, saleable and so on – unbalances this relationship. The conception of 'society' (or community) is reduced to an economic relation between the individual, education and a network of economic institutions. The educational process becomes a qualification process; qualifications become the synonym for education. The state indeed takes increasing charge of this qualification and certification process becoming specialized in the evaluation of structures for the production of qualifications. But while this is logically coherent and an integral extension of the philosophy of the market – institutions compete to attract consumers who wish to gain qualifications – no state can tolerate the full logic of this stance as a basis for educational policy.

All states require some cultural continuities with the histories of their societies: some political and social cohesion must be maintained (Mauch and Sabloff, 1995: 13–24). Thus the state needs to assess, and will probably intervene in, those areas of the curriculum which transmit important cultural messages. The teaching of English, for example, in England will not be reduced to a technical skill. Shakespeare or Dickens or Coleridge will have to be read. The teaching of Bulgarian, and Bulgarian literature must continue. Similarly, the existence of minorities within a state means that a minority language – but also a minority history – will continue to be taught. Spanish or Belgian, and some Scottish, educational policy is built on these minima.

Paradoxically, then, no state can afford to be logical, fully logical, in the application of the philosophy of the market. A conception of a society comes before economics. Philosophies of the market are constructed and implemented in a *societal* framework, and the cohesion of society – the sociological problem – is the minimum condition, and a minimum arena, for a specification of the educational implications of the economy. Here, history and sociology, in a reversal of the Marxist proposition, are determining or at least framing economics. Culture, social cohesion, the idea of 'national treasures', unifying myths, histories – the grand narrative of what makes societies – come before, and must be sustained, for philosophies of the market and educational management to have a secondary, if powerful, social position.

The full cultural implications of philosophies of the market are not yet clear. But some of the implications can be discerned. The initial paradox is that the state remains at the centre of social action; not the individual. The state needs to create a double market and thus is not the preferred non-interventionist state of Thomas Jefferson, who feared the tendencies of governments everywhere towards tyranny. This is an interventionist state, insisting on the tyranny of the market. The autonomy of the individual who is written into this one-sided social contract is peculiarly limited. This individual is the asocial individual, the individual abstracted from society, certainly abstracted from *Gemeinschaft*, the individual who is economically rational. This individual makes economic choices, is autonomous but autonomous on only one dimension: the economic. As a correlate, this individual has no political identity. The individual for example is not a member of a *polis*; nor is the individual one of those 'statesmen, legislators or judges on whom the commonwealth so much depends', in Thomas Jefferson's phrase. This economically autonomous individual has few social obligations, except the obligation to make rational economic and educational choices, within the frame of the market established by the state. This individual is free precisely because once economic choices are made there are no other choices to be made or obligations to be met. The individual is autonomous and socially and politically unrooted.

This emerging situation contrasts strongly with the formal stabilities in the Asian educational systems (for example of Japan, Taiwan, Singapore and even Hong Kong). Following the work of Lee (1991) on Singapore, Hong Kong and Japan, it is possible to identify the strong and peculiar mixture of curriculum which combines insertion into modernity (via science, mathematics and technology) with the parallel emphasis on the formation of social and social-moral identity. In most of the Asian societies there is a distinct reaffirmation of the moral, the hierarchical and even the political in the education system (Selvaratnam, 1994: 173–92). Clearly the tradition is rooted in Confucius, and by extension, in the exportation of Confucian ideas to Japan, Korea and in the Chinese communities overseas. Clearly, the Confucian-driven – as well as market-driven – educational systems are in crisis, currently. Japan is concerned with increasing the potentials of its educational system for creativity; Taiwan is engaged in gradualist political reform and is concerned about the pedagogic modes and curriculum contents which might lead to an increase in individual autonomy; Deng's China is uneasily poised between an educational system based around socialist principles and one which is beginning to follow socialist-market principles. In contrast, perhaps, Singapore is so enmeshed in its modernity and knowledge economy paradigm that it has not yet realized there is a crisis of all modernity narratives.

However, the Asian tradition of the role of the man of knowledge is different from that of the West. The scholar mandarin was also, often, a state servant, selected on the basis of a competitive examination for positions of power. There is still considerable prestige in the fact of being a teacher, especially a university teacher, in Japan and South Korea and in many Chinese-speaking parts of Asia. But this tends to mean that the point about university autonomy is not always as clearly made in Asia, as for example in Europe and in North America (Selvaratnam, 1994). The resistance to the introduction of systems of evaluation in higher education which is occurring in Japan, for example, flows around the traditional status of the professor in the university as someone who is an authority figure. It is the potential loss of 'face' which gives as much pause as the potential loss of 'academic freedom' in the Japanese university. It is accepted that the university is part of the modernity project; that academic autonomy is bounded by the needs of development; and that the scholar has, as part of his or her social responsibilities, responsibility to the state. It seems likely that the Asian societies, locked into a narrow debate about the nature of their own late modernity, will have to review the evaluation systems which they are on the edge of borrowing.

In the late modernity of some of the post-industrial nations, it is clear that the liberal political traditions of Jefferson, of Locke, of the social contract theorists including the early Marx, are weakening. They, with their views of citizenship, were the political guarantors of the autonomy of individuals. Jefferson, with his views on governments and the need for a new university in Virginia, was one of the supporters of academic freedom. His separation of the state, and education in the State of Virginia, from religion was a good example. What remains to be clarified is whether universities, and the creative parts of their work cultures, can continue to function in a context of the routinization of creativity. Older forms of academic governance, a combination of medieval guild practices and the power of the German model of the professional chair, had their peculiarities. They were occasionally corrupt, as in Mexico and Argentina earlier in this century, they were everywhere slow, and they sometimes went badly wrong becoming, without checks and balances on the professoriate, tyrannical. But they had evolved to deal with an awkward problem: how do you govern institutions devoted to the creation of that which is not yet known? Charismatic intellectual leadership, judgement by guild members, careful obfuscation of who was, and the reward directly due to, the paymaster, and a willingness to accept that scholarly production and preparation for it is a life-work, were parts of the answer. Quite so; a lifetime is not a useful managerial concept (except in Japan until recently).

There is a great deal of evidence to show the tight nexus between a concern for economics and the newly urgent concern of states for knowing about the output and productivity of 'their' higher education systems (Kogan, 1989; Neave and van Vught, 1991; 1994; Smyth, 1995; Salter and Tapper, 1994; UNESCO, 1991). Certainly in many countries political legitimacy has been urgently negotiated for the new policies of evaluation of higher education of higher education systems in laws and appropriate public political arenas. It is politically mandated and it will be instructive, to measure, for a while, the productivity of higher education systems; perhaps in four-year cycles. It will be a different kind of productivity from that historically associated with universities (Shattock, 1991: 57–86); its short-term costs will be known; and the managerial rules can be changed as frequently as is required. There remains the danger that at some point higher educational systems will, as their academic cultures change, be unable to respond to demands for more than routine research and predictable, and measured, creativity. By then they may have lost the confidence and the micro-cultures which produce critique and sustained and documented reflection. By than they may have lost the distinction between scholarship and applied research. They may have been, very successfully, inserted into national research and development industries, as major or minor productive, economically useful, units. That might be a pity. Reinventing the wheel (or recreating the university) every three or four generations would seem, *a priori*, to be a waste of resources, and narrowing the cultural mission of higher education institutions, through crude and crudely used evaluation criteria, to their immediate economic contribution may be dangerously short-sighted.

References

Bourdieu, P (1971) 'Systems of education and systems of thought', in Young, M (ed.) *Knowledge and Control in the sociology of Education*, London: Macmillan, 161–88.

Cowen, R (1991) 'The management and evaluation of the entrepreneurial university: the case of England', *Higher Education Policy*, 4(3)

Cowen, R (1994) 'The social construction of "barbarians" and their education in Europe, Japan and Brazil', in Gundara, J and Twaddle, M (eds) *Multiculturalism and the State*, Vol. I, Institute of Commonwealth Studies, London: London University.

Halsey, A H (1995) *Decline of Donnish Dominion, The British Academic Professions in the Twentieth Century*, Oxford: Clarendon Press.

Jordan, T E (1989) *Measurement and Evaluation in Higher Education*, London: Falmer Press.

Kogan, M (ed.) (1989) *Evaluating Higher Education*, London: Jessica Kingsley Publishers, 11–25.

Kogan, M (1993) 'The end of the dual system? The blurring of boundaries in the British tertiary education system' in Gellert, C (ed.) *Higher Education in Europe*, London: Jessica Kingsley Publishers, 48–58.

Lee, W O (1991) *Social Change and Educational Problems in Japan, Singapore and Hong Kong*, London: Macmillan.

Mauch, J E and Sabloff, P L W (eds) (1995) *Reform and Change in Higher Education*, New York: Garland Publishing.

Neave, G and van Vught (eds) (1991) *Prometheus Bound: The changing relationship between government and higher education in Western Europe*, Pergamon Press: Oxford.

Neave, G and van Vught (eds) (1994) *Government and Higher Education Relationships Across Three Generations: the Winds of Change*, Oxford: Pergamon.

PHARE/OECD (1994) *Pilot Project on Regional Cooperation in Reforming Higher Education, Seminar One: Quality Assurance and Accreditation in Higher Education*, Paris: OECD.

Salter, B and Tapper, T (1994) *The State and Higher Education*, London: Woburn Press.

Seabury, P (ed.) (1975) *Universities in the Western World*, New York: Free Press.

Selvaratnam, V (1994) 'Singapore: university autonomy versus state control: the Singapore experience' in Neave, G and van Vught (eds) *Government and Higher Education Relationships Across Three Continents: the Winds of Change*, Oxford: Pergamon, 173–92.

Shattock, M (1991) 'The evaluation of universities' contribution to society', in Dahlof, U, Shattock, M, Staropoli, A and in't Velt, R (eds) *Dimensions of Evaluation, Report of the IMHE Study Group on Evaluation in Higher Education*, London: Jessica Kingsley Publishers, 57–85.

Shumar, W (1995) 'Higher education and the state: the irony of Fordism in American universities' in Smyth, J (ed.) *Academic Work*, Buckingham: Open University Press, 84–98.

Smyth, J (ed) (1995) *Academic Work*, Buckingham: Open University Press.

UNESCO-CRESALC (1991) *Planning and Management for Excellence and Efficiency of Higher Education*, Caracas: Regional Centre for Higher Education in Latin America and the Caribbean.

World Bank (1993) *The World Education Report 1993*, Paris: Unesco.

Yeatman, A (1995) 'The gendered management of equity-orientated change in higher education', in Smyth J (ed.) *Academic Work*, Buckingham: Open University Press, 194–205.

Biographical notes on contributors

Baba, Masateru is Professor of Education, Faculty of Education, Shinshu University, Nagano. He was Honorary Visiting Lecturer at the University of Sheffield in 1976–7 and 1983. He has published widely on educational administration and finance, international and comparative education, and higher education in Japan, including 'Expenses of Higher Education Institutions and their Income Categories' *Bulletin of the Japanese Educational Administration Society*, No 20, 1994 and 'University Evaluation and its Effect on State Funding Formula in England' *Journal of the Japan Society for Educational System and Organisation*, No 2, 1995. Address: Faculty of Education, Shinshu University, 6 Nishinagano, Nagano 380, Japan.

Ronald Barnett is Professor of Higher Education and Dean of Advanced Courses in the Institute of Education, University of London. His books include: *The Idea of Higher Education, Improving Higher Education: Total Quality Care* and (most recently) *The Limits of Competence*. He was the principal author of what some have called 'the Barnett report' (report on HEFCE Quality Assessment methodology). Address: CHES, Institute of Education, 20 Bedford Way, London WC1H 0AL, England.

Cheng, Kai-ming did mathematics in his undergraduate studies and taught physics and mathematics as a secondary school teacher earlier in his career. Then he turned to educational administration, planning and policy analysis, and undertook doctoral studies in the University of London Institute of Education. His research concentrates on education policies in China. He is also known for policy research on Hong Kong. He has worked as consultant for most of the major international organizations. He is Professor of Education in the University of Hong Kong and is currently the Dean of Education. Address: Faculty of Education, University of Hong Kong, Pokfulam road, Hong Kong.

Boutheina Cheriet took her License (BA) in English language and literature at the Institute of Foreign Languages in the University of Algiers. She holds MA and PhD degrees, in comparative education, from the University of London. Currently she is the research coordinator at the Centre of Arab Women for Training and Research (CAWTAR) in Tunis where among other things she is working on a research project, jointly with Johns Hopkins University Centre for Communication, on training for Arab women in areas such as public participation, empowerment and women's rights. She has published articles in Arabic, French and English on education in the Maghreb, on literacies, Islam and socialism.

Bob Cowen is a Senior Lecturer in Comparative Education in the University of London, Institute of Education. His current research interests include the contemporary theoretical condition of comparative education; and the impact of 'philosophies of the market' on educational systems and on the creation of educated identities. Formerly a Vice-President of the Comparative Education Society in Europe, and a Professor or Visiting Professor in the University of Brasilia, the Catholic University of Leuven, Belgium, SUNY, Buffalo and the University of La Trobe, Melbourne, he is currently a member of the Editorial Board and Deputy Editor of *Comparative Education*. Address: CCS, Institute of Education, 20 Bedford Way, London WC1H 0AL, England.

Maria C M Figueiredo is Brazilian Lektor at the University of London Institute of Education. Previously, she was a Senior Lecturer in Brazil, and Dean of a School of Education. She has a first degree from Brazil in romance languages and literature. Her MSc is in educational administration and planning (University of Wisconsin, USA), and her PhD was written in the University of London. Her main research interests include higher education in Brazil and in Latin America, and politics and education. She has published in academic journals in Brazil, in the USA, and in Europe. Her most recent publication is a co-edited book (with Denise Gastaldo), *Paulo Freire at the Institute* (1995). Address: Brazilian Lektor, Institute of Education, 20 Bedford Way, London WC1H 0AL, England.

Susan Douglas Franzosa is Professor of Education and Humanities, and Chair of the Department of Education at the University of New Hampshire. She teaches and conducts research in philosophy of education, the history of educational thought, and educational equity. She serves as the associate editor of the *National Women's Studies Association Journal* and on the executive councils of the American Educational Studies Association. She is the co-author, with Karen Mazza, of *Integrating Women's Studies into the Curriculum* and editor and contributor to *Civic Education: Its Limits and Conditions*. Her current research concerns the methodological uses of educational autobiography in educational studies. Address: Department of Education, College of Liberal Arts, University of New Hampshire, Morrill Hall, 62 College Road, Durham, New Hampshire, USA.

Emmanuel Kanakis obtained his BEd from the University of Athens, Greece and his MA in comparative education at the Institute of Education, University of London, where he is currently a doctoral student. His topic is the state and higher education systems in selected countries in the semi-periphery of Southern Europe. Address: c/o CCS, Institute of Education, University of London, 20 Bedford Way, London WC1H 0AL, England.

Xanthi Karadima holds an MA from the Institute of Education, University of London and is currently researching the topic of the state and teacher education in Greece, as part of her PhD. Address: c/o CCS, Institute of Education, University of London, 20 Bedford Way, London WC1H 0AL, England.

Kim Terri did her undergraduate degree, in education, at Yonsei University in Seoul, the Republic of Korea. Subsequently she studied for an MA in comparative education at the Institute of Education, University of London. On her return to Korea in 1992, she worked in the Division of International Cooperation at the Korean Educational Development Institute (KEDI), Seoul. She is now currently working on her doctoral thesis in CCS at the Institute of Education. The topic of her thesis is the creation of the academic profession in South Korea, Malaysia and Singapore, from the Japanese and British colonial periods until the contemporary period. Address: c/o CCS, Institute of Education, University of London, 20 Bedford Way, London WC1H 0AL, England.

Denise Leite is a researcher for the National Council for Research (CNPq) and a full Professor of Education in the Graduate Programme, School of Education, Federal University of Rio Grande do Sul. She teaches and researches about higher education theory and practices. Since 1994 she has been in charge of conducting the institutional evaluation programme of the Federal University of Rio Grande do Sul. She has published many articles in her specialty and is co-author of two books analysing universities and higher education in South America (Mercosul). Address: School of Education, Federal University of Rio Grande do Sul, Brazil.

John R Mallea is a Professor and past-President at Brandon University, Manitoba, Canada. He is a widely published author with a special interest in international, ethnic and cross-cultural studies in education. A member of the OECD teams reviewing educational policies in Hungary (1992–4) and Mexico (1994–), his current research activities are focused on the internationalization of higher education and its contribution to the development of knowledge-intensive, service-based societies in Europe, North America and Asia. Address: School of Education, Brandon University, Brandon, Manitoba, Canada R7A 6A9.

Guy Neave, before becoming Director of Research at the International Association of Universities, was Professor of Comparative Education at the University of London (UK). An historian by training, his main field is policy analysis in education. Founder member with Frans van Vught and Ulrich Teichler of the Consortium of Higher Education Researchers (CHER) and editor of the quarterly journal *Higher Education Policy*, he has written extensively on higher education in Western Europe. His latest works include the *Encyclopedia of Higher Education* (4 vols, 1992) with Burton R Clark of UCLA, and with Frans van Vught, *Government and Higher Education Relationships across Three Continents*, 1994. Address: International Association of Universities, 1 rue Miollis, F75732 Paris, Cedex 15, France.

Barry A Sheehan is a Professor and Deputy Vice-Chancellor (Resources) at the University of Melbourne. His PhD is from the University of London. He has been involved in teacher education at La Trobe University and as a Director of the Melbourne College of Advanced Education. He has published widely in comparative and international education, and is director of the Australian component of a major multinational study of the academic profession, funded by the Carnegie Foundation for the Advancement of Teaching at Princeton and the Australian Department of Education, Employment and Training.

Isabel F Sobreira is presently Head of the Department of Education and former Dean of the School of Education at the State University of Montes Claros, Brazil. Previously she was, from 1989 to 1993, Municipal Secretary of Education for Montes Claros, Minas Gerais. Her interests include teacher education, education and the state, and higher education management. She has published papers in university journals (in Portuguese) on these topics in Brazil. Address: School of Education, University of Montes Claros, Montes Claros, Minas Gerais, Brazil.

Tianxiang Xue is Director of the Centre for Higher Educational Research, also Director of the Higher Education Society of China, and General Secretary of the Higher Teacher Education Society of China. He has published five monographs and many articles on higher education evaluation and administration.

The series editors

David Coulby is Professor of Education and Dean of Education and Human Sciences at Bath College of Higher Education. He has recently published, with Crispin Jones, *Postmodernity and European Education Systems*.

Crispin Jones is a Senior Lecturer in Education at the University of London Institute of Education. His main research interests are the study of diversity in inner city schools and the consequences for education of late modernity.

Bibliography

Compiled by Emmanuel Kanakis and Xanthi Karadima

The bibliography is composed of mainly English-language material. It can be used as a supplement to the references attached to each chapter. The bibliography is composed of four parts: encyclopaedias on higher education; books; book chapters and journal articles; and journals. The bibliography is biased toward material produced in the last five years.

Encyclopaedias

Altbach, P G (ed.) (1991) *International Higher Education — An Encyclopaedia*, New York and London: Garland Publishing, Inc.

Clark, B and Neave, G (eds) (1992) *The Encyclopedia of Higher Education*, Oxford: Pergamon Press.

Knowles, A S (ed.) (1977) *The International Encyclopedia of Higher Education*, San Francisco: Jossey-Bass Publishers.

Books

Adelman, C and Silver, H (1990) *Accreditation: the American Experience*, London: Council for National Academic Awards.

Adelman, C (1988) *Performance and Judgement: Essays on Principles and Practices in Higher Education Assessment*, Washington, DC: US Department of Education, US Government Printing Office.

Altbach, P (1976) *Comparative Higher Education Abroad: Bibliography and Analysis*, New York: Praeger.

Altbach, P (1977) *Comparative Perspectives on the Academic Profession*, New York: Praeger.

Altbach, P G (1980) *University Reform: An International Perspective*, Washington, DC: American Association for Higher Education.

Altbach, P G (1990) 'Perspectives on Comparative Higher Education, Essays on Faculty, Students and Reform', *Special Studies in Comparative Education No. Twenty-Two*, Buffalo, New York: Comparative Education Center, SUNYAB.

Altbach, P G, Kelly, G P and Weis, L (1985) *Excellence in Education: Perspectives on Policy and Practice*, Buffalo, NY: Prometheus Books.

American Council on Education, Education Commission of the States (1988) *One Third of a Nation*. A Report of the Commission on Minority Participation in Education and American Life, Washington, DC: US Government Printing Office.

American Council on Education (1988) 'Memorandum to the 41st President of the United States', *Report from the Commission on Minority Participation in Education and American Life*, Washington, DC: US Government Printing Office.

Ashworth, A and Harvey, R (1994) *Assessing Quality in Further and Higher Education*, London: Jessica Kingsley Publishers.

Association of American Colleges (1991) *Liberal Learning and the Arts and Sciences Major: Reports from the Fields*, Washington, DC: American Association of Colleges.

Association of Universities and Colleges of Canada (1988) *Inventory of Research on Post-secondary Education*, Ottawa: Department of the Secretary of State of Canada.

Astin, A W (1993a) *Assessment for Excellence: The Philosophy and Practice of Assessment and Evaluation in Higher Education*, New York: American Council on Education, Macmillan Publishing Company.

Astin, A W (1993b) *What Matters in College: Four Critical Years Revisited*, San Francisco: Jossey-Bass.

Australian Senate Standing Committee on Employment, Education and Training (1990) *Priorities for Reform in Higher Education*, Canberra: Australian Government Publishing Service.

Ball, C and Eggins, H (eds) (1989) *Higher Education into the 1990s*, Buckingham: Open University Press.

Barnett, R (1990) *The Idea of Higher Education*, Guilford: Society for Research in Higher Education.

Barnett, R (1992) *Improving Higher Education*, Buckingham: Open University Press.

Barnett, R (1994) *The Limits of Competence: Knowledge, Higher Education and Society*, Buckingham: Society for Research into Higher Education, Open University Press.

Becher, T (ed.) (1994) *Governments and Professional Education*, Buckingham: Society for Research into Higher Education, Open University Press.

Becher, T, Henkel, M and Kogan, M (1994) *Graduate Education in Britain*, Higher Education Policy Series 17, London: Jessica Kingsley Publishers.

Becher, T and Kogan, M (1992) *Process and Structure in Higher Education*, 2nd edn, London: Routledge.

Becher, T, Henkel, M and Kogan, M (1994) *Graduate Education in Britain*, London: Jessica Kingsley Publishers.

Becher, T (ed.) (1987) *British Higher Education*, London: Allen and Unwin.

Bennett, W J (1984) *To Reclaim a Legacy: A Report on the Humanities in Higher Education*, Washington, DC: National Endowment for the Humanities.

Berdahl, R O, Peterson, M W, Studds, S and Mets, S A (eds) (1987) *The State's Role and Impact in Improving Quality in Undergraduate Education: A Perspective and Framework*, College Park, MD: National Centre for Post-secondary Governance and Finance.

Berdahl, R O (1959) *British Universities and the State*, Berkeley: University of California Press.

Berdahl, R O (1970) *Statewide Co-ordination of Higher Education*, Washington, DC; Council on Education.

Berg, B and Östergren, B (1977) *Innovations and Innovation Processes in Higher Education*, Stockholm: National Board of Universities and Colleges.

Bjorklund, S (1992) *Leadership and Accountability in the Republic of Scholars: Studies of Higher Education and Research*, Stockholm: Council for Studies of Higher Education.

Bloom, A (1987) *The Closing of the American Mind: How Higher Education has Failed Democracy and Impoverished the Souls of Today's Students*, New York: Simon and Schuster.

Bogue, E G and Saunders, R L (1992) *The Evidence for Quality: Strengthening the Tests of Academic and Administrative Effectiveness*, San Francisco: Jossey-Bass.

Boyer, E L (1990) *Scholarship Reconsidered: Priorities of the Professoriate*, Princeton, NJ: Carnegie Foundation for the Advancement of Teaching.

Boyer, E L (1987) *College: The Undergraduate Experience in America*, New York: Harper and Row.

Brennan, J E A (1992) *European Higher Education Systems: Germany, the Netherlands, the U.K.*, London: Council for National Academic Awards.

Brennan, J, El-Khawas, E and Shah, T (1994) *Peer Review and the Assessment of Higher Education Quality: an international perspective*, London: QSC Higher education Report No 3.

Brennan, J, Kogan, M and Teichler, U (1994) *Higher Education at Work*, London: Jessica Kingsley Publishers.

Bull, G M, Dallington-Hunter, C, Epelboin, Y, Frackmann, E and Jennings, D (1994) *Information Technology: Issues for Higher Education and Management*, London: Jessica Kingsley Publishers.

Burgess, R G (ed.) (1994) *Postgraduate Education and Training in the Social Sciences: Processes and Products*, London: Jessica Kingsley Publishers.

Calder, J (1994) *Programme and Quality*, London: Kogan Page.

Cave, M, Hanney, S and Kogan, M (1994) *The Use of Performance Indicators in Higher Education*, London: Jessica Kingsley Publishers.

Cave, M, Hanney, S, Kogan, M and Travett, G (1988) *The Use of Performance Indicators in Higher Education: A Critical Analysis of Developing Practice*, Higher Education Policy series, 2, London: Jessica Kingsley Publishers.

Center for Educational Competitiveness (1992) *Knowledge for All Americans*, Arlington, VA: Knowledge Network for All Americans.

Centre for Higher Education Studies (1994) *Assessment of the quality of Higher Education: a review and an evaluation: Report from the Higher Education Funding Councils for England and Wales*, London: Institute of Education, University of London.

Cerych, L and Sabatier, P (1986) *Great Expectations and Mixed Performance: The Implementation of Higher Education Reforms in Europe*, Trentham: European Institute of Education and Social Policy.

Chapman, J W (ed.) (1983) *The Western University on Trial*, California: University of California Press.

Cheney, L (1988) *Humanities in America: A Report to the President, the Congress, and the American People*, Washington, DC: National Endowment for the Humanities.

Chernay, G (1990) *Accreditation and the Role of the Council on Post-secondary Accreditation (COPA)*, Washington, DC: COPA.

Chinapah, V (1992) *Evaluation of Higher Education in a Changing Europe*, Stockholm: UNESCO and the Institute of International Education, University of Stockholm.

Clark, B (1983) *The Higher Education System: Academic Organization in Cross-National Perspective*, Berkeley: University of California Press.

Clark, B R (ed.) (1984) *Perspectives on Higher Education*, Berkeley and Los Angeles: University of California Press.

Committee of Vice Chancellors and Principals (1986) *Academic Standards in Universities (Reynolds Report)*, London: CVCP.

Council for National Academic Awards (1992) *The Measurement of Quality in Post-Secondary Education: International Working Conference Proceedings*, London, 15–16 April, 1992.

Council for National Academic Awards (1989) *Handbook*, London: CNAA.

Craft, A (ed.) (1992) *Quality Assurance in Higher Education*, London: Falmer Press.

Craft, A (1994) *International Developments in Assuring Quality in Higher Education*, London: Falmer Press.

Cuenin, S (1988) *Performance Indicators in Higher Education*, Paris: OECD.

CVCP Academic Audit Unit (1991) *Notes for the Guidance of Auditors*, Birmingham: CVCP Academic Audit Unit.

Daalder, H and Shils, E (eds) (1982) *Universities, Politicians, and Bureaucrats: Europe and United States*, New York: Cambridge University Press.

Dahllöf, U *et al.* (1991) *Dimensions of Evaluation: Report of the IMHE Study Group on Evaluation in Higher Education*, London: Jessica Kingsley Publishers.

Dahllöf, U, Löfgren, J and Willén, B (1979) 'Evaluation, Recurrent Education and Higher Education Reform in Sweden', *Uppsala Report on Education*, 6, Sweden: Uppsala University.

Danish Centre of Quality Assurance and Evaluation. (1994) *Conference on frameworks for European Quality Assessment of Higher Education: a report*, Copenhagen: Norre Volgade.

Dawkins, J (1987) *Higher Education: A Policy Discussion Paper*, Canberra: Australian Government Publishing Service.

Dawkins, J (1988) *Higher Education: A Policy Statement*, Canberra: Australian Government Publishing Service.

Department of Education and Science (1985) *Academic Validation in the Public Sector Higher Education (Lindop Report)*, London: Her Majesty's Stationary Office.

Department of Education and Science (1990) *Report of the Council for National Academic Awards (Bird Report)*, London: Department of Education and Science.

Department of Education and Science (1991) *Higher Education: A New Framework*, London: HMSO.

Dochy, F J R C, Segers, M S R and Wijnen W H F W (eds) (1990) *Management Information and Performance Indicators in Higher Education: An International Issue*, Assen/Maastricht: Van Gorcum.

Dockrell, W B (1990) *Evaluation procedures used for measuring the efficiency of higher education systems and institutions.* Paris: UNESCO.

Eaton, J (1991) *The Unfinished Agenda: Higher Education in the 1980s*, New York, NY: Macmillan Publishing Company.

Ellis, R (1993) (ed.) *Quality Assurance for University Teaching*, Buckingham: Open University Press.

Everman, R, Svensson, L G and Soderqvist, T (eds) (1987) *Intellectuals, Universities, and the State in Western Modern Societies*, Berkeley: University of California Press.

Ewell, P T and Lisensky R L (1988) *Assessing Institutional Effectiveness: Redirecting the Self-Study Process*, Washington, DC: Consortium for the Advancement of Private Higher Education.

Gellert, C (1993) *Higher Education in Europe*, London: Jessica Kingsley Publishers.

Gellert, C (1994) *Innovation and Adaptation in Higher Education*, London: Jessica Kingsley Publishers.

Ginsberg, M (ed.) (1991) *Understanding Educational Reform in Global Context: Economy, Ideology, and the State*, New York: Garland Publishing Inc.

Gove, S K and Beyle, T (eds) (1988) *Governors and Higher Education*, Denver: Education Commission of the States.

Green, D (1994) *What is quality in Higher Education?* Buckingham: Society for Research into Higher Education and Open University Press.

Halsey, A H and Trow, M (1971) *The British Academics*, London: Faber & Faber.

Harcleroad, F F (1963) *Accreditation: Voluntary Enterprise*, San Francisco: Jossey-Bass.

Harris, R M (1976) *A History of Higher Education in Canada 1663–1960*, Toronto: University of Toronto Press.

Henkel, M (1991) *Government, Evaluation and Change*, London: Jessica Kingsley Publishers.

Heywood, J (1989) *Assessment in Higher Education*, New York: Wiley.

Higher Education Quality Council (1994) *Learning from Audit*, London: HEQC.

Higher Education Quality Council (1994) *Checklist for quality assurance systems 1994: A briefing from the Higher Education Quality Council*, London: HEQC.

Hinkson, J et al. (1986) *Review of Efficiency and Effectiveness in Higher Education*, Canberra: Commonwealth Tertiary Education Commission.

Hirsh, E D (1987) *Cultural Literacy: What Every American Needs to Know*, Boston: Houghton Mifflin.

Hogarth, C P (1987) *Quality Control in Higher Education*, Lanham MD: University Press of America.

Holmes, B and Scalon, D S (eds) (1971) *Higher Education in a Changing World; World Yearbook of Education – 1971–72*, New York: Harcourt Brace Jovanovich.

Hussain, K M (1976) *Institutional Resource Allocation Models in Higher Education*, Paris: OECD.

Industrial Research and Development Advisory Committee of the European Commission (IRDAC) (1994) *Quality and Relevance, The Challenge to European Education, Unlocking Europe's Human Potential*, Brussels: IRDAC.

Jaraussch, K H (ed.) (1983) *The Transformation of Higher Learning, 1860–1930: Expansion, Diversification, Social Opening, and Professionalization in England, Germany, Russia and the United States*, Chicago: University of Chicago Press.

Jarratt, A (1985) *Report of the Steering Committee for Efficiency Studies in Universities*, London: CVCP.

Jones, J and Taylor, J (1990) *Performance Indicators in Higher Education*, Buckingham: The Society for Research into Higher Education, Society for Research into Higher Education, Open University Press.

Jordan, T E (1989) *Measurement and Evaluation in Higher Education: issues and illustration*. London: Falmer Press.

Kallen, D (1991) *Academic Exchange in Europe: Towards a New Era of Co-operation*, Bucharest, Romania: UNESCO European Centre for Higher Education, pp. 10–80.

Karmel, P (Chairman) (1989) *Reflection on a Revolution: Australian Higher Education In 1989*, Canberra: Australian Vice-Chancellors' Committee.

Kells, H R (1984) *Self Study Processes: A Guide for Postsecondary Institutions*, Washington, DC: American Council on Education.

Kells, H R (ed.) (1990) *The Development of Performance Indicators for Higher Education: A Compendium for Eleven Countries*, Paris: Programme on Institutional Management in Higher Education, OECD.

Kells, H R (1992) *Self-regulation and higher education: a multinational perspective on collaborative systems of quality assurance and control*, Vol. 15, Higher education policy series, London: Jessica Kingsley Publishers.

Kells, H R and Van Vught, F A (eds) (1988) *Self-regulation, Self-study, and Program Review in Higher Education*, Culemborg: Lemma BV.

Kerr, C (1994) *Troubled Times for American Higher Education: The 1990s and Beyond*, Albany, NY: State University of New York Press.

Knight, P T (ed.) (1994) *University-Wide Change, Staff and Curriculum Development*, paper 83, Birmingham: SEDA.

Kogan, D and Kogan, M (1983) *The Attack on Higher Education*, London: Kogan Page.

Kogan, M (1986) *Education Accountability: an Analytic Overview*, London: Hutchison Press.

Kogan, M (1989) *Evaluating Higher Education*, London: Jessica Kingsley Publishers.

Kogan, M, El-Khawas, E and Moses, I (1994) *Staffing Higher Education: Meeting New Challenges*, London: Jessica Kingsley Publishers.

Labour Party (1991) *Quality Assured: A Consultative Document on Labour's Proposals for Quality Assurance in Higher Education*, London: The Labour Party.

Lee, H (1992) 'An Analytic Study of the Social Dynamics Determining Higher Education Enrolment Quota', unpublished doctoral dissertation, Seoul: Seoul National University.

Levine A (1993) *Higher Learning in America, 1980–2000*, Baltimore, MD: The Johns Hopkins University Press.

Loder, C P J (1990) *Quality Assurance and Accountability in Higher Education*, London: Kogan Page.

Lynton, E A (1984) *The Missing Connection Between Business and the Universities*, New York: Macmillan.

Maassen, P A M and Van Vught, F A (eds) (1989) *Dutch Higher Education in Transition*, Culemborg: Lemma BV.

Miller, H D R (1994) *The Management of Change in Universities: Universities, State and Economy in Australia, Canada and the United Kingdom*, Buckingham: SRHE, Open University Press.

National Educational Goals Report (1992) Washington, DC: US Government Printing Office.

National Governors' Association (1988) *Results in Education, State-Level College Assessment Initiatives – 1987–1988: Results of a 50-State Survey*, Washington DC: National Governors' Association.

Neave, G and Van Vught, F A (ed.) (1991) *Prometheus Bound: The Changing Relationship Between Government and Higher Education in Western Europe*, Oxford: Pergamon Press.

New England Association of Schools and Colleges (1986) *Accreditation Handbook*, Winchester, MA: NEASC Commission on Institutions of Higher Education.

New Zealand Qualifications Authority (NZQA) (1994) *Quality Assurance in Education and Training*, Wellington: NZQA.

Nichols, J O (1989) *Institutional Effectiveness and Outcomes Assessment Implementation on Campus: A Practitioner's Handbook*, New York: Agathon Press.

Nightingale, P and O'Neil, M (1994) *Achieving Quality Learning in Higher Education*, London: Kogan Page.

Perkin, J A and Baird Israel, B (eds) (1972) *Higher Education: from Autonomy to Systems*, New York: International Council for Educational Development.

Premfors, R (ed.) (1984) *Higher Education Organization*, Stockholm: Almqvist & Wiksell International.

Pritchard, R M O (1990) *The End of Elitism? The Democratization of the West German University System*, New York/Oxford/Munich: Berg.

Psacharopoulos, G and Kazamias, A (1986) *Education and Development in Greece: A Social and Economic Study of Tertiary Education*, Athens: National Centre for Social Research.

Public Policy Center, SRI International (1986) *The Higher Education-Economic Development Connection: Emerging Roles for Public Colleges and Universities in a Changing Economy*, Washington, DC: American Association of State Colleges and Universities.

Sadlak, J (1990) *Higher Education in Romania, 1860–1990: Between Academic Mission, Economic Demands and Political Control*, Buffalo: State University of New York.

Scott, P (1984) *The Crisis of the University*, Beckenham: Croom Helm.

Scottish Higher Education Funding Council and Higher Education Quality Council (1994) *Joint Statement on Quality Assessment and Quality Audit*, Edinburgh: Higher Education Funding Council.

Semrow, J J et al. (1992) *In Search of Quality: The Development, Status, and Forecast of Standards in Postsecondary Accreditation*, New York: Peter Lang Publishers.

Shattock, M (ed.) (1983) *The Structure and Governance of Higher Education*, Guilford: Society for Research into Higher Education.

Shattock, M (1994) *The UGC and the Management of British Universities*, Buckingham: Society for Research into Higher Education, Open University Press.

Sheldrake, P and Linke, R (eds) (1979) *Accountability in Higher Education*, Sydney: Allen and Unwin.

Smith, S L (1991) *Report: Commission of Inquiry on Canadian University Education*, Ottawa: Association of Universities and Colleges of Canada.

Spee, A and Bormans, R (eds) (1991) *Performance Indicators in Government-Institutional Relations*, Paris: OECD.

Svensson, L G (1987) *Higher Education and the State in Swedish History*, Stockholm: Almqvist & Wiksell International.

Tapper, T and Salter, B (1992) *Oxford, Cambridge and the Changing Idea of the University*, Buckingham: Society for Research into Higher Education, Open University Press.

Teichler, U (1988) *Changing Patterns of the Higher Education System: the Experience of Three Decades*, London: Jessica Kingsley Publishers.

Tierney, W G (1991) *Culture and Ideology in Higher Education: Advancing a Critical Agenda*, New York: Praeger.

US Department of Education, US National Commission on Excellence in Education (1983) *A Nation at Risk: The Imperative for Educational Reform: A Report to the Nation and the Secretary of Education*, Washington, DC: US Government of Printing Office.

Van de Graff, F A, Clark, H, Furth, D, Goldschmidt, D and Wheeler, D F (1978) *Academic Power: Patterns of Authority in Seven National Systems of Higher Education*, New York: Praeger Publishers.

Van Vught, F (1989) *Governmental Strategies and Innovation in Higher Education*, London: Jessica Kingsley Publishers.

Vlaceanu, L (1992) *Trends, Developments and Needs of the Higher Education Systems of the Central and Eastern European Countries*. Bucharest: European Centre for Higher Education.

Vroeijenstijn, A I (1994) *Navigating between Skylla and Charybdis*, London: Jessica Kingsley Publishers.

Warren Pipper, D (1993) *Quality Management in Universities* (2 Vols), Canberra: Department of Employment Education and Training.

Warren Pipper, D (1994) *Are Professors Professional? The Organisations of University Examinations*, London: Jessica Kingsley Publishers.

Westerheijden, D F, Brennan, J and Maassen, P A M (1994) *Changing Contexts of Quality Assessment, Recent Trends in Western European Higher Education*, Utrecht: Lemma.

Wheelwright, E (ed.) (1978) *Capitalism, Socialism or Barbarism: Essays In Contemporary Political Economy*, Sydney: Australia New Zealand Book Company.

Wiltshire, B (1990) *The Moral Collapse of the University: Professionalism, Purity, and Alienation*, Albany, NY: State University of New York Press.

World Bank (1991) *Hungary: The Transition to a Market Economy, Critical Human Resources Issues*, Washington, DC: World Bank.

Yorke, M (1991) *Performance Indicators: Observations on Their Use in the Assurance of Course Quality*, London: Council for National Academic Awards.

Zemsky, R (1989) *Structure and Coherence: Measuring the Undergraduate Curriculum*, Washington, DC: Association of American Colleges.

Book chapters and journal articles

Acherman, H A (1990) 'Quality Assessment by Peer Review: A New Era for University Cooperation', *Higher Education Management*, 2 (2), pp. 179–92.

Adelman, C (1992) 'Accreditation', in Clark, B and Neave, G (eds) *The Encyclopedia of Higher Education*, Oxford: Pergamon Press, pp. 1313–18.

Åhgren-Lange, U, Carlsson, M *et al.* (1993) 'Evaluation – A Process with many actors', *Higher Education Management* 5 (1), pp. 40–8.

Ainsworth, M (1988) 'Monitoring, Evaluation and Validation of Courses: A Case Study', *International Journal of Educational Management*, 2(1) pp. 26–31.

Alexander, R and Gent, B (1983) 'A Case for International Validation', in Church, C H (ed.) *Practice and Perspective in Validation*, Guilford: Society for Research into Higher Education, pp. 123–31.

Almeida-Lajes, M A (1995) 'Management and Quality Assurance in Higher Education in Portugal', *Higher Education Management*, 7 (1), pp. 131–6.

Altbach, P G (1991) 'Patterns in Higher Education Development: Towards the Year 2000', *Prospects*, 21 (2), pp. 189–203.

Ashby, E (1967) 'The Future of the Nineteenth Century Idea of a University', *Minerva*, 6, pp. 3–17.

Ashenden, D (1988) 'Using Our Graduates Is The Real Problem', *Australian Universities' Review*, 31(1), pp. 24–6.

Ashworth, K (1994) 'Performance-based Funding in Higher Education', *Change*, 26 (6) pp. 18–22.

Bacchetti, R F and Weiner, S S (1991) 'Diversity is a Key Factor in Educational Quality and Hence Accreditation', *The Chronicle of Higher Education*, 8 May.

Ball, R and Wilkinson, R (1994) 'The Use and Abuse of Performance Indicators in UK Higher Education', *Higher Education* 27 (4), pp. 417–27.

Barlow, K (1989) 'The White Paper and Restructuring the Academic Labor Market', *Australian Universities' Review*, 32 (1), pp. 30–37.

Barnett, R (1983) 'The Legitimation of Validation', in Church, C H (ed.) *Practice and Perspective in Validation*, Guilford: Society for Research into Higher Education, pp. 148–61.

Barnett, R (1987) 'The Maintenance of Quality in the Public Sector of UK Higher Education', *Higher Education*, 16 (3), pp. 279–301.

Barnett, R (1992) 'The Idea of Quality: Voicing the Educational', *Higher Education Quarterly*, 46 (1) pp. 3–19.

Barnett, R (1994) 'Power, Enlightenment and Quality Evaluation', *European Journal of Education*, 29 (2), pp. 165–79.

Bartos, M (1990a) 'Further Steps To A New Educational Order', *Australian Society*, March, pp. 12–13.

Bartos, M (1990b) 'The Education Exports Fiasco', *Australian Society*, September, pp. 12–13.

Baurer, M (1988) 'Evaluation in Swedish Higher Education: Recent Trends and the Outlines of a Model', *European Journal of Education*, 23 (1 and 2), pp. 25–36.

Beju, I (1993) 'Quality Assessment and Institutional Accreditation in the Romanian Higher Education System', *Higher Education in Europe*, 18 (3), pp. 110–16.

Benedict, M, Brady, D and Wallace, W (1991, October) 'A Measure of Excellence', *Maclean's*, pp. 12–68.

Berg, C (1993) 'University Autonomy and Quality Assurance', *Higher Education in Europe* 18 (3), pp. 18–26.

Berg, L (1992) 'Vocationalism in Norwegian Higher Education, Rhetoric or Reality?', *European Journal of Education*, 27 (1 & 2), pp. 79–87.

Bergquist, W H and Tenbrink, G J (1977) 'Evaluation of Administration', in Knowles, A S (ed.), *The International Encyclopedia of Higher Education*, San Francisco: Jossey-Bass Publishers, pp. 1473–98.

Billing, D (1983) 'Practice and Criteria of Validation under the CNAA', in Church, C H (ed.) *Practice and Perspective in Validation*, Guilford: Society for Research into Higher Education, pp. 33–58.

Bormans, M J G, Brouwer, R, Veld, R J and Mertens, F J H (1987) 'The Role of Performance Indicators in Improving the Dialogue Between Governments and Universities', *International Journal of Institutional Management in Higher Education*, 11 (2), pp. 181–94.

Bourke, P (1988) 'The Green Paper: Towards An Evaluation', *Australian Universities' Review*, 31 (1), pp. 2–5.

Brennan, J, Goedegebuure, L C J, *et al.* (1993) 'Comparing Quality in Europe', *Higher Education in Europe* 18, (2), pp. 129–46.

Bresters, D W and Kalkwijk J P Th (1990) 'The Role of the Inspectorate of Higher Education', in *Peer Review and Performance Indicators (Quality Assessment in British and Dutch Higher Education)*, Utrecht: Lemma BV, pp. 59–70.

Brunner, J J (1993) 'Chile's Higher Education: Between Market and State', *Higher Education*, 25 (1), pp. 35–43.

Brunner, J J (1993) 'Higher Education in Chile from 1980–1990', *European Journal of Education*, 28 (1), pp. 71–84.

Buchbinder, H (1993) 'The Market Oriented University and the Changing Role of Knowledge', *Higher Education* 26 (3), pp. 331–47.

Burchell, D (1986) 'Tertiary Education For Sale', *Australian Society*, pp. 22–4.

Burgar, P (1994) 'Enforcing Academic Rules in Higher Education: A Total Quality Management Approach', *Research in Higher Education* 35 (1), pp. 43–55.

Callan, P M (1993) 'Government and Higher Education', in Levine, A (ed.) *Higher Learning in America: 1980-2000*, Baltimore: The Johns Hopkins University Press, pp. 3–19.

Caston, G (1993) 'Higher Education in the South Pacific: a political economy', *Comparative Education*, 29 (3), pp. 321–32.

Čermáková, Z, Holda, D and Urbánek, V (1994) 'Changes in Funding of Higher Education in the Czech Republic', *European Journal of Education*, 29 (1) pp. 75–83.

Cerych, L (1989) 'University-Industry collaboration: a research agenda and some general impacts on the development of Higher Education', *European Journal of Education*, 24 (3), pp. 309–14.

Cerych, L (1989) 'Higher Education and Europe after 1992: the framework', *European Journal of Education*, 24 (4), pp. 321–32.

Cerych, L (1990) 'Renewal of Central European Higher Education: Issues and Challenges', *European Journal of Education*, 25 (4), pp. 351–8.

Chaston, I (1994) 'Are British Universities in a Position to Consider Implementing Total Quality Management?', *Higher Education Quarterly*, 48 (2), pp. 118–34.

Church, C H (1988) 'The Qualities of Validation', *Studies in Higher Education*, 13 (1), pp. 27–44.

Church, C H and Murray, R (1983) 'Of Definitions, Debates and Dimensions', in Church, C H (ed.) *Practice and Perspective in Validation*, Guilford: SRHE, pp. 6–31.

Cizer, J, Spee, A *et al.* (1992) 'The Rôle of Performance Indicators in Higher Education', *Higher Education*, 24 (2), pp. 133–55.

Cooney, P R and Paqueo-Arrezo, E (1993) 'Higher Education Regulation in the Philippines: Issues of Control, Quality Assurance and Accreditation', *Higher Education Policy* 6 (2), pp. 25–8.

Cowen, R (1991) 'The Management and Evaluation of the Entrepreneurial University: The Case of England', *Higher Education Policy*, 4 (3), pp. 9–13.

Cross, K P (1983) 'Improving the Quality of Instruction', in Levine, A (ed.) *Higher Learning in America 1980-2000*, Baltimore, MD: The Johns Hopkins University Press, pp. 287–308.

Cuenin, S (1987) 'The Use of Performance Indicators in Universities: An International Survey', *International Journal of Institutional Management in Higher Education*, 11 (2), pp. 117–39.

Dahllöf, U (1975) 'Problems and Pitfalls in Assessing Internal Efficiency in Higher Education by Means of Mass Statistics. Some Experiences from Sweden', *Scandinavian Journal of Educational Research*, 19 (4), pp. 175–89.

Dainton, F (1977) 'University Grants Committees', in Knowles, A S (ed.) *International Encyclopaedia of Higher Education*, San Francisco: Jossey-Bass, pp. 1724–9.

Darling-Hammond, L (1992) 'Educational Indicators and Enlightened Policy', *Educational Policy*, 6 (3), pp. 235–65.

Darvas, P (1988) 'Reform Policy and Changes in the Educational System', *Higher Educational Policy*, 1 (13), pp. 38–43.

Davies, M (1980) 'The CNAA as a Validating Agency', in Billing, D A (ed.) *Indicators of Performance*, Guilford: SRHE, pp. 31–42.

De Rudder, H (1994) 'The Quality Issue in German Higher Education Policy', *European Journal of Education*, 29 (2), pp. 201–19.

De Weert, E (1990) 'A Macro-analysis of Quality Assessment in Higher Education', *Higher Education*, 19 (1), pp. 57–72.

Dillemans, R (1989) 'Autonomy, Responsibility and Responsiveness of Higher Education Institutions after 1992', *European Journal of Education*, 24 (4), pp. 333–44.

Dohn, H (1987) 'Recent Trends in Research on Higher Education in Denmark', *Higher Education in Europe*, 12 (2), pp. 66–9.

Dressel, P L (1977) 'Evaluation' in Knowles, A S (ed.), *The International Encyclopedia of*

Higher Education, San Francisco: Jossey-Bass Publishers, pp. 1480–93.

Eginitou, M (1991) 'Facing the Challenges of 'Europeanisation'. Some reflections on the Greek University System', *Higher Education in Europe* 16 (4), pp. 63–9.

Elsworth, G R (1994) 'Confronting the Biases in Connoisseur Review and Performance Indicators in Higher Education: A Structural Modelling Approach', *Higher Education*, 27 (2) pp. 163–90.

Eltan, L (1992) 'Quality Assurance in Higher Education: With or Without a Buffer?' *Higher Education Policy*, 5 (3) pp. 25–6.

Escolano, A (1987) 'Recent Trends in Research on Higher Education in Spain', *Higher Education in Europe*, 12 (1), pp. 70–72.

Evers, F T and Gilbert, S N (1991) 'Outcomes Assessment: how much value does university education add?', *The Canadian Journal of Higher Education*, 7 (2), pp. 53–76.

Ewell, P T (1991) 'Assessment and Public Accountability: Back to the Future', *Change*, 23 (6), pp. 12–17.

Ewell, P T (1994a) 'A Matter of Integrity: Accountability and the Future of Self-Regulation', *Change*, 26 (6), pp. 24–9.

Ewell, P T (1994b) 'Total Quality: The Idea We've Been Waiting For?' *Change*, 25 (3), pp. 49–55.

Farrant, J H (1987) 'Central Control of the University Sector', in Beecher, T (ed.) *British Higher Education*, London; Allen and Unwin, pp. 29–52.

Frackmann, E (1987) 'Lessons to be Learnt from a Decade of Discussions on Performance Indicators', *International Journal of Institutional Management in Higher Education*, 11 (2), pp. 149–62.

Franke-Wikberg, S (1990) 'Evaluating Education Quality on the Institutional Level' *Higher Education Management* 2 (3), pp. 271–92.

Frederiks, M M H, Westerheijden, D F *et al.* (1994) 'Effects of Quality Assessment in Dutch Higher Education', *European Journal of Education*, 29 (2), pp. 181–99.

García, P, Mora, J G, Rodrigues, S and Pérez, J J (1995) 'Experimenting with Institutional Evaluation in Spain', *Higher Education Management*, 7 (1), pp. 101–18.

Gellert, C and Rau, E (1992) 'Diversification and Integration: the Vocationalisation of the German Higher Education System', *European Journal of Education*, 27 (1 & 2), pp. 89–99.

Glytsos, N P (1990) 'Anticipated Graduate Job Mismatches and Higher Education Capacities Inadequacies in Greece', *Higher Education*, 19 (4), pp. 397–418.

Goedegebuure, L C J (1992) 'Grapes, Grain and Grey Cats: Binary Dynamics in Dutch Higher Education', *European Journal of Education*, 27 (1 & 2), pp. 57–68.

Goedegebuure, L C J and Meek, V L (1991) 'Restructuring Higher Education. A Comparative Analysis between Australia and the Netherlands', *Comparative Education*, 27 (1), pp. 7–22.

Goldschmidt, D (1984) 'The University as an Institution: Present Problems and Future Trends', *Higher Education In Europe*, 9 (4), pp. 65–73.

Gordon, M (1993) 'The Economy and Higher Education', in Levine, A (ed.) *Higher Learning in America: 1980-2000*, Baltimore, MD: The Johns Hopkins University Press, pp. 20–35.

Green, F M (1995) 'Transforming British Higher Education: A view across the Atlantic', *Higher Education*, 29 (3), pp. 225–39.

Halasz, G (1986) 'The Structure of Educational Policy-Making in Hungary in the 1960s and 1970s', *Comparative Education*, 22 (2), pp. 123–32.

Harris, R W (1990) 'The CNAA Accreditation and Quality Assurance', *Higher Education Review*, 23 (3), pp. 34–53.

Hernandez, A G (1991) 'The Autonomy of Spanish Universities: A problem of three powers', *Higher Education Policy*, 4 (1), May, pp. 37–44.

Hochleitner, R D (1990) 'The Private University and the Private Sector in Higher Education: A Spanish Perspective', *Higher Education Policy*, 3 (2), June, pp. 18–20.

Hüfner, K (1991) 'Accountability' in Altbach, P G (ed.) *International Higher Education – An Encyclopaedia*, New York and London: Garland Publishing, Inc, pp. 47–58.

Hutchings, P and Marchese, T (1990) 'Watching Assessment: Questions, Stories, Prospects', *Change*, 22 (4), pp. 12–38.

In 't Veld, R (1991) 'The Future of Evaluation in Higher Education', *Higher Education Management*, 3 (2), pp. 178–83.

Ivić, I (1992) 'Recent Developments in Higher Education in the Former Federal Republic of Yugoslavia', *European Journal of Education*, 27 (1 & 2), pp. 111–20.

Jaschik, S (1994) 'A Modest Retreat on Accreditation', *The Chronicle of Higher Education*, May 4, pp. A31–4.

Jastrzab-Mrozicka, M (1994) 'Autonomy of Colleges and Selection for Higher Education in Poland', *European Journal of Education*, 29 (1), pp. 85–95.

Jenkins, A (1995) 'The Research Assessment Exercise, Funding, and Teaching Quality' *Quality Assurance in Education* 3 (2), pp. 4–12.

Johnes, G (1994) 'Research Performance Measurement: what can international comparisons teach us?', *Comparative Education*, 30 (3), pp. 205–16.

Johnston, A D, Brady, D and Sabastini, G (1991, November) 'Measuring Excellence', *Maclean's*, pp. 20–79.

Kauffman, J F (1993) 'Governing Board', in Levine, A (ed.) *Higher Learning in America 1980-2000*, Baltimore, MD: The Johns Hopkins University Press, pp. 222–42.

Kazamias, A and Starida, A (1992) 'Professionalization or Vocationalization in Greek Higher Education', *European Journal of Education*, 27 (1 & 2), pp. 101–9.

Kells, H R (1989) 'University Self-regulation in Europe; the need for an integrated system of programme review', *European Journal of Education*, 24 (3), pp. 299–308.

Kells, H R and Kirkwood, R (1979) 'Institutional Self-Evaluation Processes', *Educational Record*, Winter, pp. 25–45.

Kells, H R (1990) 'The Inadequacy of Performance Indicators for Higher Education: The need for a more Comprehensive and Development Construct', *Higher Education Management*, 2 (3), pp. 258–70.

Kells, H R (1992) 'An Analysis of the Nature and recent Development of Performance Indicators in Higher Education', *Higher Education Management*, 4 (2), pp. 131–8.

Kenway, J and Blackmore, J (1988) 'Gender and the Green Paper: Privatization And Equity', *Australian Universities' Review*, 31 (1) pp. 49–57.

Kitzinger, U (1991) 'Higher Education: An International Dimension', *Oxford Review of Education*, 17 (1), pp. 33–44.

Kivinen, O and Rinne, R (1990) 'How to Steer Student Flows and Higher Education: the Headache Facing the Finnish Ministry of Education', in Neave, G and Van Vught, F (eds) *The Changing Relationship Between Government and Higher Education in Western Europe, Prometheus Bound*, Oxford: Pergamon Press, pp. 51–63.

Kogan, M (1990) 'Policy making and Evaluation in Higher Education', *Higher Education Policy*, 3 (4), pp. 30–32.

Koucky, J (1990) 'Czechoslovak Higher Education at the Cross-roads', *European Journal of Education*, 25 (3), pp. 361–78.

Kozma, T (1990) 'Higher Education in Hungary: Facing the Political Transition', *European Journal of Education*, 25 (4), pp. 379–90.

Krotseng, M V (1990) 'Profiles of Equality and Intrusion: The Complex Courtship of State Governments and Higher Education', *Review of Higher Education*, 13 (4), pp. 557–66.

Kwiatkowski, S (1990) 'Survival Through Excellence: Prospects for the Polish University', *European Journal of Education*, 25 (4), pp. 391–8.

Lajos, T (1993) 'Perspectives, Hopes and Disappointments: higher education reform in Hungary', *European Journal of Education*, 28 (4), pp. 403–11.

Lamoure, J and Lamoure R J (1992) 'The Vocationalisation of Higher Education in France: Continuity and Change', *European Journal of Education*, 27 (1 & 2), pp. 45–55.

Lane, J E (1979) 'Power in the University', *European Journal of Education*, 14 (4), pp. 389–402.

Larson, M (1980) 'Proletarianization And Educated Labor', *Theory And Society*, 9 (2), pp. 131–75.

L'Écuyer, J (1995) 'Quality Assurance Procedures in Quebec Universities', *Higher Education Management*, 7 (1), pp. 7–14.

Linke, R D (1992) 'Some Principles for Application of Performance Indicators in Higher Education', *Higher Education Management* 4 (2), pp. 194–203.

Linke, R D (1995) 'Improving Quality Assurance in Australian Higher Education', *Higher Education Management* 7 (1), pp. 49–62.

Lucier, P (1992) 'Performance Indicators in Higher Education: Lowering the Tension of the Debate', *Higher Education Management* 4 (2), pp. 204–14.

Lysons, A (1993) 'The Typology of Organisational Effectiveness in Australian Higher Education', *Research in Higher Education*, 34 (4), pp. 465–88.

Lysons, A and Hatherly, D (1992) 'Cameron's Dimensions of Effectiveness in Higher Education in the UK: A cross-cultural comparison', *Higher Education*, 23 (3), pp. 221–30.

Mackenna, J B (1985) 'University Reform in Spain: New Structures for Autonomy and Accountability', *Comparative Education Review*, 29 (4), pp. 460–70.

Meek, V L, Gedegebuure, L C, Kivinen, O and Risto, R (1991) 'Policy Change in Higher Education: Intended and Unintended Outcomes', *Higher Education*, 21 (4), pp. 451–9.

Meisenhelder, T (1983) 'The Ideology of Professionalism in Higher Education: Another Axe Being Ground', *Australian University Review*, 31 (1) pp. 60–65.

Middlehurst, R (1992) 'Quality: An Organising Principle for Higher Education?' *Higher Education Quarterly*, 46 (1) pp. 20–38.

Moodie, G C (1983) 'Buffer, Coupling and Broker: Reflections on 60 Years of the UGC', *Higher Education*, 12 (3), pp. 331–47.

Moodie, G and Acopian, J (1988) 'New Instrumentation In Higher Education: Another Axe Being Ground', *Australian Universities Review*, 31 (1) pp. 60–65.

Morrison, H G, Magennis, S P, *et al.* (1995) 'Performance Indicators and League Tables: A Call for Standards', *Higher Education Quarterly*, 49 (2), pp. 128–45.

Moscati, P (1991) 'University Autonomy: Models and Perspectives' *Higher Education in Europe*, 16 (3), pp. 87–90.

Nast, M (1986) 'On the Problems of Comparisons of Curricula, Examinations, Graduation from Higher Education and Academic Programmes and Degrees', *Higher Education in Europe*, 11 (2), pp. 13–18.

Neave, G (1982) 'On the Edge of the Abyss: An Overview of Recent Developments in European Higher Education', *European Journal of Education*, 17 (2), pp. 123–44.

Neave, G (1982) 'The Changing Boundary between the State and Higher Education', *European Journal of Education*, 17 (3), pp. 231–41.

Neave, G (1983) 'The Changing Face of the Academic Professions in Western Europe', *European Journal of Education*, 18 (3), pp. 217–27.

Neave, G (1986) 'On the Cultivation of Quality, Efficiency and Enterprise: an Overview of Recent Trends in Higher Education in Western Europe, 1986-1988', *European Journal of Education*, 23 (1 & 2), pp. 7–22.

Neave, G (1986) 'European University Systems', *CRE-information*, 1, 75, pp. 5–53.

Neave, G (1989) 'Foundation or Roof? The qualitative, structural and institutional dimensions in the study of Higher Education', *European Journal of Education*, 24 (3), pp. 211–23.

Neave, G (1992) 'On Instantly Consumable Knowledge and Snake Oil', *European Journal of Education*, 27 (1 & 2), pp. 5–27.

Neave, G (1994) 'The politics of Quality: Developments in Higher Education in Western Europe 1992–1994', *European Journal of Education*, 29 (2), pp. 115–34.

Neave, G and Rhoades, G (1987) 'The Academic Estate in Western Europe', in Clark, B (ed.) *The Academic Profession: National, Disciplinary, and Institutional Settings*, Berkeley, CA: University of California Press.

Nedwek, B P and Neal, J E (1994) 'Performance Indicators and Rational Management Tools: A Comparative Assessment of Projects in North America and Europe', *Research in Higher Education*, 35 (1), pp. 75–103.

O'Buachalla, S (1992) 'Self-regulation and the Emergence of the Evaluative State: Trends in Irish Higher Education Policy', *European Journal of Education*, 27 (1 & 2), pp. 69–78.

Omari, I M (1991) 'Innovation and change in Higher Education in Developing countries: experiences from Tanzania', *Comparative Education*, 27 (2), pp. 181–205.

O'Neil, R M (1994) 'Quality and Higher Education: Australia and the United States', *Journal of Tertiary Educational Administration*, 16 (1), pp. 135–40.

Ornelas, C and Post, D (1992) 'Recent University Reform in Mexico', *Comparative Education Review*, 36 (3), pp. 278–97.

Ory, C J (1992) 'Meta-assessment: Evaluating Assessment Activities', *Research in Higher Education*, 33 (4), pp. 467–81.

Ory, C J and Parker, S A (1989) 'Assessment Activities at Large Research Universities', *Research in Higher Education*, 30 (3), pp. 375–85.

Papandreou, A (1987) 'Greek University – Yesterday and Tomorrow', *Western European Education*, 19 (1), Spring, pp. 13–15.

Patrinos, H A (1990) 'The Privatization of Higher Education in Colombia: Effects on Quality and Equity', *Higher Education*, 20 (2), pp. 161–73.

Peace-Lenn, M (1993) 'Quality Assurance in Higher Education: A Global Tour of Practice and Resources', *Higher Education in Europe* 18 (3), pp. 71–80.

Perkin, H (1984) 'The Historical Perspective', in Clark, B R (ed.) *Perspectives in Higher Education*, Berkeley and Los Angeles: University of California Press, pp. 17–55.

Peters, R (1994) 'Some Snarks and Boojums: Accountability and the End(s) of Higher Education', *Change*, 26 (6), pp. 16–23.

Pišút, J (1993) 'Higher Education Reforms in the Slovak Republic', *European Journal of Education*, 28 (4), pp. 421–8.

Polin, R (1983) 'Freedom of the Mind and University Autonomy', in Chapman, J W (ed.) *The Western University on Trial*, Berkeley, CA: University of California Press, pp. 39–45.

Pratt, J (1992) 'Unification of Higher Education in the United Kingdom', *European Journal of Education*, 27 (1 & 2), pp. 29–44.

Prokopchuk, A (1993) 'The Control and Evaluation of Higher Education Institutions', *Higher Education in Europe* 18 (3), pp. 134–6.

Psacharopoulos, G (1990) 'Education and the Professions in Greece in the Light of 1992', *European Journal of Education*, 25 (1), pp. 5–22.

Qiping, Y and White, G (1994) 'The 'Marketisation' of Chinese Higher Education: a critical assessment', *Comparative Education*, 30 (3), pp. 217–37.

Ramsden, P (1991) 'A Performance Indicator of Teaching Quality in Higher Education: The Course Experience Questionnaire', *Studies in Higher Education*, 16 (2), pp. 129–50.

Recent Trends in Research on Higher Education (1987) 'Proceedings at an International Conference on Research in Higher Education, Salamanca, Spain, October 1987', *Higher Education in Europe*, 12 (1), pp. 111–19.

Róna-Tas, A (1993) 'Accreditation in Hungary and the Hungarian Accreditation Committee', *Higher Education in Europe*, 18 (3), pp. 100–109.

Rossides, D (1987) 'Knee-Jerk Formalism: The Higher Education Reports', *Journal of Higher Education*, 58 (4), pp. 498–514.

Ryan, L (1993) 'Prolegomena to Accreditation in Central and Eastern Europe', *Higher Education in Europe*, 18 (3), pp. 81–90.

Sadlak, J (1990) 'The Eastern European Challenge: Higher Education for a New Reality', *Educational Record*, 71 (2), pp. 30–37.

Sadlak, J (1994) 'The Emergence of a Diversified System: the State/Private Predicament in Transforming Higher Education in Romania', *European Journal of Education*, 29 (1), pp. 13–23.

Saitis, C A (1988) 'The Relationship between the State and the University in Greece, *European Journal of Education*, 23 (3) pp. 249–60.

Schmitz, C C (1993) 'Assessing the Validity of Higher Education Indicators', *The Journal of Higher Education*, 64 (5), pp. 503–21.

Setényi, J (1994) 'Regional Human Resource Development and the Modernisation of the Non-University Sector in Hungary', *European Journal of Education*, 29 (1), pp. 25–36.

Šebková, H (1994) 'Institutions of Higher Education and the Czech Academy of Sciences in the Transitional Period', *European Journal of Education*, 29 (1), pp. 97–107.

Sharp, G (1988a) 'Reconstructing Australia', *Arena*, 82, pp. 70–97.

Sharp, G (1988b) 'The University And After?', *Arena*, 82, pp. 117–33.

Shattock, M and Berdhal, R D (1984) 'The British University Grants Committee, 1919–1983; Changing Relationships with Government and The Universities', *Higher Education*, 13 (5), pp. 471–500.

Shils, E (1991) 'Academic Freedom', in Altbach, P G (ed.) *International Higher Education – An Encyclopaedia*, New York and London: Garland Publishing, Inc, pp. 1–22.

Sizer, J (1992) 'Accountability', in Clark, B and Neave, G (eds) *The Encyclopedia of Higher Education*, Oxford: Pergamon Press, pp. 1305–13.

Skolinik, M L (1989) 'How Academic Programme Review Can Foster Intellectual Conformity and Stifle Diversity of Thought and Method', *Canadian Journal of Higher Education*, 60 (6), pp. 619–43.

Slaughter, S (1985) 'The Pedagogy Of Profit', *Higher Education*, 14 (2), pp. 217–22.

Slaughter, S (1991) 'The "Official" Ideology of Higher Education: Ironies and Inconsistencies', in Tierney, W G, *Culture and Ideology in Higher Education: Advancing a Critical Agenda*, New York: Praeger, pp. 59–85.

Smith, B, Burke, G, Smith, G and Wheelwright, T (1988) 'Proposals For Change in Australian Education: A Radical Critique', *Discourse: The Australian Journal Of Educational Studies*, 9 (10), pp. 1–38.

Smyth, J (1991) 'Theories of the State and Recent Policy Reforms in Higher Education in Australia', *Discourse: The Australian Journal of Educational Studies*, 11 (2), pp. 48–69.

Staropoli, A (1987) 'The Comité National d'Evaluation: Preliminary Results of a French Experiment', *European Journal of Education*, 22 (2), pp. 123–31.

Stolte-Heiskanen, V (1992) 'Research Performance Evaluation in the Higher Education Sector: A Grass-roots Perspective', *Higher Education Management*, 4 (2), pp. 179–93.

Stretton, H (1989) 'Life After Dawkins: Teaching and Research with Diminishing Resources', *Australian Universities' Review*, 32 (2), pp. 9–14.

Strydom, A H and Noruwaua, J (1993) 'Academic Standards in South African Universities and Proposals for Quality Assurance', *Higher Education*, 25 (4), pp. 379–93.

Szebenyi, P (1992) 'Change in the System of Public Education – East Central Europe', *Comparative Education*, 28 (20), pp. 9–31.

Tan, L D (1992) 'A Multivariate Approach to the Assessment of Quality', *Research in Higher Education*, 33 (2), pp. 205–26.

Tannock, J D T and Burge, S E (1992) 'A New Approach to Quality Assurance for Higher Education', *Higher Education Quarterly*, 46 (1), pp. 108–23.

Teichler, U (1989) 'Research on Higher Education and Work in Europe', *European Journal of Education*, 24 (3), pp. 223–48.

Tight, M (1985) 'Academic Freedom Re-examined', *Higher Education Review*, 18 (1), pp. 7–23.

Tornquist, K M and Kallsen, L A (1994) 'Out of the Ivory Tower: Characteristics of Institutions Meeting the Research Needs of Industry', *Journal of Higher Education*, 65 (5), pp. 523–39.

Trow, M A (1970) 'Reflections on the Transition from Mass to Universal Higher Education', *Deadalus*, 9, pp. 1–42.

Trow, M A (1974) 'Problems in the transition from elite to mass higher education', in *Policies for Higher Education*, Paris: General Report of the Conference on the Future of Post-Secondary Education, OECD, pp. 51–101.

Trow, M A (1976) 'Elite Higher Education: An Endangered Species?', *Minerva*, 14 (3), pp. 355–76.

Trow, M A (1987a) 'The National Reports on Higher Education: A Sceptical View', *Educational Policy*, 1 (4), pp. 411–27.

Trow, M A (1993b) 'Federalism in American Higher Education', in Levin, A (ed.) *Higher Learning in America: 1980-200*, Baltimore, MD: The Johns Hopkins University Press, pp. 39–66.

Tuijnman, A (1990) 'Dilemmas of Open Admissions Policy: Quality and Efficiency in Swedish Higher Education', *Higher Education*, 20 (4), pp. 443–57.

Välimaa, J (1994) 'A Trying Game: experiments and reforms in Finnish higher education', *European Journal of Education*, 29 (2), pp. 149–63.

Välimaa, J (1994) 'Academics on Assessment and the Peer Review – Finnish Experience', *Higher Education Management*, 6 (3), pp. 377–90.

Van Meel, R and De Wolf, H (1994) 'Major issues for educational innovation in Higher Vocational Education in the Netherlands', *European Journal of Education*, 29 (2), pp. 135–47.

Van Vught, F A (1988) 'A New Autonomy in European Higher Education? An Exploration and Analysis of the Strategy of Self-Regulation in Higher Education Governance', *International Journal of Institutional Management in Higher Education*, 12 (1), pp. 16–25.

Van Vught, F A (1989) 'Creating Innovations in Higher Education', *European Journal of Education*, 24 (3), pp. 249–70.

Van Vught, F A and Westerheijden, D F (1994) 'Towards a General Model of Quality Assessment in Higher Education', *Higher Education*, 28 (3), pp. 355–71.

Vessuri, H (1993) 'Higher Education, Science and Engineering in Late 20th Century Latin America: Needs and Opportunities for Co-operation', *European Journal of Education*, 28 (1), pp. 49–59.

Villanueva, J R (1985) 'The Evolution of the University Teaching Staff in Spain', *Higher*

Education in Europe, 10 (2), April–June, pp. 19–27.

Vroeijenstijn, I T (1990) 'Autonomy and Assurance of Quality: Two sides of one coin. The Case of Quality Assessment in Dutch Universities', *Higher Education Research and Development*, 9 (1), pp. 21–38.

Watson, D (1995) 'Quality Assurance in British Universities: Systems and Outcomes', *Higher Education Management*, 7 (1), pp. 25–37.

Whitman, I (1993) 'Quality Assessment in Higher Education: Issues and Concerns', *Higher Education in Europe*, 18 (3), pp. 42–5.

Williams, G (1984) 'The Economic Approach', in Clark, B R (ed.) *Perspectives on Higher Education*, Berkeley and Los Angeles: University of California Press, pp. 79–105.

Wolff, R A (1993) 'The Accreditation of Higher Education Institutions in the United States', *Higher Education in Europe*, 18 (3), pp. 91–9.

Worgan, P (1995) 'The Change in relationship between the State and Higher Education in the Czech Republic', *Higher Education Management*, 7 (2), pp. 241–52.

Yeatman, A (1988) 'The Green Paper On Higher Education Remarks Concerning Its Implications for Participation, Access and Equity for Women as Staff and Students', *Australian Universities' Review*, 31 (1), pp. 34–41.

Yorke, M (1991) 'Performance Indicators: Towards a Synoptic Framework', *Higher Education*, 21 (2), pp. 235–48.

Yorke, M (1992) 'Quality in Higher Education', *Journal of Further and Higher Education*, 15 (1), pp. 3–16.

Yorke, M (1993) 'Quality Assurance for Higher Education Franchising', *Higher Education*, 26 (2), pp. 167–82.

Yorke, M (1995) 'Siamese Twins? Performance Indicators in the Service of Accountability and Enhancement', *Quality in Higher Education*, 1 (1), pp. 13–30.

Zeleny, P (1994) 'Vocational Higher Education: A Vital Path to the Prosperity of Czech Higher Education', *European Journal of Education*, 29 (1), pp. 61–73.

Zeng, K (1995) 'Japan's Dragon Gate: the effects of university entrance examinations on the educational system and students', *Compare*, 25 (1), pp. 58–84.

Relevant journals

General

Higher Education	*Journal for Higher Education Management*
Higher Education in Europe	*Journal of Further and Higher Education*
Higher Education Exchange	*Journal of Higher Education*
Higher Education Management	*Research in Higher Education*
Higher Education Policy	*Research into Higher Education (Abstracts)*
Higher Education Quarterly	*Universities Quarterly*
Higher Education Research and Development	*Quality in Higher Education*
Higher Education Review	*Quality Assurance in Education*

Special issues

European Journal of Education, 29 (2), 1994
Trends in Higher Education: The Politics of Quality Assurance
Contains:
Neave, G 'The Politics of Quality: developments in higher education in Western Europe 1992–1994', pp. 115–34.
Van Meel, R and De Wolf, H 'Major issues for educational innovation in Higher Vocational Education in the Netherlands', pp. 135–47.
Välimaa, J 'A Trying Game: experiments and reforms in Finnish higher education', pp. 149–63.
Barnett, R 'Power, Enlightenment and Quality Evaluation', pp. 165–79.
Frederiks, M M H, Westerheijden, D F, *et al.* 'Effects of Quality Assessment in Dutch Higher Education', pp. 181–99.
De Rudder, H (1994) 'The Quality Issue in German Higher Education Policy', pp. 201–19.

Quality Assurance in Education, 3(2), 1995
Contains:
Jenkins, A 'The Research Assessment Exercise, Funding, and Teaching Quality', pp. 4–12.
Bolton, A 'A Rose by any other Name: TQM in Higher Education', pp. 13–18.
Chadwick, P 'Academic Quality in TQM: Issues in Teaching and Learning', pp. 19–23.
Lee, J and Fitz, J 'Inspection and Policy Making: Some Initial Ideas', pp. 24–31.
Tovey, P 'Context Specificity and Quality Continuing Professional Education. Part 1: Beyond the Market', pp. 32–8.
Withers, R 'Quality Assessment: Two Traditions' (A Review Article), pp. 39–46.

Quality in Higher Education, 1 (1), 1995
Contains:
Yorke, M 'Siamese Twins? Performance Indicators in the Service of Accountability and Enhancement', pp. 13–30.
Harker, B 'Postmodernism and Quality', pp. 31–9.
Johnston, R G, Jones, K and Gould, M 'Department Size and Research in English Universities: Inter-university Variations', pp. 41–7.
Bitzer, M E and Malherbe, W S 'Internal Quality Assurance in University Teaching: A Case Study' pp. 49–57.
Fearnley, S 'Class Size: The Erosive Effect of Recruitment Numbers on Performance', pp. 59–65.
Hill, R 'A European Student Perspective On Quality', pp. 67–75.

Higher Education Quarterly, 46 (1), 1992
Quality and the Management of Quality
Contains:
Barnett, R 'The Idea of Quality: Voicing the Educational', pp. 3–19.
Middlehurst, R 'Quality: An Organising Principle for Higher Education?', pp. 20–38.
King, R 'The Funding of Teaching Quality: A Market Approach', pp. 39–46.
Becher, T 'Making Audit Acceptable: A Collegial Approach to Quality Assurance', pp. 46–66.
Johnes, J and Taylor, J 'The 1989 Research Selectivity Exercise: A Statistical Analysis of Differences in Research Rating between Universities at the Cost Centre Level', pp. 67–87.
Johnes, J 'The Potential Effects of Wider Access to Higher Education on Degree Quality', pp. 88–107.

Tannock, J D T and Burge, S E 'A New Approach to Quality Assurance for Higher Education', pp. 108–23.

Higher Education Management, 4 (2), 1992
Contains:
Kells, H R 'An Analysis of the Nature and recent Development of Performance Indicators in Higher Education', pp. 131–8.
Spee A and Bormans R 'Performance Indicators in Government-Institutional Relations: The Conceptual Framework', pp. 139–55.
Sizer, J 'Performance Indicators in Government-Higher Institutions Relationships: Lessons for Government', pp. 156–63.
Middaugh, M F and Hollowell, D E 'Developing Appropriate Measures of Academic and Administrative Productivity as Budget Support Data for Resource Allocation Decisions', pp. 164–78.
Stolte-Heiskanen, V 'Research Performance Evaluation in the Higher Education Sector: A Grass-roots Perspective', pp. 179–93.
Linke, R D 'Some Principles for Application of Performance Indicators in Higher Education', pp. 194–203.
Lucier, P 'Performance Indicators in Higher Education: Lowering the Tension of the Debate', pp. 204–14.
Johansson, R 'Students from Different Campuses in Economics and Engineering Programmes: An Application of a Formative and Longitudinal Evaluative Model', pp. 215–26.
Bell, S and Sadlak, J 'Technology Transfer in Canada: Research Park and Centres of Excellence', pp. 227–44.
Fenger, P 'Research Councils: Buffers under Cross Pressures', pp. 245–55.

Higher Education Management, 7 (1), 1995
Contains:
L'Écuyer, J 'Quality Assurance Procedures in Quebec Universities', pp. 7–14.
Milot, L 'Relevance and Limitation of Periodic Programme Evaluation: A Case of Laval University', pp. 15–25.
Watson, D 'Quality Assurance in British Universities: Systems and Outcomes', pp. 25–37.
El-Khawas, E 'External Review: Alternative Models Based on US Experience', pp. 25–37.
Linke, R D 'Improving Quality Assurance in Australian Higher Education', pp. 49–62.
Meade, P 'Managing Quality by Devolution', pp. 63–80.
Massaro, V 'Quality Measurement in Australia: An Assessment of the Holistic Approach', pp. 81–99.
García, P, Mora, J G, Rodrígues, S and Perez, J J 'Experimenting Institutional Evaluation in Spain', pp. 101–18.
Van der Weiden, M J H 'External Quality Assessment and Feasibility of Study Programs', pp. 119–30.
Almeida Lajes, M A 'Management and Quality Assurance in Higher Education in Portugal', pp. 131–6.

Index